Eve's story

Eve's Story

A true-to-life story of one Christian
woman's search for fulness and equality

Eric and Joyce Lane

 EVANGELICAL PRESS

EVANGELICAL PRESS
16/18 High Street, Welwyn, Hertfordshire, AL6 9EQ, England

© Evangelical Press 1984
First published 1984

ISBN 0 85234 181 4

Typeset in Great Britain by Herts Typesetting Services Ltd., Hertford.
Printed by Anchor Brendon Ltd., Tiptree, Essex, England.

Contents

Preface

This book is the fruit of a growing realization of the vital need for clear thinking on the part of all Christians about the position of women in the Christian church. It is probably true that women have a majority holding in our churches and that without their presence and contribution many churches would simply fold up. Yet when we try to define their place and contribution in biblical terms we come up against problems. The emphasis seems to fall more on what they must not do than on what they may do, with the result that a negative attitude tends to be taken towards them. Meanwhile, women's emancipation is forcing us to re-examine the role of women, not only in society but in the life of the church. Do evangelicals just opt out of this, or do we face the challenge and look again at some of these vexed questions? For they affect independent and local churches, as well as denominations and national churches. For example, what offices in a church are open to women? May they preach? May they be pastors or elders, or even deacons or deaconesses? Are they allowed to speak at all in church gatherings? What about praying in the prayer meeting? And there are questions about clothing, particularly the appearance of the head and hair.

Our problem is not that the Bible does not answer these questions, but that the passages relating to them are among the most difficult of all to interpret, partly because of big cultural changes between the first and twentieth centuries. Misinterpretations of these passages have built up traditions about the place of the woman, which tend either to bring her into bondage or to create resentment and discontent. Such a situation calls for a sensitive and sympathetic approach, rather than for preaching and dogmatism. This is the main reason why we have adopted a fictitious approach here, based on the experience of an imaginary but, we hope, a believable character. This is not a complete biography of her, but is confined to those periods of her life in which she encounters the main questions relating to godly women that the Bible itself raises. Eve is a representative character, in the sense that the things that happened to her are shared out among Christian women generally; hence the choice of her name, from the first Eve, the mother of all living. Perhaps you will find help in those areas that affect you personally, and also have a better understanding of those who are involved in some of the other situations depicted. As we have tried to face the questions afresh without too many preconceptions, we hope you will listen to the answers similarly with 'an innocent ear'.

Just a word on the matter of Bible quotations. You will find that in the bulk of the book these are mainly from the Authorized Version. This is because it is set in the immediate post-war years, before most of our modern translations had appeared. The main alternative at that time was the Revised Version, and our characters have made use of that version where appropriate. The New International Version came out in the late 1970s, and the chapters that relate to this period, that is, mainly the first and last, have largely adopted this version. This seemed the happiest arrangement, especially since many of the texts referring to women's matters are best known in the Authorized Version.

Eric and Joyce Lane

1.
A woman's place

Sarah put down her cup and saucer and looked across at her aunt. 'It's not that I don't like them or that they treat me badly,' she said. 'Rather the reverse – they overdo the care and attention. I feel stifled, claustrophobic. I'm afraid if I don't get away something will explode – probably me! It would be better if I moved out now before it comes to a row.'

Aunty Eve's face registered concern but not shock. 'Is it really as serious as that?' she asked, more to get Sarah to enlarge than because she doubted her. Sarah duly obliged.

'Father doesn't seem to think that women have any real place outside the home. All positions of leadership are for men only. Women should stop at home and look after them and their children. When I point out that the two chief jobs in Britain are held by women he just says that proves how disordered our society has become: we've turned our backs on God and the Bible. I feel like a character in Jane Austen, to be kept in cotton wool until I'm ready to be married off – to a parentally approved husband, if not an actually arranged one. Why can't I be free to live as I wish? I want to choose my own career, decide whether or not I want to marry – and when, and whom, then run my home differently if I like. All this goes on in my mind, but I never actually get to the point of doing anything about it, or even of saying these things openly. It's not just fear, partly conscience, I suppose. Perhaps I'm not really certain what I do believe. Perhaps I'm brainwashed with the same attitude. Mother seems to accept it all right. What shall I do?'

There was a long silence before her aunt spoke. 'Forgive me for hesitating. I've got the feeling I've been here before – "*déjà-vu*", I think it's called. I might have been listening to a tape recording of my own thoughts from forty years ago! In a

way I'm not all that surprised. I can see that what your father
is doing is reproducing the kind of home he and I were
brought up in. Not that that's wrong in principle, and like
your grandad he believes it's biblical and therefore God's
will. What I mean is that this happens quite a lot: the father
thinks only about maintaining his position as head of the
house, and doesn't think too much about its effect on the
other members of the family, particularly the females, who
are supposed to be "in subjection", as he would say.'

The look on Sarah's face prompted her aunt's next
remark. 'Many people are surprised when they hear me say
that. They see me as I am now (or as I appear to them!) – a
saintly old matron who has spent her life in the service of God
– abroad, in this country, in my home and church. And they
put it all down to my Christian upbringing. But what they
don't know is that it nearly produced the opposite effect to
what was intended. They know nothing of the problems, the
stresses and even rebellions that went on inside me. It could
all have been a disaster, and for a time it was. It was only
because God overruled it and taught me his way very gently
that in the end I was perhaps able to be more useful than I
would have been if I hadn't gone through all that.'

Sarah's eyes were wide open, and watering a little. All this
was news to her. She had never for a moment thought of her
aunt as someone with a 'past', or even a childhood, come to
that. If she had thought that far back she would have
pictured her as a model child, with never a suspicion of the
questions that were going through her own mind. She
wanted to hear more. Hardly able to speak, she leaned
forward, and Aunty Eve took the hint.

'Like you I couldn't complain of ill-treatment or neglect,
such as some children in non-Christian homes experience. I
suppose I could complain about deprivation – not being
allowed to do everything other children did. But this affected
us all, the boys and the girls alike. Your father couldn't have
gone to the pictures if he'd wanted to! Anyway, as we grew up
this changed, or else we grew out of wanting these things. But

what didn't seem to change was the attitude to me as a female; in fact I became more conscious of it as I grew up. I was a member of the "weaker sex", which was supposed to mean I was physically smaller and with very limited muscle-power. But was this organic? Or was it just that we weren't allowed to develop it? These questions were never thought of, let alone discussed. The games we played and the jobs we did all had to be "feminine". If we were being trained for life in any sense at all, it was for exclusively female functions, such as childbearing and serving the family. Even those vocations which were open to women – like teaching and nursing – were only seen as temporary, something to keep us occupied until marriage came along. But if possible we were to be kept sheltered. After all, weren't we more easily tempted? Didn't we take after the first Eve?'

Sarah's mind was racing, but she was unable to say anything, so her aunt continued, 'I'm not saying we weren't respected. In fact, as we grew up we were shown more politeness and courtesy. Doors were opened, seats given up, escorts provided. But it all seemed a bit overdone, as if we were too weak to open doors ourselves or to stand on our own feet. It was an unreal world, a hark back to the age of chivalry. I came to feel it wasn't really done out of regard for us, but as part of a scheme to uphold male supremacy. We had to pay for this consideration by rendering obedience. We had to recognize that man is the head of woman; he gives the orders and must be obeyed down to the last detail. And in a Christian home the man had the Bible on his side, or so we were told. It was drummed into us that the man was created first, and the woman was made for him, to be his "helpmeet". And we were to be warned by what happened when she went against this – the whole race was ruined! It was all our fault! And we were punished by being put into subjection to the man. Nor could we write all this off as Old Testament or pre-Christ. Texts in the New Testament were produced to show it still applied. Women were to be "modest and sober, learning in silence with all subjection", because

"Adam was formed first, then Eve. And Adam was not deceived, but the woman was deceived and fell into transgression." She can be saved – yes, "through childbearing"! You see, I got to know it all by heart!'

'All that sounds very familiar!' said Sarah. 'I can see now where it came from. But what's the answer? Is there an answer? The Bible does say these things, doesn't it? I can't deny that. But I can't help resenting it. It seems to mean we're inferior just because we're women – second in creation but first in sin, made out of man, for man, in the image of man. All we're fit for is to serve men, bear their children, cook their meals, wash their clothes, keep their houses clean. We must never forget we are women and only fit for women's work, as if we were servants, not people.'

Sarah sounded bitter, but her aunt responded sympathetically: 'I have to confess I reacted rather like that myself. On reflection, I don't think they really thought of us as inferior, but at the time that was how it came across to me. And it was worse because out in the world, with the war and everything, women were becoming liberated from their traditional restriction to a domestic role. But because we were Christians we had to toe the old line. It was the Bible that had put us into this position, and the Bible does not change. So whatever happened in the outside world, we had to go on the same. And I'm afraid this even made me go so far as to question the Bible.' Eve dropped her voice as she said this, but Sarah raised hers to reply.

'You!' she exploded. 'You question the Bible! I don't believe it!'

'It didn't happen all at once,' her aunt explained. 'At first I tried to separate those things that were meant to be permanent from those that seemed to belong to the cultural background of the times. I felt that perhaps the teaching on women was not meant to be put on the same level as truths like the nature of God, the deity of Christ, justification by faith and so on. Maybe the subjection of women was a Jewish arrangement from which Christ was going to set them free.

After all, he'd spoken about liberating the oppressed, and women certainly came into that category! This idea seemed to be confirmed by Paul's teaching that in Christ there is neither male nor female, but all are one. I took this to mean the equality of the sexes, and thought the church had just failed to live up to it, probably because it has always been dominated by men.'

'Yes, but isn't it *also* Paul who teaches that women are to be in subjection? He won't let them teach in the church but says they've got to keep quiet. You can't say that's just Old Testament or Jewish, can you?'

'No, but I thought of it as a hangover from the Old Testament, which would gradually disappear, or rather should have done. After all, Paul had been a strict Jew, a Pharisee in fact, and he continued to observe Jewish ceremonies and laws which the church threw off as it became more Gentile. In any case, this attitude to women as inferior was general throughout the Roman Empire, just like slavery. The church didn't oppose slavery at the time – in fact it taught Christian slaves to be obedient to their masters. But as times changed slavery disappeared and the New Testament passages about slaves and masters no longer applied, at least not literally. I thought the same was meant to happen with the passages about women. The one that would really last and judge all the others was "In Christ there is neither male nor female" (Galatians 3: 28).'

'Well, what did you do about it? It must have made things worse at home, for everyone.'

'I did *try* to keep my thoughts to myself as far as I could. But the lines I was thinking along gradually came out. I didn't actually attend Women's Lib. meetings – I couldn't have done, anyway – but I did start reading feminist literature, secretly, of course. I couldn't help agreeing with many of the arguments, although some of the methods proposed horrified me! But, for example, I could go along with the charge that the Bible was used to support male chauvinism – after all, I had experienced that at first hand!

But quite apart from the Bible it had become written into the very language. The word "man" does duty for both sexes, and even though the female of the species has her own word, "woman", that word is derived from "man" – it's just "man" with a couple of letters tacked on, confirming that she's an appendage. And then there are words like "manpower" to describe the whole workforce. And we always speak of "man's achievements" even when they're women's! Even God is male! What chance did we stand when the very language was against us?'

'Did you just keep all this to yourself, or did you get involved in the movement?' Sarah asked.

'I didn't get actively involved until I went to university. My parents weren't too happy about letting me go there at all, especially with the change in the moral climate that was taking place. But I was quite determined, and since the place had been offered and the grant made, there was not a lot they could do to stop me. I knew they were worried and that restrained me a bit, but my feelings were so strong it was not long before I joined up with a group of "libbers". I'm afraid I spent more time with them than I did with churches or at Christian Union meetings. I didn't go as far as some and try to change the world, or lead a kind of female Trotskyist revolution. Really I was only concerned with myself. I suppose basically I wanted to work off my repression and reach equality with men. So I went in for things like judo, which was unheard of for women at that time. I also tried my hand at specifically male sports, turning my nose up at the traditional hockey-netball-tennis idea of female sport. I opposed the chivalrous attitude of men (what was left of it by then!), in fact I was quite rude when they did things like opening doors or standing up. "I'm perfectly capable of doing it myself," I used to shout! But my chief aim was to get into a male-dominated career. This was not easy. I did quite well in the economics course, but the idea of a girl getting into the Stock Exchange was just a joke at that time. I took it seriously, though. I even aimed at getting through the doors of some of those exclusive male clubs!'

She laughed at herself and Sarah joined in, although in her case it was the laughter of admiration, not ridicule. She was eager to hear more, and her aunt sensed this, for she went on, 'But that's another story and it's a long time ago – a different life. I can see now that I went too far down that road. The Women's Lib. movement, like some other reformist groups, is really based on evolution. Women have now evolved out of their primitive weakness and subservience (so the argument runs) and must assert themselves. Survival no longer depends on physical strength, as it did in the early days of the human race. There is no longer any rational ground for society being male-dominated. The only way this structure is kept standing is by indoctrinating women from childhood into the idea of submissiveness. But society has reached a stage in its evolutionary development which makes this no longer necessary. The roles of male and female can now be reversed, and the whole structure of marriage and the family be overthrown. It can't survive without the co-operation of women and if they withhold this, the whole thing will collapse. At the time I swallowed this outlook. It seemed so liberating, which was the idea of it, of course. But I came to see that you couldn't do this without overthrowing the whole of society, too, which in fact was what some of the more extreme ones wanted. But what they didn't realize was that by doing this they would lose more than they gained – there would be chaos. Strangely enough, this was what led me back to faith in God. I could see we need some order, and God is a God of order. Order is one of his gifts to ensure we have enough peace to enable us to enjoy life. But wherever there is revolution you get suffering and misery. And one revolution tends to spark off another, or else produces an authoritarian reaction which is so severe it's just as bad. At the same time I came to see that the place where we learn to live in peace and order is the home and family. For a home to run smoothly everyone has to fit into place and there has to be some kind of leadership. This was where my Christian background gave me some advantage. Even if it had been a bit repressive and over-protective, at least it had run smoothly. We knew our places and kept to them, and this was something.'

As her aunt paused, Sarah put in a question: 'So what you really did was to go round in a circle and end up more or less where you started?'

'Not altogether. I admit that I did over-react when I first left home, but I still believe, even after all this time, that some reaction was justified. I came to accept the *idea* of the headship of the husband and father over the family, but at the same time felt it had been wrongly interpreted and applied. You see, Christ taught that his idea of authority was very different from that exercised by the people of the world, where they "lord it" over each other when they get the chance. In the world authority means the right to command. The head is the one who issues the orders, and the others have to obey them – that's what subjection means. I think Christians have tended to assume that headship in the home and church is something like that. But when I came back to the New Testament after my time in the wilderness, I saw headship in a different light. If you look closely at what the New Testament says, there's very little, if anything, about commanding and giving orders. But there's a great deal about the head's responsibility for those under him, and particularly his duty to love them. It's interesting that headship in the home is always compared with Christ's headship in the church, never with any institution in the world. That seems to me to be the most important thing of all, because what the New Testament is always stressing is what Christ has done for his church and is continuing to do for it, just as in the Old Testament God called himself the husband of his people.

'Of course, we have our duties to Christ, and he has the right to require us to submit to him. But gospel submission begins with faith, what the apostles called "the obedience of faith" or "obeying the gospel". This is where we first learn to submit when we accept the terms of salvation. Then we go on to obey his other commands, but we keep them, not because we're forced to, against our will, but because we want to please him. This is how we feel – we *want* to obey him because of the loving way he has dealt with us. We don't do it slavishly, as if it were a new code of law, more rigorous than the old one. This is supposed to be the pattern both for authority and obedience in the home. The patriarchal home comes dangerously close to denying the very gospel on which it professes to be based.'

Sarah pondered these words for a few moments before saying, 'That certainly puts it in a fresh light. I suppose that's what I've been uneasy about, and groping for. You've helped me see it clearly. But there are still lots of questions. If things really are as you say, then what does it mean when it says the woman is "the weaker vessel" and that she must "learn in silence with all subjection"? I can't seem to fit that in to your way of putting it. And then there's all the business about the woman being second in creation but first in sin, then cursed for this by being placed in subjection to the man. All that doesn't seem to square with your idea about headship and submission.'

'The trouble', replied Eve, 'is not in the passages, it's in the way they're used to justify a preconceived attitude, one which comes not so much from the Bible as from tradition.'

'You mean a kind of Old Testament attitude, based on the Old Testament laws? They put restrictions on women, didn't they?'

'That's another common fallacy on the matter. In fact there isn't that much difference in principle between the two Testaments on this subject. The differences are not between the Old and New Testaments, but between the Bible as a whole and those who derive their thinking from outside of it. Did you know that the Old Testament had laws to protect women from men who abused their authority? Did you know that in some cases the Old Testament gave women the right

to inherit property? It was discovering things like this that
liberated my mind more than anything else – more even than
Women's Lib! The view that women are inferior, that they're
incapable of leadership or roles of that kind, doesn't come
from the Bible at all. It comes originally from the way the
rabbis interpreted the Bible and the things they added to it.
If Christ found women in a downgraded position, it was not
because the Scriptures had put them there. It was their
teachers who had done that. It was they who relegated
women to a position of inferiority – not Moses and the
patriarchs, not the kings and prophets. And there's a vast
array of Old Testament women who did pretty well all the
things men did in public life, and succeeded. So even to claim
the authority of the Old Testament for making women
inferior is wide of the mark.'

'And when Jesus came along he put all this right again,
did he?' Sarah asked.

'In a way, yes. He was not being a revolutionary on this
matter; he just sought to restore the position to what it had
been before the rabbis came along. Unfortunately their ideas
had rather caught on and weren't easy to break. And the rest
of the world was infected with the Greek view that women
were mere chattels. Later on came Islam, which virtually
banned women from public life altogether. It's these three
strands all woven together that have made up the view we
have inherited – oh, and I forgot! – plus medieval chivalry,
which put women on a kind of pedestal, whether they wanted
it or not. This didn't really elevate them any more than the
Miss World contest does – in fact it was only a more romantic
and mystical view of the same thing. These attitudes have
even permeated our Protestant Christianity and affected our
understanding of the Bible, just as they did in the past. What
the rabbis did in their time is still happening. Unfortunately,
these attitudes have become equated with Scripture, which is
interpreted in their light. So there's a lot to be done if the
wheat is to be separated from the chaff. So, to answer your
original question, no, I can never go right back to the old
ways.'

But Sarah was still not satisfied. 'All right. Let's say we've got our attitude right, and we've disentangled ourselves from the clutter of tradition. The texts are still there which say that the man was made first and the woman was made out of the man. And Paul himself says this proves the woman is under man's authority and must be quiet and submissive. You haven't told me what you think about these texts from the standpoint of your fresh outlook. Do you think maybe he had to gear his teaching to the culture of his day? You did say this was the general view among Jews and Greeks alike, so perhaps he was just a child of his times, and now that people's attitudes have changed we are free from these restrictions. Is that what you think?'

'The answer to those questions is "No". It wasn't Paul who was bound to the culture of his day. It's other people who have interpreted him in the light of *their* culture. People have assumed these passages mean certain things and have built up a view of the relationship between the sexes on these assumptions. If we can only disentangle ourselves from these assumptions, we can see the passages in a different light. But it would be good if we looked at the words themselves instead of just going on our memories. Memories can be rather convenient – they can forget the bits that embarrass us! There's a Bible on the shelf just behind you, Sarah. Bring it over here and sit next to me and we'll look at it together.'

Sarah reached the Bible down and came and sat with her aunt on the sofa, waiting to be instructed. 'Let's begin with that famous phrase of Peter's which has become almost a slogan for male chauvinism – misquoted, like most slogans. It doesn't say "the weaker sex" but "the weaker vessel". Paul is called a "vessel", in fact "a chosen vessel", so there's nothing derogatory about it. Now where is it? Chapter 3 of the first epistle, I think . . . yes, here we are, in verse 7: "Treat them with respect as the weaker partner." This New International Version does not use the word "vessel", as you see. But the important word is "weaker". Now why is it assumed that "weaker" means "inferior"? Couldn't it mean the exact opposite? Isn't a fragile glass or porcelain ornament better and more valuable than an unbreakable plastic one? Not that I'm suggesting a woman is an ornament! That idea is part of the trouble! Nor that she is superior because physically weaker! I suppose we could even argue about whether she *is* physically weaker. Bearing children requires much strength. And I believe it's true that on average women outlive men. In any case he doesn't say he is talking about *physical* weakness. He is talking about a married woman's relationship with her husband, so perhaps he means she is in a weaker *position* because she is not the head of the relationship. Good preachers always tell us to see texts in their contexts. The first six verses are about the wife being submissive, because it's her duty to God. She's to be like . . .'

'Like Sarah! So that's why they gave me my name!'

'Well, perhaps that comes into it a bit, but they do like the name for other reasons, I know that. However, the bit we're looking at is addressed to the husband, although it's against the background of what is said to the wife. The husband is not to take advantage of his position as head. He is not to bully her, but respect her: "Treat them with respect as the weaker partner." Peter says that a wife who behaves in the way he describes is highly valued by God. Look at verse 4: "A gentle and quiet spirit which is of great worth in God's sight". So the husband is to realize what a treasure he has in such a wife and not abuse her by dominating her, nor, on the other hand, by adopting a condescending attitude to her. He is to look on her as a fellow-heir with him – "heirs with you of the gracious gift of life", which means that from the spiritual standpoint she is his equal. It's only for domestic purposes that the one is put above the other.'

'I see what you're getting at,' said Sarah, 'and I like it. It's much easier to accept put like that.'

'I'm not saying dogmatically that this is what Peter meant. After all, I'm no expert, nor am I entitled to be. I've never had ambitions to occupy a pulpit – it's not my place. But that doesn't stop me learning from books and even assessing them critically. I'm not claiming that this is original thinking on my part, either. But it appeals to me, and it makes as much sense as the other view which sees in it the superiority of the husband. I think it makes more sense. And we've only taken the words as they stand in the passage: we haven't imported any thoughts or attitudes from outside, at least I don't think we have.'

'No, I think you've been entirely fair. So far, so good. But I'm still in trouble about the question of the order of creation. That sounds very chauvinistic to me!'

'Well then, let's have another look at it. But we'll have to go right back to the beginning, to Genesis chapter 1.'

'It's with Genesis 2 that my problems begin, where it describes the creation of the woman. Of course, there *are* problems in Genesis 1, but not sexist ones!'

'This is where so many go wrong. It's the old mistake of not starting far enough back, and so not getting the whole story. Genesis 2 is not the first reference to the creation of woman. Look at chapter 1, verses 27 and 28.'

So Sarah read out: 'So God created man in his own image, in the image of God he created him; male and female he created them. God blessed them and said to them, "Be fruitful and increase in number, fill the earth, and subdue it. Rule over . . ."'

'That'll do, thanks. You see the point? Before it describes the creation of the two separately, it describes them together. It says that "man" is created male and female in the image of God. So in a sense woman *is* man. There's no need to get steamed up over who has the name – it belongs to both! And then there's the commission to "fill the earth and subdue it" – they are to do it *together*. And together they "rule", which means the woman does have authority in many realms. Are you with me so far?'

Sarah nodded and her aunt went on, 'Now we're ready to look at chapter 2, which we must read in the light of what we've just been saying, not as if it were a completely fresh account, as is sometimes done. Much of this chapter is a

description of the man on his own, without the woman. God
draws attention to this in verse 18 – do you see? "It is not
good for the man to be alone." Then it describes him
beginning to rule over the other creatures by giving them
names. But when it comes to the task of increasing in number
and filling the earth with his own kind, he's quite unable to
do it without help. You see?'

'Yes, I do. The fact that the woman is created second
doesn't mean she is less necessary. In fact it means the
opposite – man cannot do his job without her. Now I see why
you took me back to Genesis 1 and pointed out that God's
purpose was a partnership between the two.'

'Right. And if you go in the other direction, on to the end
of chapter 2, this confirms it. "Adam said, 'This is now bone
of my bones and flesh of my flesh; she shall be called
"woman", for she was taken out of man.' For this reason a
man will leave his father and mother, and will be united to
his wife, and they will become one flesh." So man is not
complete in himself; he can't fulfil God's commission on his
own, he's got to cleave to his wife. By the way, that doesn't
mean that everyone has got to marry or else they're only half
human! But I think we'd better leave that subject to another
occasion or we'll only get confused! Are you still with me?'

'Yes, that's all very clear and logical so far. But there's still
the problem that Paul seems to understand it in a different
way. You know, that passage where he talks about the order
of creation. I forget just where it comes.'

'I know the one you mean. It's in 1 Timothy. I think it's at
the end of chapter 2.'

Sarah turned the pages over. 'Yes, here we are – verse 11:
"A woman should learn in quietness and full submission. I
do not permit a woman to teach or to have authority over a
man; she must be silent. For Adam was formed first, then
Eve." There it is, you see, Paul doesn't talk about equality
and partnership but authority and submission. It sounds like
a different view of Genesis from the one you've just given me.'

'Wait a minute. Again we must look at the whole chapter.

What's it all about?'

'Well, it seems to be about aspects of church worship, and who does what.'

'That's right, in fact the whole book is on church matters. It's not about the home, or society, just the church. And Paul is not giving a full exposition of Genesis, only appealing to it to confirm his point about order in the church. He is saying that women should not preach in the church, nor have positions which give them authority over men. I fully accept that. But what I don't accept is what is often added, or at least implied, that this makes women inferior. That is not the reason for this regulation. It is simply that God in his wisdom has decided there is to be a certain order, and to emphasize it he has written it into our very creation. But remember these are only rules for the church; they don't mean women are to be denied other roles traditionally associated with men, such as posts in management or politics. That's where the sexism comes in and builds more on the passage than it actually says.'

'Well, that's cleared that up,' said Sarah, 'but there's still the vexed question of Eve being first in sin, which is what Paul says here: "Adam was not the one deceived; it was the woman who was deceived and became a sinner." And doesn't this tie up with the bit in Genesis 3 about the curse on the woman?' Sarah fumbled with the pages until she found the place. Then she read out: ' "To the woman he said, 'I will greatly increase your pains in childbearing; with pain you will give birth to children. Your desire will be for your husband and he will rule over you.' " This means a bit more than just keeping her out of the pulpit, doesn't it?'

'Just a moment. Neither Genesis nor Paul say that the Fall was all the fault of the woman. Paul is not assigning the blame here. The place where he does that is Romans 5. That's where he answers the question of who brought sin into the world. And his answer is, "Sin entered the world through one man". And "man" here is "man" in the sense of Genesis 1, verses 26 and 27 – male and female together.'

'Then isn't he being inconsistent with himself when he blames the woman here in 1 Timothy?'

'Not at all. Take another look at it. Is he blaming Eve, or is he in fact excusing her? He says she did it because she was deceived, that is, she was tricked by the serpent's craft. That is exactly what Genesis 3 describes. And don't forget Genesis 2: when God issued the prohibition against the tree Eve was not in existence. That was why she was more open to deception – she had not heard the prohibition direct from the mouth of God. But Adam had, which is why Paul says he was not the one deceived. How could he be? He knew exactly what it was all about. Yet he still did it, with his eyes wide open, knowing full well what the consequences would be.'

'Well, what's the point of this, then? I don't get it. I don't see why Paul brings it in here at all.'

'Well, remember what Paul is talking about here – order in the church, nothing else. He is giving an example of what happened the first time that order was reversed, when the man let the woman take the lead in the things of God, instead of leading her himself. Adam had obviously taught Eve about the tree and how God had forbidden them to eat of it. Eve disregarded his teaching, and instead taught *him* how nice it was and how good it would be for him. He listened to her and upset the applecart. This is what happens in the church if we reverse God's appointed order.'

'I see. Yes, that figures. But what does this mean about her being kept safe, or saved through childbirth? Has that got something to do with the curse in Genesis 3?'

'Yes, I think it has, although I can't be absolutely certain what the connection is. When the authorities don't agree and find it difficult, who am I to lay down dogmatically what a passage of Scripture means? I'm not a theologian or professional Bible scholar, and these passages, especially this one about being saved in childbirth, are a problem to the most learned scholars. But I'll tell you how I see it at the moment. Let's take Genesis 3: 16 first of all. We'll set aside for the moment the bit about the pains of childbirth, except just to notice it's there, since it may help us when we come on to 1 Timothy. There are many interpretations of these words: "Your desire will be for your husband, and he will rule over you." A book I read pointed out how similar these words are to what God said to Cain in the next chapter. Where is it, now?'

'Do you mean this in verse 7: "If you do what is right, will you not be accepted? But if you do not do what is right, sin is crouching at your door; it desires to have you, but you must master it"? '

'Yes, that's it. This translation makes the matter much clearer than the old one. That sounded as if it meant Cain would rule over Abel, who would submit to him. This one makes it clear that God is speaking about Cain mastering his own sin while sin is trying to master him. The book explained it like this: "Sin desires to master you" – rather like what Jesus said to Peter: "Satan desires to have you" – "sin desires to master you, but you must master it." Now if we apply this to Genesis 3: 16, we come up with the following meaning: "As a result of your action, Eve, the balance of nature has become upset. The result is that instead of gladly accepting your position in relation to your husband, you will desire to usurp it – to upset the balance and reverse the order, just as you did with the fruit of the tree, when you led your husband, instead of letting him lead you. Now it will be part of your nature to want to take the lead and have the authority. But you won't succeed, because I'm going to reimpose his authority: "He will rule over you." Only from now on it won't be such a happy arrangement. Instead of glad submission on your part there will be bitter rebellion, and instead of loving, gentle, wise leadership on his part, there will be tyranny." I thought this interpretation made excellent sense, and so far as I know no one has come up with a better one.'

'I agree,' said Sarah, 'and it's certainly true to life. This is exactly how the relationship between the sexes seems to work out. It's a kind of vicious circle: women resent men being over them, and they rebel. This makes the man reimpose his authority with greater force. The women rebel even more, and so it goes on.'

'That's it exactly! You've got the message. Now I suppose you want to know what this reference to childbirth means at the end of 1 Timothy 2?'

'Yes please. Here it says, "Women will be kept safe through childbirth if they continue in faith, love and holiness, with propriety." In the Authorized Version it says, "saved in childbearing" which I've always thought sounds peculiar. And I'm not completely happy with the explanations I've heard so far. Does it mean "saved" spiritually – saved from sin? If so it seems to fortify the view that women must marry and have children if they want to please God; there doesn't seem to be any other place or role for them. I think the folks at home incline to this view. And the only alternative seems to be that it means being kept safe or "preserved" physically. This seems to be the view of this translation. If they obey God, or, as it says here, "if they continue in faith, love and holiness with propriety," then they won't die in childbirth. But the trouble is they do – even Christian women. And on the other hand non-Christian women who don't fulfil the conditions are also kept safe. There isn't any distinction as to who survives. So I'm a bit baffled.'

'Quite understandably! You're not alone either. I don't pretend to have the final answer, but I think there is an alternative to the other two views. Going back to Genesis 3, we noticed that verse 16, about the curse on woman, refers in particular to childbirth. This was to be the woman's contribution to carrying out God's command to fill the earth, which the man can't do without her. Now the Fall has affected the woman's task of childbearing, just as it has affected the man's task of cultivating the earth because the ground has become cursed with thorns and so on. But in spite of its laboriousness he still performs his task. It's the same with the woman: in spite of the pain and sorrow involved she still carries out her function. What Paul seems to be saying is that if she accepts all this from God, trusts him and obeys him by "continuing in faith, love and holiness" she will be saved from this curse. This is not so much the curse of pain as the curse of rebelling against her position in relation to her husband. If she honours God by accepting the situation from him and trusting him in spite of it, then God will honour her by keeping her from being resentful and jealous. Instead of that she co-operates by carrying out the task he gave her and the man at creation. If she does that she can still experience the *glory* of childbearing which God wrote into her very name – "Eve, mother of all living". How will that do?'

'It still sounds as though it just means we've got to marry and have children and generally knuckle down. I can't see that it leaves us much better off than we were before. It certainly doesn't help my situation.'

'I was rather afraid you might look at it like that. The thing to remember is that Paul is speaking about women who are married or thinking in terms of marriage. Actually there are several passages which clearly show that marriage is by no means the only function of a woman or the only acceptable course open to her. And no one teaches this more than Paul; he's even accused of discouraging marriage! But he obviously accepts that the majority of women marry and have children, so he is generalizing. But there is a sense in which this teaching at the end of 1 Timothy 2 is relevant to everybody. What I mean is this: what happens when women rebel against male authority? As I discovered, they attack the institutions of marriage, the family and the home, and seek to overthrow them, because that is where women are made most dependent and submissive. Paul is saying that this negative attitude won't solve the problem of male domination. What it will do is to overthrow society altogether; then everyone suffers. So what we should do is to support these God-given institutions, whether we marry or not. If there are abuses we must try to deal with them from within, not destroy the whole thing because some misuse it.'

'And is this what you did yourself, Aunty?'

'Yes, it was. Once I had accepted the principle of a God-given order, I began to understand the Scriptures afresh. On the one hand, I saw that the feminist approach went too far, because it is atheistic and evolutionary. On the other hand, I came to see that the Bible does not after all give any support to sexism and male domination, not even to chivalry! The real answer is the partnership approach which was present at the beginning – that both are indispensable and should co-operate, not compete. And Paul's words to Timothy give us the hope that it can happen, in spite of the curse. But only where there is faith and obedience, which is why the gospel is the only real answer to Women's Lib. Christians must follow God's way in their homes. God in his wisdom has ordained that the man should be over the woman. We can't get away from that. But it is not like a tyrant or a boss: it's a headship of responsibility and love.'

Eve breathed in and out deeply. 'That's about the best I can do, Sarah. I hope it's been of some help.'

'It really has. Things are beginning to fall into place now. I'm beginning to see a pattern and this is helping me to fit in the awkward pieces, rather like a jigsaw. But I don't know what I can do about it. Even if I manage to see things like this, it doesn't mean my parents will. So I don't know if things will really be any better.'

'I think they will be better because there is nothing more liberating than a clear understanding. You can see all sides now. You can understand why your parents are as they are. Their understanding of the Bible's teaching on these matters is to an extent due to a traditional way of looking at them and practising them. One generation tends to follow the one before, instead of thinking things out for itself and searching the Scriptures to see whether things are as they have been told. But you are free from this and can think more positively. This will help you in the future even though you're not in a position to do a lot about it now. At least it should make you more tolerant in the present and more hopeful about the future. And that's a lot. I wish someone had told me the

things I have been able to tell you, which I had to learn the
hard way. But perhaps God allowed me to go through so
many experiences so that one day I could help others with
similar problems. And what we've discussed is really only
one of them. There are so many problems peculiar to women.
And what isn't always realized is that the Bible has the
answer to all of them. The trouble is that this is not being
brought out as it should be. Books and sermons on women
seem so often to be negative. But I mustn't go on all night.
You've got enough to keep your mind busy for the time
being.'

'You can say that again! But I've enjoyed our talk, and
thank you, Aunty, for being so free with me. I'd better go. I
was only supposed to be popping in for half an hour!'

2.
Whom God hath joined

It was not only Sarah whose mind was racing that evening after the long conversation over tea between her and her aunt. Eve was still standing at her front door a long time after Sarah had disappeared from sight. She had been taken back some forty years to relive her past life, almost as if it were a rerun film. Sarah could have been herself at much the same age.

'I only hope', she said to herself as she made her way back to the room in which they had been having tea, 'that what we talked about will help her to come to terms with these things and avoid the mistakes I made.'

Whenever she thought about her 'mistakes', the one that towered above all the others was her first marriage. It had come about in the face of a long and bitter dispute with her parents. The very thought of it, even after all these years, sent a shudder through her body. Then she collected herself. 'I certainly learned a lot from that, although at the time I was in no mood to learn anything.' In the end it had been reduced to a battle of wills: who has the right to choose who does what and especially who marries whom? Who runs my life? What right have parents to impose their wills on their children? There had been other battles of will, as she had just been telling Sarah, but they had been mere skirmishes compared with this one.

Underneath, however, it had been far more than that, as she had come to realize with more mature reflection. It had been two contradictory approaches to marriage on a collision course. 'We should have discussed these approaches at greater depth, more calmly and objectively, and less personally and passionately. But, like so many, we weren't very good at that. I suppose we were so personally involved and afraid of losing what seemed so important, that we were blinded. We were all so sure we were right. I knew I was right, and that meant they were wrong. They knew they were right, which meant I was wrong. The idea that it might be possible to be both right and wrong at the same time never occurred to us. It was all so simple. They had their biblical and Christian view, and I my liberated and enlightened view. One must be right and the other wrong. We had to defend our positions at all costs. And so instead of discussion it was charge and countercharge, backed up with whatever arguments and proofs lay to hand.

'It was all rather like a court case – one speaks on one side, mustering all the evidence in support of its case while ignoring or playing down anything that could throw doubt on it. The other proceeds to pick holes in the case, producing its witnesses to back it up. Then at the end the jury has to pronounce one right and the other wrong, for whoever heard of a jury saying there were arguments on both sides? It was like that with us, except that we had no judge to see fair play! It was like the House of Commons without the Speaker. Both sides have made up their minds how they're going to vote before the debate starts, and so don't listen to the arguments except to note how they're going to answer them. There is no question of trying to see one another's point of view. Why is it always like this? It's the same with industrial disputes – two sides, each knowing it's right and determined that the other gives way, never questioning its own position. Is there something peculiar about the British, that we seem to conduct all our important business in this adversarial fashion? Does everyone in the world go on like this? Surely Christians ought to rise above it, especially as the matters we deal with are so deep and go beyond mere reason, observation and experience. We need each other to check or expand our own thinking. But if we do it at all, we do it too late, as I know to my cost.'

She began to go over in her mind the ground they had had to cover to make their points. It had been no less than the whole nature of marriage – in fact it went deeper than that, to the whole relationship between the sexes. What was marriage anyway? How did it come about? Was it a permanent relationship, 'till death do us part'? Was it exclusive? Must there never be anyone else ever, even temporarily? Was it wrong to break up and start again with someone else? And there had been other issues: was it necessary to go through a formal ceremony? Did it all have to be signed and sealed? Must it be public? Wasn't it a private matter between two people? Couldn't they just live together and split up if it didn't work out, avoiding the trauma of the divorce court? And did the couple have to hold the same beliefs, whether religious, social or whatever? Wasn't it enough to love each other? This had in fact been the catalyst in her own case, although at the time she had maintained that the difference was between her beliefs and her parents', rather than between hers and her husband's, for she had abandoned most of her parents' beliefs for the Women's Lib. position.

'Yes,' she said to herself, 'our attitudes did seem irreconcilable. Probably they were, but we should never have made it so obvious by the way we went about it. It was all too deep and important to reduce to a court case – they accusing me of sinful rebellion against God and themselves, and I countering by accusing them of being narrow-minded and having old-fashioned ideas which they had no right to impose on me. Instead of just pronouncing judgements we should have tried to think it out, asking ourselves, "What is the truth about these things?" Well, I learned this in time, but it was the hard way.'

Her reverie deepened and the whole incident began to pass through her mind. It had all arisen, she considered, out of the restrictions of her home. This had not been unhappy in itself. She had got on well with her brothers and sisters. Her parents, although strict, had never been physically cruel. They had taken great interest in her activities, especially at school. Nor had they been averse to a bit of romping and fun.

They had spent enjoyable family holidays and the occasional outing. It was just that they seemed to have a very small circle of acquaintances, which consisted almost entirely of Christians of a particular type. If they had people in their home they were always from the church or some similar church to their own. If they as a family visited another home, it was the same thing in reverse. As Eve passed through her teens she realized that apart from her school companions she had hardly ever met anyone who was not a Christian. Nor was she encouraged to socialize out of school, even with her school friends – rather the reverse. This stifled her. She felt she wanted to break loose and meet fresh people with other topics of conversation than church matters. This was not so that she could copy them, but simply to discover what they were like, and why they were kept at arm's length, as if they were somehow infectious.

Consequently, when she went away to university, she resolved not to keep herself to the group of Christians with whom she had been put in touch. She would mix freely with all and sundry, join societies and participate in a variety of activities. She had at all costs to meet new people – interesting people. In particular she wanted closer contact with the feminist movement, which had begun to attract her before she left home, as she had been explaining to Sarah. These people were voicing the questions that had been gradually formulating themselves in her mind during her adolescence – questions to which they had very definite and exciting answers. These answers she very quickly came to accept herself, and *for* herself. She was not going to be content with a place in society inferior to that of men. She was determined that any work she undertook, any activity she engaged in, any relationship she entered into, would be on the basis of equality. All her feminist friends were agreed on those principles. It gave her a sense of freedom she had never known before.

She soon began to make new friends, few of whom were Christian in the sense in which she had been taught to understand the term – friends of both sexes. Eventually she became involved in a close relationship with a male student also on the Economics course. Frank had come from a background very different from her own – not socially, but inasmuch as he had not been given any particular religious orientation. His parents had no convictions and made no attempt to practise either Christianity or any other faith. Frank had nothing against which to react and consequently was tolerant of all religious persuasions, and of people with none at all. The only ones he could not tolerate were the intolerant ones! To him religion was an entirely personal affair. Beliefs and observances should not be imposed, even by parents. The idea of a 'Christian country' or any kind of state religion, in which it was assumed that one particular code was the truth, was anathema to him. The same applied to the home. Parents had no right to channel their children's thoughts in a particular direction, nor even tacitly to expect them to follow in their own footsteps. This was nothing short of brainwashing. It applied even where they were only expected to conform to the externals. To Frank the sight of family cars drawing up outside churches and expectorating mum and dad and the kids all in their Sunday best horrified him. It made him feel quite sick, he said, to see them smiling and shaking hands with the other religious types as they went inside, and he usually went out of his way to avoid passing churches on a Sunday morning.

Frank took an anti-authoritarian line in general. He was not an anarchist as such but felt there were far too many laws which inhibited freedom of movement, choice and even thought. People should be taught to think things out for themselves, to work out the consequences of their decisions and actions. This, he believed, would be a far more effective deterrent to crime and disorder than large numbers of laws with all the paraphernalia required to enforce them – police, lawyers, courts, judges, prisons, to say nothing of politicians! Unwritten laws he liked even less. The idea of people following each other like sheep, reproducing the customs of previous generations as if tradition were something genetically inherited, depressed him more than almost anything else.

As Eve had met him when her own thinking was undergoing a radical revolution, she was quite strongly influenced by him. His company felt like a breeze blowing through the open door of a greenhouse. Perhaps what meant most to her was his sympathy with her own position – something she had no hope of finding at home, even from her brothers. Being opposed to the idea of imprisoning people in rigid strait-jackets of thought and behaviour, Frank was happiest when he could help to set someone free from such restrictions. To him Eve was struggling to break out of the cocoon of her religious upbringing, and he could teach her to fly. He was all for the feminist movement. To him it was ridiculous, if not actually criminal, that a few biological differences should affect virtually everything in the life of a woman. The sooner all that was changed, the better. He was too occupied with radical political groups in the university to be active in any Women's Lib. organizations, but he was all for what Eve's friends were doing. In fact there was a cross-fertilization, not only of ideas, but also of methods of implementing them, between the two groups and several students belonged to both.

The mutual sympathy between Eve and Frank ripened into love and by the time the end of their courses came into view and they were looking to the future, they thought increasingly in terms of sharing it together. Up to this time she had tried to keep Frank at arm's length from her parents, feeling they would not approve of him even as a friend for her, let alone as a potential husband. They had met him a few times on their visits to Eve, but had not found much common ground with him and had seemed rather awkward in his company. What they would have thought had they known the depth and seriousness of the relationship, she hardly dared imagine, and so far she had managed to avoid revealing it. However, as the time drew near for her to leave

the university the matter became more pressing. In order to
break them in gently it would be best if something could be
said well in advance. The opportunity for this came when, on
the night before she left home for her last term, her father
asked about her plans for the future. At first she talked
vaguely about the options – further education, research,
career training or immediate application for a post in a bank
or business. But in the end, taking her courage in both hands,
she said, 'Quite a lot depends on whether Frank and I decide
to team up.'

It was obviously a bombshell, not because it was totally
unexpected, but because it was the thing they had more and
more come to fear. They knew a certain amount about how
her views had developed and about the friendship with
Frank. The rest they just imagined in day-dreams and
sometimes in nightmares. The worst thought had always
been, what would come of it? Would it all fizzle out at the end
of the course, or would it ripen into a permanent
relationship? They knew that if the latter happened it would
be the end of her life as a Christian. This was the cloud that
had hung over them for the past two years and had thickened
week by week. Their worst fear was that Eve would say
something like what she had just said. And now it had
happened they reeled under it. The realization of long-felt
fears is far more painful than sudden shocks. A fear that
comes to pass is the climax of a long period of uncertainty.
This has the effect, on the one hand of exaggerating the
significance of the issue out of all proportion to its real
importance, and on the other of weakening the emotional
resistance to it. Far from enabling the system to prepare
itself, it does the opposite – it breaks down all the defences
and leaves the person in a state of emotional collapse. Still
being young and inexperienced at the time, Eve knew
nothing of this process and therefore had too little sympathy
for the drastic effect this news had on her parents. Although
she had only put it forward as a possibility, the very fact that
one fear had come to pass gave them a sense of inevitability
that the rest would soon follow.

And so the great debate had begun. It was her mother who first broke the shocked silence that had greeted her words. 'But you can't possibly marry him! He's an atheist, isn't he?'

'Well,' replied Eve, 'more of an agnostic. But he's not against religion. He just thinks everyone should be allowed to make up their own mind and not have things forced on them by others. He doesn't insist on my sharing his beliefs, so why should I expect him to share mine?' ('Whatever they are,' she had thought to herself, although not said aloud for fear of making things worse.)

Her father's reply therefore took what she said at its face value – that she still held the beliefs in which she had been brought up: 'That isn't the point. To agree to differ on these things is not enough in marriage. You need to be united at every level, especially the deepest one of all – the spiritual. Marriage is partnership, union, you have to be able to share everything. God is the most important person in your life, yet you won't be able to share this with Frank. That's why these marriages never really work, or, if they work as marriages, it's always at the expense of the Christian partner's spiritual life. They can't pray together, don't go to church together. So one has to give way to the other. The unbeliever can't suddenly start being a Christian if he hasn't got it in him, so the believer is the one who has to give way, especially if this is the woman. Then, what about the children? How are they going to know what is right? They're going to be pulled in two directions at once, and that's not fair on them.'

By this time her mother had had time to collect her thoughts and added, 'The Bible says we shouldn't be unequally yoked together. It says we should marry in the Lord. You would be disobeying God and couldn't expect his blessing. And don't think you can expect to win him over. That hardly ever happens, especially where it's the woman who is the Christian. Don't forget you have to promise to obey your husband. How can you obey someone who doesn't obey God? You can't serve two masters. How could you possibly be happy in such a situation?'

This was not the first time Eve had heard these

arguments, of course. The idea of a Christian marrying
someone outside the fold was taboo in her church, and she
remembered how one or two girls had gone off in disgrace
when their engagements had been announced. It always
seemed to be the girls who were affected, she had noticed,
perhaps because they outnumbered the boys by about three
to one, and some of them had little chance of marrying
Christians anyway. She had felt vaguely unhappy about this
but hadn't known the answer. Neither did she have any
answer to the points her parents had just put to her. Her
reaction was simply that these things no longer applied to
her; they only applied if the marriage was 'mixed' – between
a Christian and a non-Christian. If neither was a Christian
the case collapsed. There was only one line of reply she could
make, and with a thumping heart and trembling all over she
said, 'What you have said may be quite right, but it's not for
me. I don't think I am a Christian in the way you've been
talking about it – perhaps I'm not in any sense. At any rate, I
don't want to be bound by doctrines or the Bible. I want to be
free to think things out for myself. And I shan't want to be
committed to church-going or a stereotyped pattern of
behaviour. I would never expect my children to follow me as
you obviously expect us to follow you. And Frank thinks the
same way, so we aren't unequally yoked – quite the opposite,
in fact.'

Whether or not they had feared something of this sort, Eve
did not really know. They must have had some idea of the
change in her attitude to Christian matters over the past few
years, especially since going up to university. True, she had
continued to attend services with them during vacations, but
she had been different. Perhaps they had hoped it was just a
phase she was passing through, a reaction to her somewhat
sheltered upbringing, a period of adjustment to the outside
world. Perhaps they were beginning to realize they had not
prepared her sufficiently for it and therefore were partly
responsible for what was happening. So maybe they had
been leaving her to work it out of her system. But the context

in which it had now come up was unexpected and came as a second bombshell. For instead of it wearing off, she was going to make it permanent by marrying Frank. It was their turn now to be stumped for an answer, and some moments elapsed before her father broke the silence.

'You think like that now because you're under the influence of Frank and the Women's Liberationists. But you may change again before long; then you would regret having taken such a big step. Don't you think it would be better to give it more time before you do something so irrevocable? Wouldn't it be better to sort your ideas out and get them straight, rather than give it all up just like that? It's all a bit sudden, isn't it?'

'It's not sudden at all. You must have had some idea what's been going through my mind for several years now. It isn't only since I've been at university that I've been unhappy about the place of women in society. It's this impression we're given that we're second-class human beings, only fit for certain jobs and activities, always under man's authority. Either they dominate us, or they treat us gently because we're so delicate. Either way, we're made to feel inferior. And it begins at school. We're put into different schools because we can't compete with boys mentally and physically. I know I went to a mixed school, but that was worse in some ways because it underlined the differences. We couldn't do "male" subjects like woodwork, or play football. Boys were always called by their surnames, but girls only by their Christian names, in case their delicate feelings were hurt, I suppose! Then what jobs are open to us? Things like secretaries, waitresses, shop assistants – working under men and serving men! So we get driven into marriage to get away from the drudgery. And what then? We have to "obey and serve" men again – for life! And it's Christianity that's to blame by teaching this is all "God's will". And what can women do in the church? Make the tea, arrange the flowers, clean the building – and perhaps have a few small children to teach if they're very good girls. If that's Christianity I don't

think I want it. It's only in the last few years I've begun to feel
free at all, meeting people who think in the same way. And
Frank regards me as his equal. He encourages me to get into
some management job, and he doesn't just mean work my
way up to a headmistress or matron. He's not going to ask me
to obey him if we get married; we'll be on equal terms. So can
you blame me?'

This outburst of Eve's put her mother on the defensive.
She had just heard a description of her own life as a woman,
about which she felt completely differently from her
daughter. 'The trouble with you, Eve,' she said, 'is that
you're putting the cart before the horse. It's true this is God's
will for women, although not in the way you've described it,
but, as in everything else, we can only accept God's will and
see its wisdom if we trust and love him. We all hate God's
commands by nature and rebel against them. Our nature has
to be changed, then we see things differently. These ideas
you've got come from people who reject God; that's why they
think as they do. Perhaps I would have been the same, but
God graciously worked in my heart to show me his will is
best. So if he says I should be subordinate, I don't resent it.
Obeying your father is just another way of obeying God. I'm
quite happy to do it and I don't feel bitter as you and your
friends seem to.'

'Yes, but we're *all* expected to do it, whether we're
Christians or not, whether we want to or not. Even if it's right
for Christians to be like that, why should we all have to? That
only serves to put us off Christianity and God. This is
another objection I've got to being a Christian: everybody
seems to be expected to live as they do and obey the same
laws. It's easy for Christians to do this because their hearts
are in it. As you've just said, Mother, human nature is
against God's laws and has to be changed. Yet we're
expected to conform even without that change of nature. It
doesn't seem fair that God should only give some people the
will to obey him, yet expect everyone else to follow the Bible

in exactly the same way. If God is like this, I'm not sure I really want to know him.'

The deep theological problem Eve had raised stumped them both, but they seized on the more personal point she had made at the end. 'It's terribly hurtful for your mother and me to hear you speak like that after all we've tried to do for you. It's not just because we're Christians we want you to follow this way, but because it's best for you. We've . . .'

Eve was by now full of indignation, which had driven out the reticence and timidity with which she had begun, and she now interrupted her father. 'I wish you hadn't spent all my life doing what *you* think is best for me, instead of letting me find out for myself. You've always made my decisions for me: "Don't do *this*, or *that* will happen." If I did anything off my own bat, it was "There you are, I told you so, you should have listened to me." It might have been better if I'd been allowed to make a few mistakes, to explore and experiment, to learn by trial and error. Anyway, that's what I'm going to do this time, and you won't stop me. If I'm wrong, I'll find out in my own way and time. I'm fed up with everyone doing everything for me for my own good.'

Eve had not intended to go as far as that. She had made it sound as though the marriage was as good as settled, which was very far from being the case. But she was determined to declare her independence. This was her first campaign for Women's Lib. and she wasn't going to lose it. She had to prove a point – to her parents, her friends and, above all, to herself. That was her dominant thought as she went out of the room and made her way upstairs, half wondering if this would be the last time she would make that journey. As she lay sleepless in bed she had very little sympathy for the middle-aged couple she had left broken-hearted downstairs, weeping, talking and praying far into the night.

But now, all these years later, with two marriages behind her, as well as a variety of other experiences, she could look back at it more objectively. Although she had not regarded

herself as a Christian at the time, in her parents' minds this
had been the main issue. They had never really been able to
bring themselves to believe that one of their own children
should be completely cast away by God, after all their
prayers, instruction, training and example. To them, a child
brought up in a Christian home was well on the way to
salvation, and in normal circumstances the rest would come
in God's good time and way. Certainly Eve was in a
completely different position in their eyes from someone like
Frank who had had no opportunity to discover what the
gospel really was. Although the two of them seemed to be
agreed in their outlook, Eve's parents doubted whether the
agreement went very deep and were afraid things would not
really work out. The strength of Eve's background and
upbringing would in time emerge as the chief influence.
Then she would realize her mistake, but too late.

Events had proved they were only too right, since when
Eve had done a good deal of thinking on the whole subject.
Over the years she had seen others come to grief through
intermarriage with non-Christians. In some cases, where one
of the partners had come from a Christian home, families had
been split. In others, where the Christian partner had no
evangelical background, it had been the end of their spiritual
pilgrimage. Eve could now see the wisdom of what her
parents, and others, had said on this matter. Yet her
experience and study had taught her to look at it in a
somewhat different way. She had thought it over many
times, and now tried to collect her thoughts together.

'I can't help feeling,' she mused, 'that the way it's taught
gives the impression, even if unintentionally, that only
marriage between Christians is true and full marriage. But
surely in the Bible there is only one kind of marriage – the one
that goes back to creation before there was any division in the
human race over religion. Every couple that comes together
for union and companionship is truly and fully married in
God's sight, even if they don't believe he even exists.
"Christian marriage" is not the highest grade, with mixed
marriage a poor second and marriage between non-

Christians third rate. Marriage is marriage, whatever beliefs are held – even about marriage! "Christian marriage", if there is such a thing – since the Bible doesn't speak of it – means marriage between Christians. Of course, there is Christian teaching on marriage and a Christian view of marriage, and it would be wonderful if all who came into marriage were Christians and held that view. But that doesn't make their marriages more valid. It doesn't even mean their marriage is more certain to succeed,' and she sighed as she recalled Christians she knew whose marriages had come to grief. 'Love and marriage are God's gifts to all his creatures, like the works of creation, such as art and music. He was good enough to give us this gift, and normally will be good enough to bless it.'

She reflected again on the way in which Christians tended to put over their condemnation of intermarriage. 'They seem to suggest that it's almost bound to fail – doomed from the start. They assume it is prohibited by God and therefore to go into it is sinful disobedience which God will not bless. They put it on a par with the Ten Commandments or the deity of Christ as an absolute. I'm not sure that it comes among the biblical absolutes and that it is therefore always totally wrong. I have looked carefully at all the passages which are normally advanced and I can't really see that this is so. Much of the reasoning is based on Old Testament texts – the people of Israel not being allowed to marry into tribes not in the covenant. There is the example of Abraham in seeking a wife for his son from his own kindred and not from the Canaanites; and Isaac doing the same for Jacob, in contrast to Esau, whose Hittite wives brought grief to Isaac and Rebekah – but was it *only* because they were Hittites? Then there is God's prohibition on all the Israelites not to marry Canaanites when they entered the promised land. Solomon's marriages to foreign women turned him away from the Lord. Then after the exile they started to intermarry and Ezra and Nehemiah had to force them to divorce their foreign wives.

'But then there's the other side – Moses marrying a

Midianite and then an Ethiopian (that is, if they weren't one
and the same person); Samson marrying a Philistine woman,
which is said to be "of the Lord"; Boaz marrying Ruth, a
Moabitess, who became an ancestor of David. It's not quite
so simple as it's made out to be – there are lots of questions.
In any case, wasn't all this something to do with the nature of
the old covenant? God took one nation to himself out of all
the other nations. If they had intermarried this national
distinction would have become blurred. Of course, it
provides a warning to Christians about the dangers of mixing
religion in marriage. But is the prohibition as absolute for us
as it was for them? Don't we need some New Testament
back-up?'

So she began to recall New Testament passages which
were usually brought into the argument. One came
immediately to mind: 'Be not unequally yoked together with
unbelievers.' Quoting that was supposed to end all
discussion. But did it? Was it not a classic case of getting hold
of a text to back up an argument, while ignoring its context?
Isn't the passage, taken as a whole, a call to Christians to
separate from idolatry? As she saw it, the Corinthians had to
be warned against keeping associations which involved them
in recognizing the idols they were supposed to have
renounced on becoming Christians, particularly by
attending banquets in honour of idols. Now, of course, if a
Christian married an idolater there would be a likelihood of
becoming mixed up in idolatry in some way. The same would
apply today if a Christian married someone of an entirely
different religion. But would it be the same if the other person
had no religion at all, especially where they were
open-minded on the whole question? She doubted whether
Paul had that sort of person in mind; such people did not
exist in the world of his day. Everyone was committed to
some religion or god. The days of free thought and religious
toleration had not dawned. 'What would Paul have said to us
today?' she wondered.

Then, of course, there was the other famous text about marrying 'only in the Lord'. She opened the Bible that was still lying on the arm of the chair where she and Sarah had looked at it together and turned to 1 Corinthians chapter 7. 'There it is in verse 39, almost at the end of this long chapter on marriage questions. There's quite a lot in this chapter, including the case of an actual mixed marriage. He tells them to stay together because the unbelieving partner and the children are "holy" (whatever that means!). Paul's advice is "Don't marry at all" rather than "Don't intermarry"! However, he does allow it to those whose feelings are so strong there would be a danger of immorality if they didn't. And he allows it for a widow, "only in the Lord". What does this mean? Only to a believer in the Lord? If so, it's a pity he didn't make it clearer. The NIV thinks that's what it means, saying, "but he must belong to the Lord". But this is the translators' interpretation of the word "in". He might have meant "in the fear of the Lord" or "by faith in the Lord", meaning she should look to God for his blessing. However, supposing he did mean "to another believer", is he saying it in a legalistic way, laying it down as an absolute command, or is he giving wise pastoral counsel? Surely when the argument is good and the counsel is wise, absolute commands are not really necessary. A true believer who seeks to follow God and glorify him, as well as to satisfy his own wishes, will surely see the difficulties and dangers of marrying out of the Lord. All those things mother and father said to me were quite right – a Christian can't share the deepest things of life with an unbeliever, so they won't be truly united, and so on. All this is true and any Christian should see it. The reason I couldn't accept it at the time was simply because I was unconverted and it didn't seem to apply to me. Had I been marrying a Christian, *he* would have been guilty of marrying out of the Lord.

'Nevertheless, the advice was still good in itself. Yet that doesn't seem to be the only advice the New Testament gives

on marriage. It even has advice for the believing partner of a
mixed marriage, not only from Paul in 1 Corinthians 7 but
from Peter in 1 Peter 3. Of course, it is usually said these
marriages were contracted before the conversion of one
partner took place, which may be so, but we don't know for
certain. Can we really be so dogmatic about this matter?
What brings two people together and keeps them together is
a very mysterious thing, and may sometimes be quite
independent of their religious beliefs. The Bible is clear that
what constitutes marriage is physical union, becoming "one
flesh" rather than "one mind" or "one soul". God is wise
here too, for how far is it possible to be "one mind", even with
another Christian? Sometimes' (and here there came to her
mind some instances of Christians marrying and splitting
up) 'I think this teaching is put across so dogmatically as to
suggest the only thing required for a Christian to have a
successful marriage is that the partner be another Christian –
any Christian will do. It's assumed that because they're
Christians they're bound to be happy, so they don't consider
anything else. But they might be incompatible in other ways.
In fact they may choose a person simply because he or she is a
Christian, letting the head decide rather than the heart.
There may be very little feeling, even physically, and so it
doesn't work. What was it Paul said? "Better to marry than
burn"? Suppose someone burns towards an unbeliever, but
is cold in relation to a Christian? It's not quite so simple as it
sounds. And then is it always possible to be absolutely
certain of the other Christian's spiritual standing? Because
they claim to be a Christian and seem to behave like one
doesn't mean they are really so, or will go on being so. Aren't
the lines a bit blurred here, too? Who decides whether the
other person is truly Christian or not? They themselves? The
one they propose marrying? The parents? The minister?'

Eve was beginning to become confused again, and so put
her train of thought into reverse, coming back to the
arguments against intermarriage. 'The main thing,' she
decided, 'is to put these arguments forward as wise counsels

rather than absolute rules. We have such an inbuilt revulsion against authority, especially when we're young and our heart is set on something or someone, that we automatically reject being dictated to, and refuse to consider a case, simply because we're told we've got to accept it. Rules seem designed to make us abandon the use of our reason – except to make us seek reasons for disregarding them! We need reasoning with, rather than commanding. And why is it only the Christian partner who has to be persuaded? It's always assumed that if anyone loses out it will be the believing partner. The other one is supposed to be on to a good thing, getting someone whose trust can be guaranteed because of their fear of God. But isn't it also bad for the unbeliever to join up with someone of a basically different outlook? Aren't the use of Sunday and things like that going to affect that partner, in the opposite way? And there's the embarrassment of seeing the other person praying and reading the Bible. It isn't only the Christian whose life-style is threatened! The problems are on both sides, so that there's all the more reason for calm thought and discussion to bring all these things to light.'

Of course, in Eve's case at the time this aspect had not been the main issue since she hadn't regarded herself as a Christian entering on a mixed marriage. Yet there had been a problem in this respect since her parents at least treated her as if she were a Christian. This was one of the problems – that Christian parents tend to assume their children are Christians because they themselves are. But they're not really consistent about it. They make it plain on the one hand that they don't inherit salvation and therefore must be born again, but on the other hand expect them to act and think like Christians. They seem to want it both ways – to have their cake and throw it away! There's still a great deal of thinking to be done on this matter of the children of Christian parents. It isn't only paedo-baptists who have problems. It lies under the surface for years and then comes into the open when marriage looms up. They aren't allowed baptism or communion until they're converted, but they're expected to contract Christian marriage. 'I think this was what I was really trying to say all those years ago.'

Her thoughts went back to the events which followed that night when she had stalked out of the room in anger. It had meant that she returned for her last term in a state of cold war against her parents. She remembered how she had gone to see Frank the moment she arrived back at her college to tell him what had transpired.

'This is typical of the arrogance of religious people,' had been his fairly predictable response. 'What right do they have to dictate to us in these matters? Aren't we grown-up people? It's *our* decision about *our* lives, not theirs. They've chosen how they want to live. It's for us to choose how we are going to live. I'm not getting married to *them*; I'm not going to live with *them*. They hardly come into it.'

'I said all that to them, and a lot more. But the question is not what we *think* about it, but what we're going to *do*. It isn't easy to marry when your parents disapprove, especially for the girl. I shall feel torn in half. I can't imagine what it's going to be like telling our relations and church friends and seeing the disapproval in their eyes when they learn that you're not one of them. And what about the wedding day? Is it going to take place in church? You won't want that; they will, unless they wash their hands of me altogether, which will be worse. Someone is going to be upset, and this will create a bad atmosphere. I don't know if I can go through with all that.'

'This is what seems so unfair. It's as though people got married for the benefit of their parents and friends, not for their own happiness. And this wedding business – lots of people you hardly know who just want to get a good time out of it. Where do the feelings and wishes of the couple come in, I'd like to know?'

'I know all that. The thing is what can be done about it?'

Frank's solution to the problem was one he may have been thinking about for some time, but it had certainly never even occurred to Eve. 'There is a way,' he said. 'We just move in together and don't involve anyone else. That gets round all these problems at one stroke. We wouldn't be the first to do that. And after all it isn't the wedding ceremony that makes the marriage. It isn't making vows and signing a register, it's living together when all that's over and forgotten. We can do that and bypass all the red tape. What is there to stop us?'

'Only that it would make things even worse with my family. It's bad enough that I'm thinking of marrying a non-Christian. But to go and "live in sin" with one would be the very last word. It's not that they would make it hard for me out of spite or anything; it would really hurt them. It wouldn't just be a disappointment they would get over; it would really break their hearts. They would feel they'd failed. Their whole aim has been to bring me up prepared for a good Christian husband who with me would raise up another family like their own. I would dash all this to the ground. And they would feel ashamed to look their friends in the face. They would be known as parents of a girl who was living as another man's mistress. I don't think I could do that to them.'

'Perhaps they need something to break them. It might do them good.'

'I don't know. Sometimes I do feel like that. But I don't think I'm brave enough to be the one to do it.'

'You've got to make up your mind where you stand and stick to it, come what may. For the last two years or so you've been saying you believe in personal freedom, especially for women. Well, here's your test, the parting of the ways. It's got to come sometime. You've got to make your choice and have the courage of your convictions.'

Although she felt the force of Frank's arguments enough to be unable to answer them, there was still something that held her back from going along with his suggestion. It wasn't just the fear of how it would affect her family, but something deeper. She wasn't really convinced that 'shacking up' was the answer to the problem. It might have got round the immediate situation but it didn't seem to be a good long-term solution. At the time she didn't really know why she felt like this, it was just a gut reaction. But later she realized what it was that gave her pause. Cohabitation avoided commitment: it left the back door open for escape with the minimum of fuss. Many Christians looked on cohabitation merely as a symptom of permissiveness, a licence for promiscuity, a way of flitting from one partner to another at will. This was not necessarily so. Many such couples remained together longer than some who married. From the company she had kept at university Eve had come to see there was something behind it far deeper than a craze for sex. Many she knew who did this desired stable relationships as much as those who went through marriages. It was not an abandonment of marriage as such, but a feeling that its demands were too great for them. They realized what marriage expected from them more than many who married, especially with the escape route of the divorce court before them. It was because they realized that marriage involved permanency that they shrank from it. Marriage meant monogamy and that was where they drew back. Marriage involved loving someone until death. How could anyone promise to do that when it might mean fifty or sixty years? How could a person guarantee their feelings wouldn't change? How could they guarantee to 'keep themselves only unto' this one person and 'forsake all other'? How could they promise they would stay together whatever happened, through sickness and health, riches and poverty, and everything implied by those words 'better or worse'? Fewer and fewer who took on these things were carrying them out anyway. When things failed to work out there was adultery and they broke up with the inevitable separation and eventual divorce. Where was the difference between this and a couple living together without marriage?

Eve had known of this line of thinking and had been quite strongly drawn to it. But something had always held her back. It was only much later that she had come to realize what it was. Deep down in her, due no doubt to her long acquaintance with the general teaching of the Bible, she saw that monogamy was not some restriction imposed on the human race by a spoil-sport God. It was the only form of sexual relationship in keeping with human nature. This was where her friends were deficient. Most of them were evolutionists and looked on man as a glorified animal, with no essential distinctions from the brute creation, simply more developed. Human sexual behaviour was therefore only a glorified form of animal behaviour. But the biblical view of man as essentially different from and superior to animals meant he needed an altogether higher mode of sex relationship. Monogamy was given him as most appropriate to his nature – ennobling, not restrictive. She was able to go back to the early chapters of Genesis and see them in a fresh light. Man was made in two kinds, not just for sensual pleasure or the propagation of the species, but for the pleasure of companionship in all its aspects, and to provide stability for his offspring, who took so much longer to develop because they had such greater heights to which to attain.

When she had come to see that, other things began to fall into place. There was the teaching of Jesus Christ on marriage. He was not putting forward a Christian standard, a new and higher way for his followers. In fact he said nothing new at all about marriage: he simply got behind all the corruptions and qualifications with which generations of lawmakers and interpreters had hedged it round and went back to the original institution in Genesis 2. Jesus did not set out a form of marriage for Jews or Christians, but for all – for human beings as human beings. Hence he went back to the time they were at their most human – before the Fall. ('Strange, she thought, 'how that word "human" is used to mean someone who accepts weaknesses and faults as if they didn't matter, someone who settles for being very imperfect, who expects nothing better. We ought to be tolerant, of course, but is 'human' the right word for this? "He is a very human person" has come to mean the opposite of what it should mean. It has come to mean less human than Adam before the Fall!') So to follow Jesus' teaching means to base marriage on what man was when he first came into the world. This is what he came not only to teach us but to do for us; this is what redemption means – restoring us to our original state, from which we had declined. In worship we started as monotheists and declined into polytheism. In marriage we started as monogamists and declined into polygamy. This is the natural direction in which sin takes us. We can see it in England where polygamy has long been held back by the law. But this has been relaxed and we can now practise polygamy through the divorce court, or else by avoiding formal marriage. Of course, not everyone who cohabits or gets divorced is polygamous. There is so much ignorance about what is really human, and many never hear any other view than the evolutionary one. Some of Eve's friends who had cohabited she regarded as virtually married, and they had stayed together down the years.

But for herself she was glad she had rejected that way out of the dilemma. It was too individualistic. Life was not like that. Marriage and family life were not just for the parties concerned but for the stability of society as a whole. You cannot just leave everyone else out – family, friends, neighbours and so on. Being truly human means fitting in with the whole community. A recognized regularized marriage is part of this, although by no means everything. Anyway, she could make sense of the Bible's teaching on marriage now. She could see it was consistent all the way through. Everything was linked to its origin in Genesis 2. God's great concern was to safeguard monogamy. This explained those strange rules given to Israel on Mount Sinai about how men were and were not to treat their wives. Fallen man sits loose to monogamy, and when he does so it is the woman who has most to lose; hence the laws God gave to protect her. Jesus was doing exactly the same in his own day when women were once again being exploited. He saw that the best thing he could do for them was to restore the reputation of monogamy, to try to get people to see that this was God's original way, which showed man up as the noble creature he was. Then the apostles took this message with them around the world of their day, where the standards were even lower. Their letters not only expounded the gospel in the narrow sense of salvation from hell, but in the broad sense of the redemption from all sin's effects in all areas of life, including marriage. And so Paul wrote extensively about marriage in his letters, as did Peter.

Nor did the apostles only write about how to get the best out of marriage by doing it in God's way. They even used marriage to illustrate the loving relationship between Christ and his people. Christ was monogamous: he had one wife, his church, to whom he would ever be faithful and kind. And this was nothing really new; it had been the same in the Old Testament. God himself had practised monogamy: Israel was his wife, he and she belonged together in a marriage covenant. It ran through the Bible like a refrain. Unfortunately, it was rather a broken refrain, since it was the wife who was untrue to the arrangement. Israel's frequent falls into idolatry were like a woman with a succession of lovers. Idolatry was adultery, whoredom, a breach of the marriage contract, a blot on this great gift of God to mankind. But it all served to show which way was best. If it was good enough for God, it is good enough for us.

'Yes,' said Eve, as she put the Bible away and prepared for bed, 'that experience taught me a lot I needed to know.'

3.
Let not man put asunder

As Eve lay in bed that night she could not stop her mind reliving her early life, especially the events surrounding her marriage to Frank. They had eventually agreed together on a course of action. She and Frank would be married legally, but the ceremony would be performed by the registrar and not take place in church. This had seemed the best compromise. It would mean they were fulfilling their responsibility towards society by coming together publicly and according to the law of the land. At the same time they would not be involved in making far-reaching vows which they were not sure they would be able to keep. Even if they managed to observe them in the letter they could not see how anyone could guarantee keeping to the spirit of them. Loving, cherishing, honouring and so on were attitudes and feelings. How could anyone foretell what their feelings would be years hence and promise they would survive the varying circumstances and fluctuating fortunes of life? Nor were they prepared to be involved in making presuppositions about God and the Bible which Frank knew he did not believe and about which Eve was uncertain. Although her parents would scarcely be happy about this aspect of the matter, it was only the logical sequel to the course her thinking and life had taken over the previous few years.

In fact, in the event her parents had become reconciled to the arrangement. With their decided views as to the line of demarcation between church and world, believer and unbeliever, they could not have been happy that a couple who made no claim to spiritual life should take God's name on their lips and call him to witness their vows and bless their marriage. Not only would there have been no point in their exerting pressure on them for a church wedding, but it would have been wrong. They had therefore resigned themselves to the arrangements proposed and sought to make the best of them. They did, however, ask that their pastor be allowed to attend the ceremony and reception, and be granted time during the latter to speak briefly and offer prayer. Neither Frank nor Eve saw any reason to refuse this request. For the rest, her parents kept their feelings to themselves and gave themselves much to prayer, privately and together. If God's blessing was not to be sought at the ceremony, this could be done before and after by them.

Nevertheless, the occasion, when it came, had not been an altogether happy one. It was impossible to hide the fact that there were two distinct groups present. The invitations had been restricted to their immediate families plus their closest friends. Most of the latter were not only unbelievers but held fairly advanced views about religion, society, marriage and, not least, the relationship between the sexes. Although everyone had behaved pleasantly towards each other, the awkwardness of the two groups with each other had shown through. Before the meal commenced, the pastor had spoken briefly and prayed. He was listened to politely, but it was impossible not to sense the somewhat embarrassed atmosphere. Although he had chosen his words with the utmost care, they had sounded strange in the ears of the majority of the guests. The speeches which had accompanied the toasts had sustained the strained atmosphere. Neither Frank's best man – his college flat-mate and a kindred spirit – nor Eve's father had felt completely free to be himself, and the inhibitions had been noticeable.

As she lay awake thinking back over the event, Eve realized how little she had been conscious of this at the time. This was not the first time she had sought to analyse what exactly her feelings had been that day. Why had she not felt more keenly the sense of division from her parents and the anguish of their hearts? She was very aware to which of the two groups she belonged and that this meant her family was isolated, not only from her friends and Frank's family, but

even from herself. Yet she had not felt as though she were
being torn. It had taken many years and much water under
the bridge before she began to realize why this was. She had
come to the conclusion that her feelings of freedom and
triumph so dominated her emotions at that time that there
was little room left for anything else. It represented the
breaking of the last of the chains binding her to her past life.
That continual sense of female inferiority and male
dominance which had dogged her through her adolescence
and early womanhood was gone, and gone for ever.
Moreover, she had had her own way for once. This had been
her own decision, arising from what *she* wanted. She had for
the first time taken a major step in her life entirely on her own
initiative. She had not given way to the usual paternal
disapproval. She had not only asserted her own
independence but struck a blow for women's liberties
generally. It was, at least as far as she was concerned, the
dawn of a new order. She was being herself, not what
someone else wanted her to be, and she had felt really good
about it.

Looking back now, she could see how she had exaggerated
the significance of her 'victory'. Not that she regretted the
marriage in itself. Given the circumstances and the attitude
to life she held then, she would have done it again. But the
desire to assert herself had been too prominent. Her motive
in marrying Frank should have been love. The love had been
there, but it had become mixed with other motives connected
with her new views. It was almost as if she had been using
Frank as a means of flexing her new-found muscles. She
could not deny that she had been trying to prove something –
though whether to herself, her parents, her friends or
whoever, she could not be sure – but, as she looked back, the
symbolic nature of her action was undeniable. She could
have taken her parents' advice to the extent of waiting to see
whether she would continue in this frame of mind. But she
was in no mood to take anyone's advice, and to have done so
would have been to admit at least partial defeat. Had she

done so, things might have worked out differently. Her engagement to Frank could have served to make the point she wanted to make. When this had been established she could have given herself wholly to the relationship with him. Either it would have deepened during that time, or she would have realized that true love was not really there and that he had simply been a symbol of a new life. 'You can't love a symbol for very long,' she said to herself.

This mature analysis was borne out by subsequent events. She had long since ceased going over the details of the three years of her life with Frank. She was impervious now to the pleasures and pains of those years, but she never ceased to reflect on the lessons she had learned and from which she continually drew in order to help others, either to guide them away from the rocks on which she had foundered, or to rescue those who had actually been shipwrecked on them. Such deep emotions, however, can never be erased completely, and though to recall those times no longer upset her, she could easily revive the experience if she gave vent to her imagination. This being one of those nights in which sleep would be a long time coming, if it came at all, she let her mind range where it would.

'How true it is,' she thought, 'that you don't really know a person until you've lived with them! Before that, you talk and you walk, you do things together and go places, but you're always aware that there is something special about these occasions. They've usually been pre-arranged and therefore prepared for, if only subconsciously. So we are never completely natural with one another. It's when we're off guard that we act naturally and show ourselves for what we are. And this doesn't happen until we've been through the daily routine a few score of times, and the other person shows himself by the way he reacts to us, and vice versa. So gradually everything is laid bare and the secret of what we're really like is out. It might be too late by then. The "trial marriage" people certainly have a good argument on their side! The big drawback with their position is that to all

intents and purposes the trial marriage *is* marriage. And how
long is the trial supposed to last? Who decides?'

She had wondered many times in the past whether it
would have been better if she and Frank had undergone a
trial marriage. It would have given them time to discover
things about each other that no courtship, however long,
reveals. But there would have been the same artificiality that
marks courtship. Both would have been keen for the try-out
to succeed and therefore have made efforts not to irritate the
other and to do everything possible to please. It would not
have been a really natural situation, which would only have
come with marriage proper. If there are incompatibilities
they must out at some time. And in the case of herself and
Frank these began to emerge around the end of their first
year together. The early days had been heady in the extreme.
Because of her sheltered background she had not
experienced love, or at least not enjoyed it. So she passed
through many months of rapture.

Along with this went the novelty of this entirely new way
of life she was leading. She had new ideas – liberated ideas –
and there was no restriction on her expressing them and
putting them into practice. She had a new circle of friends –
exciting people with none of her inhibitions, no fear of giving
offence, no shame over their revolutionary ways, insensitive
to the shock they might give the old-fashioned. Life was an
adventure. Nor did she become a conventional wife who
stayed at home and attended to the domestic work while her
husband went out to earn their living. This would have been
a defeat for her new life-style. She had conformed to
convention to the extent of giving up her own name and
taking her husband's – a practice which some of the feminist
leaders were beginning to question, although the neutral
'Ms' had not at that time been invented. But she was not
going to yield any more to the male sex. She was determined
to strike a blow for the new women in society by invading the
male domain of the business world. She took a position in a
large company of stockbrokers, and although she began as

one of a team of female clerks, she had no intention of remaining in a recognized woman's job and would not be satisfied until she had taken over what had always been regarded as an exclusively male position. She was not too particular what it was, so long as it was a post traditionally denied to women. She would also make full use of her present lowly status by complaining about the type of job women were expected to fit into, namely, one in which they were always told what to do by a man. Pay-rates were also going to be challenged and the slogan 'full equality' was to be made to mean just that.

All this she knew would take time, but they were in no hurry to have children, as this would certainly interfere with their plans. For they were totally agreed on this strategy. Far from opposing Eve's career ambitions, Frank positively encouraged them. He did not feel in the least that she was competing with him; in fact his aim was to break down this sense of superiority among men that saw women as a threat. He wished the sex war, both in its serious and its more comic aspects, would end and the two sexes would treat each other as equals. He had married Eve partly because this was what she was striving for. Nor did it worry him if she had not done the shopping or prepared a meal when he arrived home. His student days had taught him how to live from day to day and keep domestic chores to a minimum. He did not expect to be waited on by his wife, and they had no problem in deciding day by day who did what. One of them might pick up some shopping in the lunch hour or on the way home. Then, after a rest, a drink and a chat, they tackled the household chores together. They had no hard and fast rules about who did what; they 'played it by ear'. Eve did most of the cooking, but by no means all, and Frank did not mind whether he did the washing, the ironing or the cleaning, or anything else.

So where did the incompatibilities show? This had been so subtle and gradual that it was a long time before it became apparent. This was because it depended ultimately on her coming to know her true self. For she came to see it was not

only the other person you got to know by living with them – it
was yourself also. 'You don't just *live* with a stranger; you *are*
a stranger – to yourself,' she thought. 'And I don't think
there's a quicker or more thorough way of getting to know
yourself than by living with another person. You act and
react in ways you never thought yourself capable of. This is
not necessarily always for the worst. Many people bring the
best out of each other: they discover qualities they never
knew existed, and find they have a capacity for
consideration, understanding and even sacrifice they had no
idea was in them. Others, of course, expose their basic
selfishness and then there are continual clashes.'

But it had been nothing so clear-cut as this in her and
Frank's case. It was more a question of their different
backgrounds beginning to show through, particularly in her
case. Frank remained more or less what he had always been,
for he had not undergone any great change of outlook or
life-style. But Eve had been virtually turned inside out and
upside down, or thought she had. Yet in spite of herself she
found herself beginning to say and do things she had heard
and seen at home. At first she took little notice of this. After
all, it mostly occurred with ordinary, even trivial things. She
told herself it was not necessary to cast off everything from
the past, so long as she did not compromise any of her new
principles. But as time passed she found it increasingly
difficult to feel enthusiastic about her way of life and her
ambitions for the future. The disillusionment began at work.
She found she had less stomach for competing with the men
for the management positions than she had when she first
joined the firm. There were a number of reasons for this. One
was that she had to admit that most of her male colleagues
were in fact more suited than herself to these posts. There
was a girl in the office who she thought would have fitted the
bill, but she was on the point of commencing a family and
was not particularly interested. Another reason was that she
found herself happier doing the more routine work than
undertaking bigger responsibilities. The opportunities she

had had from time to time to act on her initiative had not
been taken with outstanding success. When they occurred
she enjoyed them less and less, and secretly began to dread
them. But the main reason was a deep revulsion against
working in an atmosphere of competition and a yearning to
replace it with one of co-operation. It may have been that her
particular office, or even the whole firm, was not the ideal
place to conduct a war for the liberation of women. Possibly
men got the top jobs on merit and maybe a sufficiently
suitable woman would be selected *if she applied*. It was this
latter condition that was not being fulfilled and she was
learning rapidly that it was female apathy as much as male
chauvinism that was responsible for the existing state of
things. Her friends, no doubt, would have told her that her
first duty was to break down this apathy and infuse some of
her own fighting spirit in its place. What was actually
happening, however, was the reverse – the apathy was
getting to her. Worst of all, she found she didn't really mind
that much!

But it was one thing to reconcile herself to this outlook,
and another for it to be accepted by the others in her circle.
From time to time she and Frank would visit their old
university friends or have them to stay. There was also an
increasingly wide circle of new acquaintances with a similar
outlook with whom they had meals or parties. Eve found she
was making less and less contribution to the conversations on
these occasions. She prevaricated when asked about her
'progress with the cause' at work, and showed no great
enthusiasm about the achievements of the others. At first her
friends joked about her 'backsliding', but when she failed to
join in the hilarity over this they became a little suspicious,
and parties became something of an ordeal for her. This in
turn brought some awkwardness into her relationship with
Frank when they were alone. It was at such times she found
her thoughts reverting to her former home life, which began
to be less distasteful. In fact she started to think she would
like her present home life to be more on those lines, apart

from the religious aspect. She had no wish to introduce Bible-reading, prayer and church-going, but she found the thought of a more relaxed home life increasingly attractive. Domestic chores weren't so bad and even the prospect of children began to appeal. The picture of this she formed in her mind was not altogether dissimilar to that of the home in which she had grown up.

She said nothing about all this to Frank. The same fear that had made her keep silent at home when she was reacting against Christianity now inhibited her when she was becoming disillusioned with this new way of life and thought. In any case it could have been just a phase she was passing through, part of the process of adaptation to change. If it was, it was turning out to be an extremely long phase, and before it had a chance to burn itself out, the worst had happened. As the relationship between her and Frank became cooler, so his relationship with one of their mutual friends became closer. His occasional nights away from home became more frequent until one day he announced he would not be back – their marriage was over.

This had come as a terrible shock to Eve. Although she could not deny that she had changed somewhat of recent times, nor that her relationship with Frank had been upset by this, she had no thoughts of their breaking up. This reaction further emphasized the differences between the two. Frank had a basically different approach to marriage from Eve. He had never regarded it as a final and exclusive commitment. This had been behind his proposal that they live together without marriage, although Eve had not been fully aware of its implications at the time. Now she was being made all too painfully aware of them. To him marriage was not 'for better or worse', only 'for better'. Neither was it to the exclusion of 'all other', nor 'until death do us part'. She, of course, had thought seriously about these things and had in fact come to accept the criticism of her friends that marriage as traditionally presented in England was too demanding. She could envisage circumstances in which it would be better to end it than continue. But she had not thought of this happening to her, certainly not as soon as this. It was one thing to agree to it in theory, another to experience it for herself in practice.

She was learning that there were things in the depths of her being which she thought she had got out of her system. In general she felt things more deeply than she had realized. Her friends seemed to be able to deal with everything on the intellectual level, so that the head was in complete control of the heart. If they felt elation at success or disappointment at failure it passed very quickly. And they could transfer their affections quite painlessly, it seemed. Although Eve had to some extent shared this approach it was not really her, and she found she could not view everything on the cerebral plane or change her feelings virtually at will. In addition to this, she found she had a more developed sense of loyalty and commitment. Even if her feelings for Frank were less strong than they had once been, it would not have occurred to her to break it all off. She would, left to herself, have hoped things would improve or, failing that, would have settled for a steady but less emotional relationship and an agreement to differ over some things. Along with this went an increasing desire for a settled way of life. The manner in which they were living was all right for a few years, but she did not think in terms of continuing it for ever. The excitement of not knowing what would happen from day to day had worn off and was replaced by a growing sense of exhaustion. A more regular routine would be easier to live with. If they were to have children more stability would seem a necessity. But breaking it all off would put paid to this wish for ever.

However, probably the strongest influence was the one of which she was the least conscious and the last she would admit to – a bad conscience over the breaking of a solemn agreement. Although the promises they had made at the registry were of a far lower standard than those of a Christian ceremony, nevertheless it had been stated that marriage is a lifelong arrangement. While the state was tending to make divorce easier, it still saw it as the exception and held to lifelong marriage unless this proved unworkable. The promises she and Frank had made to each other had been made on this understanding. There was something in Eve which held her back from simply assuming that she and Frank were one of the exceptional cases allowed for by the state and therefore free to break the agreement. Nor was it just a matter of obligation to the law and society which restrained her. There was something deeper and more elemental which could not be put in words – at least not by her at that time. Later she came to realize what it was – a sense of accountability to a higher law and greater lawgiver, the sense which was known as 'conscience'. This was a word which was 'out' as far as the feminist movement was concerned. It was an ugly word – part of the whole male chauvinist vocabulary which had served to keep women in bondage for so long. It could be used to justify so many things, since it was entirely irrational. This was no longer acceptable. All ideas and practices, especially those relating to women, must come out into the open and prove their case beyond all reasonable doubt. They must be cross-examined and tested in the light of a contrary point of view. There was no place now for primitive reactions like conscience. Eve had swallowed all this and gone over to the approach of 'pure reason'. She still held this, or thought she did. *Reason* indicated that it was time for her and Frank to admit their marriage had failed and say so publicly. Why pretend they were still man and wife when they no longer lived together and hardly ever saw each other? Eve could not answer this question, neither could she produce a single strong reason for continuing with the marriage. Yet she could not come to a decision to end it. The burden was intensified by the fact that it seemed to be all down to her. Frank was not seeking divorce, because he had no plans to remarry. The new woman in his life made no demands in this direction, in fact rather gloried in the liberty of cohabitation. She almost wished he had been agitating for divorce so that the onus of responsibility would have fallen on him. But it was she who had to decide, and although everything she had come to believe in recent years pointed in that direction, she could by no means bring herself to take the step. Friends sought to persuade her and tried to help her. Several times she had been on the point of writing to a solicitor, but it just did not get done.

Gradually it dawned on her what was really happening inside her. She was beginning to question the whole Women's Lib. approach. Not so much the actual issues of women's rights in the world, for she still rejoiced in all that had been accomplished over the past century for women, and she still believed more had to be done. But she was less convinced now that this was the main fault in society, and not so optimistic that once women had obtained full equality with men and set themselves free from their traditional roles Utopia would have arrived. She was beginning to see there were deeper problems that no amount of women's liberation would solve. Suppose women were to achieve equality with men, and even go on to take over some of their roles. Suppose they came to occupy the positions of power in the world. What then? Would that mean no more wars? Would it abolish poverty and disease? She doubted it. She was coming to realize the world's disorders went much deeper and that just to alter the structure of society and change its laws, and even its attitudes, was not the final answer. You could do all this and still be left with a nagging feeling inside that things were not right. She knew in herself that if she had gone and sued for divorce at this stage simply because it was Women's Lib. teaching, it would have been wrong.

'Wrong?' That was a word she had not used in a moral sense for a long time. What on earth was happening to her? Was she beginning to realize that there was a higher authority than human codes, whoever established them and however enlightened they were? Was she accepting that this higher power actually had a voice speaking within her which could tell her what to do and what not to do? After all, that

was supposed to be what the word 'conscience' meant. She
was getting nearer and nearer to the position in which she
had to give an affirmative answer to these questions.
However persuasive and vociferous were the arguments of
her friends, 'the voice' seemed to speak louder and more
convincingly. Also it went on when the friends had gone
home. It refused to shut up. It demanded to be listened to. It
threatened worse if it was ignored or disobeyed. Moreover, it
not only spoke to Eve about the divorce issue; in fact that
gradually ceased to be an issue. It began to speak to her
about the whole course of her life in recent years. It brought
up matters she thought she had settled once and for all. It
displayed before her mind's eye scenes from her past life as
vividly as a moving film, which filled her not so much with
nostalgia as with horror. She lived again through her
arguments with her parents and everything else that had
marked her rejection of Christianity. But she no longer felt
that sense of triumph and freedom she had experienced at the
time.

Eventually she capitulated and began to reassess the
teaching she had turned against. She could see now that
what she had really objected to had been the position given to
women and the attitudes adopted towards them by
Christians. But she had now sorted her ideas out on this, and
in any case this was not the whole of Christianity, however
things had seemed at the time. Therefore, if she were to
accept Christian teaching now she did not have to accept
that part of it. Perhaps it was not really part of it in any case.
So she began to open her mind again and immediately felt
much better. The 'voice' spoke to her in a more friendly way
and she found she could agree with it. Eve, as she lay in bed
that night after Sarah's visit, lived again through the months
that had followed that crisis. She recalled her tentative
approaches to evangelical churches, her inward feelings of
regret leading her at last to speak to the one whose voice had
for so long been speaking to her, telling him how she felt, all
her wrong thoughts and actions. She recalled how she had

come to realize that the story of the cross was as central as Christians had said, for it was reading and hearing about that which at last gave her a sense of peace and well-being, a peace which had never left her since and which filled her, even on such a sleepless night as this.

But in those early days Eve had kept her spiritual experience very much to herself. She deliberately avoided attending any one church regularly enough to be drawn into giving an account of herself. She tended to change the pattern from week to week so that she would not be missed when absent. There was, however, one church where she felt more at home than the others, partly because she was never buttonholed there. The pastor was not of the type that blocks the exit and tries to obtain information from every stranger. Indeed it was possible to leave without confronting him at all, which she sometimes did. Nor did she attend gatherings of the informal 'getting to know you, getting to know all about you' brand. That Christians should 'get to know all about' her was the last thing she wanted at that time. She was very conscious of the difference between herself and the others, and knew they would be surprised – some perhaps even shocked – over the life she had lived in recent years and the views she had held. Most of all, she was embarrassed about her marital position – having an unbelieving husband living with another woman, not a very common experience for a Christian. She wondered whether to take her wedding-ring off to stop people asking after her husband, but the mark it had left would be noticed by the inquisitive and raise even more questions.

It was while shopping in a large store in the centre of the town one Saturday that she found herself in the same department as someone she recognized and who recognized her. The lady came over and introduced herself as Grace Marley, a member of the evangelical church for which Eve had a preference. Eve soon found herself sitting in the store's tea-room drinking coffee with Grace, who was a natural conversationalist, so that Eve found she was obliged to say

very little about herself, much to her relief. This made her
warm to Grace and on subsequent visits to the church she felt
less and less need to avoid her. A few weeks after their first
meeting in the department store Eve was invited to spend
part of a Sunday in the home of Grace and her husband,
Peter. Grace must have sensed something and discreetly
avoided any reference to Eve's husband. The couple were in
their middle thirties and had two young children. Eve went
to their house on a number of occasions and the warmth she
felt towards them gradually blossomed into confidence. She
had long felt the need to talk to someone she could trust
about her situation, and one evening, after the children had
gone to bed, she decided she would open her heart and life to
Peter and Grace.

After telling her story she added, 'The reason I've told you
all this is to explain my behaviour at your church. It's not
that I particularly mind people knowing about me, but that if
they ask casual questions at the church door I can't really
answer them in a couple of sentences. You've seen how long
it's taken me this evening to put you in the picture, and you
know how long it's taken me to get round to the subject at all.
It's not that I want help or advice, or anything. In fact it's not
the sort of situation anyone can do anything about, even me.
It's just that I felt my relationship with you and others would
be better if you knew about it.'

Their response to Eve's story, however, was hardly what
she expected. She had imagined them sympathizing and
comforting, promising to pray for her and so on, but beneath
the surface being perplexed and not knowing what to say.
The last thing she had expected was to be given practical and
positive advice. And she had been quite sincere in saying she
was not looking for anyone to recommend a course of action
to her. She was resigned now to living in a state of separation
and had no thoughts of obtaining a divorce. She assumed
Christians would agree with this, knowing how much they
were opposed to divorce. Imagine her feelings then, when the
line Peter and Grace took with her was that not only should

she accept divorce, but initiate the proceedings for it! This had come so unexpectedly that even now all these years later she could remember the gist of the conversation. In fact on returning home she had written down notes of it and referred back to them many times, as her understanding of the Bible's teaching on marriage and divorce deepened.

They had begun by saying it was a common fallacy that Bible Christians were against divorce altogether. Many were, but they tended to base their case on single texts such as 'What God hath joined together let not man put asunder'. Peter and Grace felt this text had become detached from the rest of the passage from which it came – a passage which in fact allowed divorce in certain circumstances, and this by Christ himself. For while he forbade *man* to put couples asunder, he did not say that *God* may not do so. The question was when and how God did so. But it was not just the relevant passage in Matthew 19 that needed considering, but the Bible's view generally. Peter explained that he had a personal interest in the subject, and when Grace raised her eyebrows at this he added that he meant in connection with his work with the social services, which brought him into contact with people who had marital problems. He had been forced to think out what the Bible actually taught, as distinct from what people said, thought and assumed it taught. This was not easy, since many of these assumptions had become ingrained into the culture.

He then went on to try to give Eve a picture of the very high regard God had for the relationship between a man and a woman, as reflected in every passage in the Bible which refers to it. It was the sexual relationship that constituted the marriage as God originally instituted it, when the two became 'one flesh'. This he had been at pains to safeguard right from the beginning. But the state of the world became so corrupt that the human race soon ceased to respect its sanctity. True, all civilizations had their codes of conduct but, apart from their disapproval of adultery, they did very little to protect the sexual relationship. Prostitution became

rife; indeed it was encouraged as a means of communion with
the gods and a way of guaranteeing fertility. Even the way
adultery was punished only made things worse, for the
adulterer's wife was made a prostitute! The fact was that
these pagan civilizations, however highly developed, were
guided by the well-being of the clan or tribe, not by that of the
particular individual or couple. The laws God gave Israel,
however, were quite different. Although he did not prohibit
divorce absolutely because he knew that even his people
would never be able to keep such a law, God did impose
restrictions on it. He was particularly concerned it should
not get so out of hand that women should find themselves
being passed from man to man at whim.

At this point Bibles had been produced and Eve had been
taken through passages in Exodus 22 and Deuteronomy 22
and 24. She had not grasped all the details at the time but she
gathered that the main point was that what God had set
himself against was sex outside of marriage, 'unlawful
intercourse', in whatever form it took place. So seriously did
God regard this that he actually prescribed the death penalty
for it. Whereas men had instituted divorce for this and other
sexual irregularities, God had gone further. He sought to
impress the sacredness of marriage on his people by using it
to illustrate his own relationship with them, in which he saw
himself as Israel's husband. By this he meant he had loved
them, chosen them and taken them to himself to cherish
them, and expected them to requite that love and be faithful
to him. For them to turn to other gods was thus adultery, and
if they engaged in the ritual prostitution that accompanied
the worship of these gods they were doubly defiling
themselves, polluting their relationship with him and their
marriages. All this proved one thing – that in God's book a
sexual relationship was something exclusive, to be enjoyed
only between two people. He absolutely forbade it to be
extended to a third party, in whatever circumstances.

As she listened to this, something struck Eve like a
thunderbolt and she felt she must interrupt Peter's

exposition. 'What you're saying affects me, doesn't it? It means that for my marriage to Frank to continue is against God's will. For since he is still my husband he has the right of intercourse with me even though he is actually living with someone else. While this is allowed to continue it is bringing the relationship of men and women generally into disrepute. But what's to be done? After all, from what you have said, in the Old Testament somebody had to be put to death, didn't they?'

'Yes, and this is where we have to come on to the New Testament and the teaching of Christ. The most complete account of the matter is Matthew 19, where he is specifically asked about divorce.' So they gave themselves to a close examination of that passage. Peter explained that, although Jesus was ostensibly answering the Pharisees, he was really directing his words to believers in himself, which was why he said in verse 11 that not everyone can accept his teachings, only those who are given special grace. It needs grace to understand them, more grace to accept them and yet more to carry them out. Jesus spoke as one who was not so much interpreting the law, as the rabbis did, as founding a new and spiritual kingdom. He was concerned most of all to help the members of his kingdom, who, because they are dedicated to him, want to know how to please him in this, as in everything.

Jesus went back beyond Moses to the original institution of marriage. Moses had been sanctioned by God to permit men to divorce their wives in certain circumstances because of the hardness of their hearts. In some instances it might have been worse for the wives to stay married than to be put away. But this was not what God had really intended marriage to be like. His purpose was that they should stay together and love each other as long as they lived. But he is wise enough to know they will not always do that, not even after he has established his kingdom among them. They may still commit adultery. What then? For one thing, because he is merciful he no longer commands them to be put to death.

In fact what he does is to take something man invented –
divorce – and use it to sanction his prohibition on unlawful
intercourse. What Jesus did was to replace the death of the
person guilty of adultery by the death of the marriage. In a
way this was not so much a punishment as a declaration of
fact – a marriage is killed by the adultery of one of the
partners. But this did not mean he was just perpetuating the
law of Moses on the matter. There are very important
differences in addition to the sweeping away of the death
penalty. In any case the Jews were no longer allowed to
inflict it because they were under the law of the Roman
Empire, of which they had become part. How wonderfully
God's sovereign providence in history had operated! He had
begun to wean the Jews away from the Sinai code in advance
of the coming of his Son with the new law of the kingdom.
There was no need for them to agitate for things like the
power to impose capital punishment for all sorts of offences;
God had finished with that, except in cases of murder, and
the Romans themselves still imposed that.

The other way, Peter went on, in which Jesus had
branched out on a new course was by placing man and
woman on the same level with regard to matrimonial
offences. Even the law of Moses had sought to protect the
woman from the man's abuse of his superior position,
something unknown in other nations. But it had given no
provision for a woman to initiate divorce proceedings against
a guilty man; it had only been the man who was allowed to
give his wife a 'bill of divorcement'. The rabbis had wrongly
interpreted this to mean that it was invariably the woman
who was the guilty party; it was always her fault if the
marriage went wrong. One school of thought followed the
teaching of Hillel – that a man could divorce his wife for any
cause at all. Probably this was what the Pharisees were
referring to when they asked Jesus, 'Is it lawful for a man to
put away his wife *for every cause*?' They were asking Jesus
whether he agreed with the libertarian view of the school of
Hillel, that if a man's wife displeased him in some way,

however trivial, he could 'put her away', divorce her. Jesus refused to take sides between Hillel and the other school which followed Shammai, and whose more rigorist view allowed divorce only for 'gross indecency' (whatever that might mean!) He went back behind the rabbis and behind Moses himself to Eden, when God had first brought man and woman together, but had not given man the right to separate them. Jesus then went on to pronounce as especially guilty the man who does this, who puts his wife away for trivial reasons in order to marry someone else who has taken his fancy. Such a man, says Jesus, is guilty of adultery. He is the guilty party and, worse still, causes another man to sin by marrying the wife he has wrongly divorced. This teaching was a long way from the contemporary view that saw the woman as always to blame. Either she was unattractive and unwomanly, so that her husband could not delight in her, or else she was too seductive and flirtatious, a temptation to others. She could not win!

However, Jesus restored the balance and made the man at least as much to blame. When he had spoken about divorce in his Sermon on the Mount he had led up to it by talking of the need for self-control and discipline in the thoughts and imaginations of the heart: 'Everyone who looks on a woman to lust after her has committed adultery already with her in his heart.' To the rabbis this was unheard of; it was always the woman's fault for being seductive. That was why on public occasions, and especially at religious services, the women had to be segregated lest they distract the thoughts of the men. But Jesus said it was rather for the men to discipline their thoughts and not give way to lust. That was where adultery began. Of course, he in no way countenanced immodest dress or seductive behaviour in women; this was equally culpable. But if women practised modesty and men self-control all would be well. Hence he both advocated and himself practised the mingling of the sexes in social and religious life. It was not law and punishment imposed from outside that were to control behaviour, but discipline imposed from within. No wonder he said his teaching could only be received by those 'to whom it was given', by those dedicated to the cause of his kingdom. Apart from the saving grace of God no one has the power to impose this discipline on himself.

Nevertheless, notwithstanding all he said and all the grace he can give, he was realistic enough to know there would be occasions when this self-discipline would break down. One or other of the partners might be led away and commit adultery. What then? Then it was in order for there to be a divorce. And here again the two sexes were on a par, for in Mark's account these additional words are recorded: 'If a woman shall put away her husband and marry another she commits adultery', that is, if she does it for any cause less than unlawful intercourse. But if it is 'for the cause of fornication', then it is in order. Thus the teaching of Jesus not only condemned the practice of his contemporaries in this matter but even that of some 'Christian countries'. In Britain the laws relating to marriage, the family and the home favoured men until the middle of the present century. Women had little if any rights or powers in relation to erring husbands. Even if they were able to raise the money for an expensive divorce case, they invariably came off worse in the subsequent settlement. Some of our traditional Christianity was less Christian than we have thought.

All this came like so much fresh air to Eve. She could see that the view she had formed of the Bible, the church and Christianity – that they favoured men and downgraded women – was incorrect. Perhaps it was true of the church, of the way Christianity was presented and practised, and of the way the Bible was interpreted, but when impartially examined and allowed to speak without prejudices and assumptions, the Bible painted a very different picture. And the one to thank for all this was the Saviour himself, Jesus Christ, a true liberator indeed. Here was women's liberation in a new outfit. How much more Eve felt drawn to him now that she saw he did not condemn her past ideas and aspirations for women, but viewed them sympathetically! Now he was beginning to channel them in the right direction and bring them into line with his own teaching. And not only that, she had seen that this stalemate which her marriage had reached was not what he wanted for her; it was not some kind of punishment she must bear for the rest of her days. It could be put right, and she herself could do something about it, with his approval and blessing. But there was a nagging thought in her brain which would not go away. She felt a bit ashamed of it but Peter and Grace had been so helpful that she decided to ask them.

Grace seemed to sense there was something bothering Eve and asked her if this were so. 'Yes, it's about Paul's teaching. Wasn't he a bit harder on women than Jesus? Didn't he regard them as a nuisance, a distraction from living spiritually? Didn't he say he wished everyone was like him, and should remain unmarried and not get involved with women?'

'I can answer that,' said Grace, 'because I had the same problem and it bothered me quite a lot. In fact there's absolutely no difference between Paul and Jesus on marriage any more than there is on any other subject. Like Jesus, Paul stresses that marriage is a permanent relationship for the whole of life, and that to go outside it is adultery. Here, look, in Romans 7, verses 2 and 3: "The woman who hath an husband is bound by the law to her husband so long as he liveth; but if her husband be dead, she is loosed from the law of her husband. So then if, while her husband liveth, she be married to another man, she shall be called an adulteress: but if her husband be dead she is free from that law; so that she is no adulteress, though she be married to another man." So there's no difference there. And since Jesus allowed divorce in cases of adultery, so would Paul have done. He doesn't actually say this here because he isn't really dealing with marriage and divorce, but with the law as a whole. He just uses marriage as an illustration.'

'But doesn't he actually forbid divorce in 1 Corinthians 7?

I've been looking into these passages lately, and I must say that one rather frightened me.'

'Yes,' said Peter, 'but that's because you haven't taken the background into account – quite understandably, because it's a bit complicated. But to cut a long story short these Corinthian Christians had got hold of some strange ideas about sex and marriage. They were over-reacting against their former life as pagans, in which ritual prostitution was one of the highest forms of worship. They thought repentance meant not just giving up the idols but sex as well, because it was so closely involved with idolatry. So they wrote to Paul and asked him what he thought about the question: "Is it good for a man not to touch a woman?" Paul replied: "Yes, that's good if you have the calling to do it and the grace to go through with it," as he believed he himself did. This was exactly what Jesus had taught about becoming a "eunuch for the kingdom of heaven's sake". You don't *have* to refrain from marriage, but if you have the gift of continency then use it for the sake of the gospel. Paul's position was the same. But he also made it clear that if a Christian were already married then he must not separate from his wife, nor must the Christian wife separate from her husband, not even if the partner is unbelieving, or perhaps still an idolater. That does not invalidate the marriage. Remain in whatever state you were in when you were converted – married or unmarried. If you stay together you may win your spouse over to Christ. As for those who aren't married, they should consider whether it would be better to remain so, like himself, because of the troublesome times which were making family life difficult for Christians. But if you don't have the grace to do this, then don't strain yourself; it's better to marry than burn. So Paul isn't really any different from Jesus; it only appears that way because he's talking to converts from Gentile pagan idolatry and not Jews. He doesn't mention grounds for divorce because that doesn't arise. The only valid ground for divorce is sexual irregularity, and this was not the Corinthians' problem.

Their problem was in fact the opposite – they were turning against sex altogether, and even thinking of getting divorced to avoid intercourse. Paul says they shouldn't do this, because it is a holy thing, created by God himself and blessed by him.'

'Thank you,' said Eve, 'that's cleared that up beautifully. So now where does that leave me? As I see it, I would be within my rights as a Christian if I were to seek divorce. In fact, it seems I almost have a duty to do it. The position I'm in means that the sacredness of intercourse is being violated. I'm still accessible to a man who is virtually married to another woman. And not only that, I'm being forced into a life of celibacy. It seems this is a special calling for which one needs special grace. I don't know whether I've got that. So I've got a lot of serious thinking to do. And then there's the question of how all this would go down in the church. Supposing I did decide to come to your church, would I be accepted? Could I be baptized? Could I attend the Lord's Supper and become a member?'

'If what we've said is all true, there is no reason why not. But it might be better if you talked with our pastor about that side of things.'

At this point Eve started to feel that events were running away with her too quickly and that she ought to stop for breath. She decided that the first thing to do was to get clear in her mind whether seeking divorce was the right thing or not. She did not want to be influenced one way or the other by the consequences, but to face those separately. It would have been easy to use the pastor's reaction as a reason for or against proceeding. But she knew she must be clear in her own mind whether or not this was the will of God, as revealed in his Word. So she went over the points made by Peter and Grace many times and examined the Bible passages carefully. She saw very clearly that God's purpose in marriage was lifelong union; that when it was broken this was done by man and was sinful; that nevertheless God, knowing human frailty, was merciful as well as righteous, so

that while he condemned the partner who broke the union by
adultery, he did not hold the innocent one in bondage to the
other who had sinned against the marriage bond. He gave
this one the freedom to break the outward bond and start
again with someone else. She also saw that this was God's
way of safeguarding the sacredness of the union of the sexes.
Thus divorce was only God's will when there was adultery;
the other grounds permitted by the state were not really
options for Christians. Far from safeguarding the sacredness
of the sexual relationship, these other grounds tended to
encourage promiscuity. There was a danger that easy
divorce would become a means of legalized polygamy. In her
case, however, the issue was quite clear. She had the grounds
for divorce sanctioned by Christ himself and it was in no way
sinful for her to pursue it. Indeed she had come to the
conclusion that it would be positively right in the sight of
God. So this was what she proceeded to do.

As she lay in bed going through all this in her mind, Eve
refused to let her imagination roam over all that the divorce
had involved. It had been a wearisome business, especially
as Frank had not been at all co-operative. Nor at that time
had the legal system been entirely fair to women. There had
been times when she had almost abandoned it, and she had
needed all the help of her friends, Peter and Grace. They had
also brought the pastor and her together, and his
sympathetic attitude had helped a great deal. Above all, it
had been the knowledge that she was acting rightly in the
sight of God that had kept her going; indeed she had felt that
because it was his will he was upholding her and gradually
weaving a way through the tangled skein. But it was all far
behind her now, and she had never regretted it. She had
suffered misunderstanding and misjudgement, not least
from other Christians, but she could not altogether blame
them. There was no doubt in her mind that this had been one
of the pivotal decisions of her life. In fact it was the first major
step she had taken since becoming a Christian. She often
wondered how many people had commenced their Christian
lives by getting divorced!

4.
Free indeed

Before finally relapsing into a somewhat disturbed sleep that night, Eve had remembered the diary and notebook she had kept as a record of these events all those years ago. Next morning as soon as she was dressed she went in search of them. This involved emptying two or three boxes of her 'archives', material she had hoarded at various stages of her life. As well as the diary for the year in question there was also a notebook with summaries of various books and articles she had read at the time of her divorce, plus a few cuttings from magazines and some leaflets. She took the lot into her arms and sat down to browse through it over her breakfast.

She turned immediately to 15 April and read, 'Tomorrow is D-day, i.e. Divorce day. How do I feel? Nervous, with spasms of panic, like someone facing an amputation. I know the limb is dead and better cut off, yet can't expel a lingering sense it might come back to life if I leave it alone. Then I remember I'm different from when I married Frank, no longer governed by how I feel or think, not living in a state of reaction to convention or under the influence of friends. "Hallowed be thy name . . . Thy will be done" is my new slogan. And he has made his will clear, not by signs or hunches, but by his Word. My mind is quite clear on what it teaches about this. However I *feel* and whatever comes of it, it must be done. In his eyes the divorce has already taken place long ago. Now I am just obeying that part of his will which requires us to carry out the state's laws and do our public duty. This is enough to see me through tomorrow.'

She had not written anything on the day itself and the next entry was three days later.

'*18 April.* Father and mother have been here for a couple of days. They attended the court and came home with me. It must have been difficult for them, but they never said, "We told you it would never work." My being a Christian now has made all the difference to their attitude to me. They obviously feel a lot happier. But they asked me much about what I will do now. How do I know? How can I make plans? In any case I still have much to put right.'

The last comment related mainly to her position in the church. Peter and Grace had also attended the hearing as they felt much involved in her action. As Eve's friendship with them had deepened, she had gone more and more to their church and now rarely visited any other. She had become acquainted with the pastor and some of the other members. Subsequent entries in the diary thus related more and more to these things.

'*4 May*.   P. and G. invited me for supper on Friday and arranged for the pastor to be there too. They feel I need some encouragement to broach the matter of church fellowship. They are probably right. I think I am far less decided about this than I was about seeking the divorce. On one hand, I feel a little out of things, especially having to slip out on communion Sundays. Also there have been two baptism services, those involved all having been converted since me. But on the other hand, I am afraid of becoming the centre of controversy. Everyone knows about me now. I don't want to be a cause of division. Perhaps I'll see things more clearly after Friday.'

'*10 May*.   Trying to collect my thoughts after last night. P. and G. handled it very well. They made no attempt to hide the reason they had invited me to meet pastor at their home. They did not waste half the evening in small talk, but prepared the way so that I could put my problem. I said I thought it was a matter of all or nothing – baptism, membership and communion as one package, not one or two without the others. Pastor agreed with this. All three involve the church, he said, and are not just individual actions. I just wondered slightly whether he was hiding behind the church, so I asked what he himself felt about baptizing and receiving into the church a divorced woman. He replied, that depended, but in my case he was completely happy. Then he said something which sent a thrill down my spine and still does: "I don't regard you as a 'divorced woman'." Seeing the puzzled expression on my face, he explained: "That is a passive expression, meaning 'a woman who has been divorced'. You have not 'been divorced'; you have divorced your husband. That is entirely different. It means he is the offender and has been given what he deserves. You were in the clear and therefore in a position to take action yourself. You have nothing to apologize for in this. You are more sinned against than sinning. You have not broken the marriage laws and have acted in accordance with the Scriptures. You are not merely eligible for the church as someone to be tolerated; you are a positive asset." A truly enlightened man! Not only does he clearly understand divorce, but accepts that a woman can take the initiative in it. It warmed my feminist (?) heart! However, when we discussed the attitude of the church, the situation is not so good. He feels there are weaker ones whose consciences might be troubled at this stage. They would have to proceed gradually and with full consultation. The elders are going to talk together about how to approach the matter.'

'*25 May.* Peter mentioned after church today that the elders had met and decided to hold two or three special church meetings to go into the Bible's teaching on divorce. This to be done without any specific reference to myself. The first one is to be on 4 June. The members have been asked in the meantime to read and think about a number of Bible passages on the subject. I think they are those P. and G. went through with me. The main one will be Matthew 19.'

'*27 May.* Today had the thought that I should not sit idle while everyone else does their homework. I propose studying some of the passages in the Bible about women. Feel I can do this with an open mind and come to it freshly now without preconceived ideas. Haven't any books to help at the moment, but can start with the little concordance I had as a

Bible class prize when I was fifteen. Glad I didn't get rid of it
after all!'

'*31 May*.   Borrowed a book from the library today, *Women
in the Bible*. Amazed to find how many there were who did
things women were not supposed to do: made decisions, took
initiatives, exercised leadership and performed other roles
associated with men. Have also been making my own
researches and coming to similar conclusions. Reading the
Gospels has shown how often Jesus was in the company of
women, used them in his work, in fact depended on them.
Not a sign of a condescending or patronizing attitude, but
acting perfectly naturally. Yet he didn't choose any as
apostles. I wonder why not? Perhaps I'll learn.'

'*6 June*.   Grace phoned and told me a little about the first
of the special church meetings. Apparently not everyone is
happy with the pastor's explanation of the subject. Oh dear!
I hope I'm not to be the cause of controversy and division.
But these things must come out some time. In coming days
there may be others like me who have marriage problems,
and come to faith in Christ.'

'*9 June*.   Having stretched my concordance to the limits,
have taken to visiting the reference library on my way home
from work and spending a couple of hours with their large
concordance, biblical encyclopaedias and commentaries.
Took a good while to get going, but tonight struck gold.'

The diary at this point referred to some notes in the
notebook made during these researches. The first page was
headed 'The position of women in the O.T.'. The notes read:
'There is no case of a woman having authority over her
husband in the home, but outside the home the position is
different. There are examples of women participating in
business on equal terms with men – e.g. Naomi (Ruth 4) and
the "model wife" of Proverbs 31. Even *civil government* is in the
hands of a woman in the case of Deborah, whose authority
was accepted by the military commander, Barak (Judg.
4:4-6). The prophetess Huldah brought a word from God to
King Josiah (2 Kings 22:11-20). In *the home*, the woman had

authority over the children (5th commandment) but it was
subject to her husband's. If the husband were dead she took
over his roles (e.g. Num. 30). In *personal religion*, women had
equal privileges in approaching God in prayer and sacrifice.
They were not excluded from *public worship*. There were also
prophetesses (Miriam, Deborah, Huldah, Anna) who led
worship, some even composing hymns (Miriam, Deborah
and Hannah). They were excluded from the priesthood, for
this grew out of the patriarchal system, in which the man, as
head of the household, offered sacrifice on behalf of the
family. But under Moses only Levites were eligible, and
among them only unblemished ones (physically). Thus the
majority of men as well as all women were barred. All this
suggests there is nothing intrinsically different about women
which unfits them for roles normally performed by men. It
was simply that God arranged things like this for the sake of
order.'

The comment on this in the diary read, 'So far, so good.
Where to next?' This question held her up for a few days, but
the next entry revealed the answer she found.

'*13 June.*   Have come to realize that the gap between Old
and New Testaments is almost 500 years – half a millennium
– and that I must find something out about this period,
during which there must have been many changes in
customs and ways of thinking. To ignore this would be like
jumping straight from the Middle Ages to the twentieth
century.'

The cross-reference system she had adopted led her to
another page of notes headed 'Women under the Rabbis':
'Remembered how Peter had explained the divorce debate
between Jesus and the Jews by referring to the various
schools of thought among the rabbis. Went in search of the
rabbis' views on women generally. There don't seem to have
been different schools of thought about this! It was agreed by
all that women were inferior, to be classed with the illiterate
and slaves! Deborah and Huldah were an embarrassment –
the Talmud either passed over them or denounced them!

One rabbi found significance in their names – Deborah means "hornet" and Huldah "weasel"! Feeble excuses are made for the men who accepted their authority (Barak and Josiah). A good example of the rabbinic method of making the facts fit the theory!

'The rabbis imposed far more restrictions on women than did the O.T. itself. They did not allow them the religious privileges enjoyed under Moses, although they were expected to obey all his rules! They had a separate court in the temple and a separate gallery in the synagogue, to keep them from distracting the men. Although allowed to listen to the teaching they were not expected to understand it. They were regarded as stupid, so that if they asked a question they were just ignored. And to cap it all they taught their sons to pray, "Blessed art thou who hast not made me a woman"!'

The diary went on to comment, 'If ever a feminist movement was justified it was under the rabbis! Yet the women seem to have accepted their position meekly. No wonder it has taken so long to stir them into action.'

'*16 June.*   Went round to P. and G.'s to tell them what I have been learning, also because I want to know where to go next. My researches have shown me that during the 500 years before Christ the Jews were becoming more and more mixed with other civilizations. But I'm pretty ignorant of what these were like; it's so long since I read anything that can remotely be called history. P. has loaned me a book on it, which has a section about female matters. They told me they will be holding their last study meeting on divorce next week and then at the July church meeting will put forward my request for membership. By that time everyone should have sorted out where they stand. It seems some are still sticking out for the view that divorce is always wrong, full stop. Others have prayed for me at the prayer meeting. I would like to go to this, but feel it would be best to know whether I am accepted first. It shouldn't be long now, and I have plenty to do sorting myself out.'

'*20 June.*   Have not gleaned a great deal about the

position of women in the world generally prior to Christ's coming, since there doesn't seem to have been much research done into it. Someone will have to do something about this! I gather that sexual morality was much looser among the Greeks and Romans, and there was a good deal of prostitution, which was not illegal like adultery. But how can there be prostitution without adultery? Possibly the answer was that they practised it in a religious form. I also gathered that the position of women generally improved under the Romans. The Greeks saw them as chattels, useful for pleasure, procreation and domestic service. But Roman women were getting opportunities to hold positions in public life, gaining legal rights and the power to own property. This explains people like Lydia, the seller of purple-dyed cloth in Philippi, and Priscilla, who seems to have acted as partner with her husband Aquila in the tent trade in Rome and Corinth. These facts have whetted my appetite to discover what Paul made of it all, with Judaism on one side and this increasingly permissive Roman civilization on the other. But before that, of course, comes Jesus himself.'

The subject of 'Women in the Ministry of Jesus' occupied several pages of the notebook and to these she now turned, reading, 'All that Jesus said and did on earth was guided by one thing above all – his awareness that his arrival in the world meant the kingdom of heaven had come. Because of this he refused to be governed by current attitudes and traditional forms. He often appealed to the original traditions of the Old Testament, but was not restricted even by these. He had an entirely fresh approach. He was not a man of his times, the product of his age; he had a new message and new forms to enshrine it. He looked beneath what people were outwardly – high or low, rich or poor, healthy or diseased, old or young, Jew or Gentile, young or old *and man or woman* – to see them in their relationship with God. He brought this to the fore as their basic need and overlooked the externals. Thus he dealt in the same way with a high-ranking religious leader like Nicodemus as with an immoral Samaritan woman. This had important consequences for the position of women in his ministry.

'1.   He treated women naturally as members of society. He made neither feminist nor anti-feminist speeches and was unselfconscious about dealing with them. He looked at their particular need, not their difference of sex. Women who were sick were healed if they came to him, just as men were – e.g. Peter's mother-in-law, the woman with the issue of blood, the infirm woman whom he called "a *daughter* of Abraham", a phrase utterly foreign to the Jews. In his parables he refers to women in their normal environment as naturally as he referred to shepherds and sowers.

'2.   He accepted their faith as being just as valid as that of men. A woman with faith was more acceptable than a man with none. The ex-prostitute who anointed him was commended and blessed, while the Pharisee was reproved (Luke 7:35-50). The Canaanite woman was praised for her faith (Matt. 15:22-28) when even the apostles were rebuked for lack of it.

'3.   Women became his disciples or followers, which no rabbi would have thought of allowing. Sex was irrelevant; what mattered was "doing the will of God" (Matt. 12:49-50).

'4.   He regarded tham as capable of receiving his teaching. Rabbis saw women as unable to understand doctrine, let alone teach it, but Jesus was happy to instruct women, even on their own, as with the Samaritan woman (John 4) and Mary and Martha (Luke 10:38-42).

'5.   He included women among his travelling companions (Luke 8:1-3; Mark 15:40-41). These were women of substance who could compensate for the lack of income of Jesus and his disciples. They were not apostles, nor credited with any office, but at least their names are given, whereas the seventy temporary missionaries of Luke 10 are unnamed. This was a break with convention, which would have regarded the presence of women in a band of itinerant teachers as not only a hindrance, but a source of temptation, bringing discredit on the movement. There is no indication of anything improper or shameful in the arrangement. Had there been scandal, it is unlikely the writers would have mentioned the women at all in their writings.

'6. Some of these women were present at the crucifixion and, more important, were witnesses of the resurrection. In fact they were the first to see him alive (Mat. 27:61; 28:1-7; Mark 15: 40-16: 7). The rabbis did not accept the witness of a woman: it had no force in law and was ineffective. Even the apostles at first rejected it and regarded their reports as nonsense (Luke 24: 11). Later they discovered them to be true.

'None of this means Jesus was a feminist or gave women office or authority. But it does mean their position in his kingdom was to be different from what was allowed in Judaism or the Roman Empire, or even by the Old Testament itself.'

Turning back to the diary, she found some comments she had added on completing the research.

'*29 June.* What a feast of good things I've had over the last week or so! To think I used to get so angry at the position I thought Christianity gave to women! How beautiful the Lord's approach to them was! It makes me feel so much closer to him to realize he came to save me as a woman, not just as a part of humanity. I almost wish I was a preacher and could share it all. But I must be content to absorb it myself. The important thing for me is to be right in my own thinking, and then live according to it. That's enough. In any case I haven't finished the study yet. There's still the rest of the New Testament – the church and the apostles.

The next reference to this was '*2 July.* Am finding the position of women in the early church rather daunting. The only passages of any length that deal with women are the difficult ones, which concern matters like dress and keeping silence. I don't know what to make of these things or the passages on them. Will ignore them for the present and concentrate on more general points. But there are rather a lot of texts to look up! Some have to be hunted for because they are individuals mentioned by name, not just general references to "women".'

However, less than a week later there was a more hopeful remark: '*7 July.* The penny has dropped! I noted down a few points and as I looked over them I was struck with how similar they were to the conclusions I'd come to about the attitude of Jesus, so I followed out this line of thinking.'

This took her to the notebook again where she found a couple of pages on 'Women in the Early Church". It read, 'The position of women in the apostolic church was basically the same as their position in relation to Jesus himself. His followers continued as he had begun. I am not clear about everything, but what is evident are the following points:

'1.   The apostles had the same natural unselfconscious attitude to women as Jesus had. Paul – often regarded as both misogamist and misogynist – spoke affectionately of a number of women and highly valued their fellowship, e.g. Phoebe (Rom. 16:1-2), Mary (Rom. 16:6), Tryphena and Tryphosa (Rom. 16:12), Julia and Nereus' sister (Rom:16.15), Rufus' mother (Rom. 16:13). And he was at least as close to Priscilla as to her husband, Aquila.

'2.   They regarded the faith of a woman as equivalent to that of a man and conferring the same privileges. In Galatians 3:28 Paul speaks of union with Christ as being on the basis of faith alone, so that racial, social and sexual distinctions are irrelevant to it. Women were evangelized, converted and baptized along with men everywhere (Acts 5:14; 8:12; 16: 14-18; 17: 4,12,34).

'3.   Just as Jesus had numbered women among his disciples, so they were included within the circle of the church, and this from the beginning (Acts 1:14; 8:3). Thus they took part in its worship and activity, including money offerings (Acts 5: 7-10; 12:12).

'4.   Women received instruction in doctrine in the church, something they had been excluded from in the synagogue (Acts 2:42; 16:13).

'5.   Women assisted the apostles, as they had Jesus. Paul

received help, support and hospitality from such as Priscilla, Lydia, Euodias and Syntyche. Women also took an active part in the work of local churches, as Paul's comments in Romans 16 show. Phoebe is called a "servant" or "deacon" of the church in Cenchrea. Women are associated with deacons in 1 Timothy 3:11.

'6. There is no specific reference to women being called as witnesses to the resurrection of Jesus in the way the apostles were. But there is no ground for excluding women from those who "were scattered abroad" who "went everywhere speaking [or gossipping] the word" (Acts 8:4) or from the groups of those to whom Jesus appeared alive, referred to in 1 Corinthians 15:6.

'*Loose ends*: a. the question of dress in general and head-coverings in particular, and in this connection the meaning of 1 Corinthians 11:2-16 and 1 Timothy 2:9-10. b. the injunction to be silent in 1 Corinthians 14:34-35 and to refrain from teaching in 1 Timothy 2:11-15.'

'*10 July.* I've been glad to have this project to occupy my mind over these past weeks, while the church has been going into the question of divorce. It has not been a distraction but really encouraging, liberating in fact. I realize how full of prejudice and misunderstanding I was about the Bible's teaching on women. Much has been cleared up and I have learned many new things. However, I gather things are moving in the church, and the pastor is coming to speak with me next week.

'*14 July.* The pastor visited me this evening and brought me up to date with events. They have held three meetings, thoroughly explaining the biblical teaching on marriage and divorce, and allowing time for questions and discussion. In spite of everything there are apparently some dissentient voices who still hold that divorce can never be right. Others are wavering; they feel attracted by the rigorist position because it claims to uphold the sanctity of marriage. This is their strength in view of the decline in sexual and marital standards since the war. The pastor feels they are governed too much by fear and the "thin-end-of-the-wedge" syndrome. If we relax the standard to allow one ground for divorce, then we shall eventually erode the whole thing. The line the elders took over this was twofold. First they challenged them to interpret the clause "except it be for fornication" in Matthew 19, and to prove it did not refer to the adultery of one of the partners. One of these brethren had got hold of a theory held by some commentators that the word can mean "marriage within the prohibited degrees", i.e. incest. Such a marriage would be invalid anyway and dissolved. When it was pointed out that this was the Roman Catholic view these good Protestants were silent, but still did not give way. The other line the elders pressed was that to refuse divorce in the case of adultery, far from upholding the sanctity of marriage, was in fact damaging it. It was allowing a person to have access to two partners – the illicit partner and the legal spouse. To cut such a person off from intercourse with the original spouse was surely a way of rescuing the institution of marriage from abuse of this kind. But the opposition replied that divorce only drove the adulterer into the arms of the new partner and also put an end to any hope of reconciliation.

'Thus a kind of stalemate has been reached. The difficulty, the pastor explained, was that these people were well motivated and guided by conscience. This made it hard to ignore them, since the New Testament teaches the need to respect conscience, even where misguided. The problem is increased because of my presence in the church and desire for membership. It cannot be left as an agreement to differ over principles; a decision has to be made in practice. This made me very disheartened, even fearful, and I offered to withdraw from the church altogether if it would help. In fact I wondered secretly whether he had come and told me all this in the hope that I would make this offer. He replied that to do so would be evading the issue for everyone and that it had to be faced. I asked if it would be wise to postpone the matter of membership and for me just to continue to attend services in the hope that they would gradually come to one mind. But he does not think that is a spiritual way to approach it, but smacks of Gamaliel, not to say Micawber. It may be an English way of doing things, but it is not a Christian way. The truth is paramount over policy and it must be obeyed. All the facts have been put forward and the matter must be resolved in line with these facts. Christians who are seeking to know and do the will of God ought to be able to resolve their differences.

'I said I couldn't help agreeing with this and told him something of my recent studies and how I had found that when facts stared me in the face it was impossible just to hold tenaciously to what I had previously thought and try to justify it somehow, anyhow. In fact I had found it really liberating to let go my preconceptions in order to grasp this new truth. I suppose what is happening now is a test as to whether I really believe this enough to see it through. He said he was glad I felt like that and assured me he had not come round to hint that I drop the matter, only to warn me that when the question of membership was put to the church there might be some who would oppose it, and he felt I should know this and be prepared for it. As far as the elders were concerned, they were determined to see it through and would proceed as they normally do with requests for membership. They would not treat my case as extraordinary but follow normal procedure. This is that the applicant meets with the elders, who then decide among themselves whether they support the application. If they don't, that is the end of the matter, but if they do they present the applicant to the church and ask them to welcome the new member. He said he would leave me for a few days and then, if I am willing, arrange for a meeting with the elders. Meanwhile we must give ourselves to prayer. Who knows? The dissentients might come round to agreeing. He prayed with me about it all, which helped me, since my mind was a bit too confused even to know how to pray. However, I feel more settled now. At least I cannot see any other course except to proceed.'

'*17 July*. The pastor phoned to ask after my feelings on

the matter, and to say that since the church meeting was to
be on 26 July I would need to meet the elders as soon as
possible. So this is arranged for Friday.'

'*20 July*.   The meeting with the elders did not go in quite
the way I had expected. I was not submitted to a close
examination about my experience and doctrine, which they
seemed to take as read. The purpose of the meeting was more
to discuss what line would be taken in presenting me to the
church members in view of my unusual situation, which
obviously could not be ignored since everyone knew that it
was my presence among them that had given rise to the
special meetings on divorce. We were all aware that some
members might prove difficult and that we should be agreed
on how to approach this. They all felt they must stand out for
two things. The first was that conversion blotted out a
person's past life, whatever it may have been. Jesus had
received prostitutes, thieves and murderers. They could not
accept any objection against my past life, such as my
association with the Women's Lib. movement, or my leaving
a Christian home to marry a non-Christian. They felt
reasonably sure of carrying the church with them on this
point. The other would be more difficult – that in some cases
divorce is an act of obedience, right in God's eyes and
therefore no disqualification from church membership. They
felt it must be put positively in this form, and not as a kind of
concession to modern deteriorating standards. It would be
easy to take the line that since the state permitted it we could
do nothing to stop it, that it was all a pity, but we should not
be too hard on someone who had made a mistake. This they
felt was a negative approach, a capitulation, which might
gain general support but would not be true to the facts, since
I had not drifted into divorce but sought it and taken the
initiative. It was a clear-cut issue and not just a gradual
marriage break-up, and should be presented thus.

'They further agreed that they would not yield on these
points, and that if any could not accept them they would
have to make their choice. If they cannot accept my

fellowship they cannot accept that of the elders who do accept my fellowship. I was horrified that they should take such a strong line, but they explained there was a principle at stake even more important than my position. This was that the church has no right to impose conditions not required by Christ or the apostles. *They* had not made divorce a bar to membership, where it was in accord with Christ's teaching, so neither should we. It was comparable to the principle on which Paul had stood out in Galatia, that circumcision should not be required for entrance to the church, only repentance and faith. If objectors used the "thin-end-of-the-wedge" argument it could cut both ways. To introduce a fresh rule for church fellowship unknown in apostolic times could also be the thin end of a wedge consisting of all sorts of other rules.

'I couldn't help admiring them for taking this line, but my admiration was interrupted by the real bombshell of the evening – that I should testify before the church! They explained that this was not an absolute necessity, nor a tradition. Some did it, most did not. They only suggested or recommended it where they thought it would help. In my case they thought it would be a good thing in view of the unusual circumstances. They would not be looking at a hypothetical "case", but an actual person who had passed through certain experiences which were real. They would all see how God had been in it all, so that their minds would be turned away from principles and matters of conscience to the living God and one of his children. If they rejected me they should have to feel they were rejecting not a "point of view" but a person whom God had received. This was the last thing I had expected and I was dumb-struck. But they said they would not press it but leave it entirely to me now. On my way out Peter whispered that he and Grace would help me over it if I needed them. I do!'

'*24 July.*   Have had some rather broken nights lately. My mind won't stop thinking about what to say on Thursday.'

However, when it came to the meeting itself, Eve scarcely

needed her diary. She could visualize the scene as if it had taken place last night. She could still see all the faces looking up at her. Even the pastor and other elders had sat facing her. Some registered sympathy, others apprehension, while many looked as they always looked, whatever the occasion or subject, whoever the speaker. None looked hostile. She could hear herself beginning nervously and speaking too loud, saying she was grateful to them for the opportunity to share with them what God had done for her. She thanked him now that she had been born into a Christian family. Although she had gone her own way it had sown a seed which was now bearing fruit. Her voice softened as she began to speak more naturally, telling them how she became aware of being treated differently because she was a girl, how she had noticed all sorts of things – at home, at school and church – which indicated the female sex was regarded as somewhat inferior by the male sex. Many of these things were trivial in themselves but were straws in the wind. She had particularly resented not being trusted to make her own decisions. There had been one or two others, older girls, who had shared these views and influenced her, lending her books and taking her to meetings. Gradually she had become involved in the Women's Liberation movement. She went on to tell them of her university career, her break with her parents and marriage to Frank, then the disillusionment with the feminist campaign and how this had led to the break-up of her marriage. Without going into details, she made it clear he had left her for another woman.

Then she came to the matter of her spiritual awakening and how God had drawn her to himself in his love, and she had willingly yielded up everything to him: her past with its wanderings, unbelief and sin; her present by coming to Christ as she was, not pretending to be either better or worse than she actually was; her future, whatever that might be. She made a point of saying that at that stage she had had no thoughts about obtaining a divorce; in fact she had been prepared to remain as she was for the rest of her life as a kind of penance, or at least a way of showing she was willing to accept the consequences of her actions. She explained how she had resumed attending church services, going to one or two churches in the town to keep in the background, but through meeting Grace by accident had been drawn more into this church. She tried to avoid involving Peter and Grace too much, and went on to talk more generally about how she had looked into the Bible's teaching on marriage and divorce and the position of women generally.

She could remember almost word for word how she had brought her testimony to a conclusion. 'I had the advantage of coming to the Bible freshly, without preconceived ideas about it. Also I came to it from feminism, very conscious of being a woman in a man's world. If I had any preconceived ideas they were that the Bible shared this sexist attitude, in fact was to a great extent responsible for it. These delusions were shattered. I came to see that these ideas came from outside the Bible, although many people read them into the Bible, and this had gone on from the times of the rabbis to the present. However, whatever other people thought and did, whether they were men or women, I know that Christ himself shared none of these prejudices of his day or ours, and in his eyes I am as precious and useful as any man who has ever lived or is alive today. I thank him for what it means to be born into his kingdom and to be lifted above the petty squabbles and divisions of people, and delivered from a negative attitude and an aggressive mentality. For many years I sought freedom. I thought I had found it when I left home – and in some ways I had – but now I *know* I have. I know the truth, or some of it, and the truth has made me free. I know I need never be afraid of letting go of my ideas and going afresh to his Word. I shan't lose anything and I shall gain freedom. I would like to think we all shared that conviction.'

Eve could still recapture the feelings she had had as she sat down that evening – how the hearts of the people seemed to melt towards her. She turned to her diary again.

'*27 July*.   Grace phoned late last night to say all is well.
My words had touched their hearts and no one opposed or
refused my entry into membership. It is not the practice in
the church to take a vote, only to allow opportunity for
anyone with objections or difficulties to voice them. No one
did so, and one who had previously expressed doubts said he
was happy to welcome me now. He saw that it was one thing
to discuss a subject in theory, another to see it in the life and
experience of a real person. He felt sure that since the Lord
had led me to himself he would not immediately lead me to
make a wrong decision. He was going away to rethink his
views.'

As she closed her diary that morning Eve reflected on that
final remark. 'I think that brother hit on one of the big
weaknesses of our evangelical churches. Are we too
theoretical? Do we think too much about our own principles
and our own consciences and too little about other people
and the way God is dealing with them? Do we try to force
people into armour that doesn't fit them, when all the time
God has received them without that armour? Perhaps we
ought to go in a *little* more for what the legal profession calls
"case-law". It could have a salutary effect on us.'

5.
Every woman who prays

Eve had been glad that her acceptance by the church had come on the verge of the summer holidays, so that her formal reception into membership had to be postponed several weeks. She was able to go away with her mind at rest that the matter had been settled and there would be no more waiting and discussing. It also meant she had time to collect her thoughts and prepare for the future. She gave much thought and prayer to the new activities in which she would soon be participating – baptism, reception into membership and attending the Lord's Supper; also joining in the members' meetings for fellowship and business and, perhaps above all, taking part in the prayer meetings. It was going to be a very new life, so different from the past few years, but she was looking forward to it. She hoped and prayed she would be able to justify the pastor's opinion that she would be 'an asset to the church'.

Her baptism took place at the beginning of September, and the rest of the programme followed from that. In spite of having spent her childhood in a Christian home and having been much involved in church activities, she had lived her formative years outside the influence of Christianity and very much under that of contemporary society. She therefore regarded herself as one coming into the church more or less fresh from the world, with no prior commitment to any particular outlook or form. She thus noticed things which to the more established Christian had become part of the background, to be taken for granted. To Eve everything was new and strange and she was very conscious of this, so that she considered each activity deeply, both before and after. At the same time she was maturing in character as a Christian and growing in her understanding of the Bible. The pulpit ministry was giving a depth to her experience of salvation, opening out to her what it meant to be redeemed from sin and made a child of God. Her own researches were enabling her to come to terms with those aspects of Christianity which had alienated her in her adolescence, in particular those which related to the place of women.

In view of this she was particularly sensitive to the relationship between the sexes in her own church. It was not that she had any ambitions to bring Women's Lib. into the church. She was as anxious to rethink that matter as she was everything to do with her life. But over the past few years it had become second nature to her to latch on to everything, great or trivial, which indicated that women might be regarded as inferior and that they even accepted that status for themselves. She could not help herself, therefore, at least subconsciously, noticing the way the women were treated in the church and how they conducted themselves. But she no longer judged them by the stance of the Women's Liberation movement. She had carefully studied the place the Bible itself gave them and this was now her point of reference. She was no longer interested in making every woman she met into an activist for feminism. On the other hand, she could not prevent herself noticing where there were discrepancies between what the Bible indicated and what actually happened. She was not plotting any kind of revolution, only seeking to arrive at the truth. It might be that her own understanding of the Bible was still immature and therefore incorrect, and that those who had been Christians and church members far longer than she had would be able to put her right. She was quite happy for that to happen. She had not arrived at a hard and fast position on particular issues, nor was she setting out to pass judgement on all who did not share her outlook. On the other hand, if questions arose in her mind she saw no reason to ignore them.

And questions did arise as she began to mingle more with the members and participate in the activities of the church. One question which bothered her increasingly was the participation of the female members in the meetings for prayer and discussion. The general position of the church was clearly to encourage all members to take part except where this was inappropriate. There were not only open prayer meetings, but other gatherings for fellowship which were totally given to the members' contributions. Church meetings were only partially concerned with business matters, since these were thoroughly gone into by the elders and deacons. The remainder of the time, which more often than not was the greater part, was given over to questions raised by members or issues put before the church by the elders. Sometimes they revolved around an experience related by one of the members or a report of something God was doing in another church or part of the world. It was a fairly flexible system which allowed for things to be brought out while they were fresh and prevented problems or disagreements from festering. It was this system that had facilitated investigation into the matter of divorce involving Eve herself.

In general she was pleased at the degree of freedom felt by the members at these gatherings, and it was not long before she herself began to make her contribution to them. She was also glad to discover that the women seemed to have no inhibitions about participating – indeed this was what had encouraged her to take part herself. But as time went by she began to realize that certain of the lady members never joined in vocal prayer or spoke in the discussion meeting. It was not that she judged them adversely for it; she just wondered why it was. It was not that they were unspiritual or immature, for she had had conversations with most of them and received encouragement and good counsel. In some cases she could see it was shyness and nervousness that held them back, which she felt was a pity, since she was convinced they would have helped themselves, one another and everybody if they had been able to overcome it to some extent. But there were others who did not fit into this category, who were very capable conversationalists and had

no inhibitions about expressing their views on church
matters. Eventually she discovered that, earlier in life these
particular ladies had belonged to churches where women
were not expected to participate in spiritual meetings, indeed
this was regarded as incorrect. They had found it difficult to
adapt to new ways. Some could still not accept that it was
right for women to raise their voice in these meetings, and
others, although they did not condemn it in others, felt
unable to break the habit of a lifetime and open their mouths.

Eve could not help feeling a certain pity for these sisters.
She recalled her own experience of the truth setting her free
from prejudice, and wished that they could share something
of the joy this brought in relation to their own particular form
of bondage. But at the same time she started to question
herself. Was she sure she was right on this point? It was true
the majority were convinced that it was in order for women to
take part in prayer and contribute to a discussion, even
raising questions. But majorities were not always right. In
their former churches these women had been in the majority
in the view they held. And they were sound and godly
women, conscientious in their desire to do the will of God.
Could it just be assumed that they were wrong and she and
the others were right? What was the truth in this matter? Eve
remembered how, when she had been doing her studies into
women in the Bible, there had been one or two loose ends she
could not tie up. This had been one of them – whether or not
women should participate vocally in gatherings of the
church, at least where men were present. There had been
certain passages she could not make head or tail of. Worst of
all, they seemed to contradict each other. She thought the
only way to resolve it in her mind was to take up these points,
look into the relevant passages and see if she could get to the
bottom of them.

But she had not been at work very long before she found
herself presented with a conundrum. She found two passages
that seemed to authorize women to participate vocally in
worship, and two which seemed to forbid it! She read in Acts

2:17-18 how Peter, preaching on the Day of Pentecost,
declared that a prophecy made long ago by Joel was being
fulfilled: 'I will pour out of my Spirit upon all flesh.' This
outpouring was to affect both sexes equally: 'Your sons and
your daughters shall prophesy.' In the same way it would
make no distinction as regards age: 'Your young men shall
see visions, and your old men shall dream dreams,' nor as
regards social class: 'And on my servants and on my
handmaidens' (literally 'bondmen and bondmaidens') 'I
will pour out of my Spirit.' The last clause indicated that it
was not only high-class or educated women who would
receive this gift, but even slave girls. That this kind of thing
actually happened was proved by the case of the four
daughters of Philip the evangelist, all of whom exercised the
gift of prophecy (Acts 21:9).

The other passage she came across was in Paul's first
letter to the Corinthians, chapter 11, verse 5: 'Every woman
that prayeth or prophesieth with her head uncovered
dishonoureth her head.' From the letter in general she
gathered that the members of the church in Corinth had
received a profusion of gifts of the Spirit, and this was
creating some disturbance. The church was tending to divide
into groups, one or other of which had written to Paul
complaining about the behaviour of some of the others and
asking for a ruling. The problem at issue here seemed to have
been about the physical appearance of the two sexes in
church worship. Evidently the men's heads should be
uncovered and women's covered (although exactly what this
meant she was not too sure at the time). But the interesting
thing was that Paul did not say the women should not be
praying or prophesying at all. If they were forbidden to
participate vocally anyway, the simplest thing would have
been to have stated this and put an end to the whole matter.
There would have been no point in discussing what they
were or were not to wear when exercising these gifts if they
were not allowed to do so anyway. Supposing the question
put to him had been, 'Is it all right for women to be

uncovered when they take part in the worship of the church?' his answer would then have been, 'They should not be speaking at all, so the question of attire does not arise.'

All this made something abundantly clear: Paul's practice was in line with the words of Peter on the Day of Pentecost and the practice of the Jewish churches as exemplified by Philip's daughters. But everything was thrown back into the melting-pot when, three chapters later, she read, 'Let your women keep silence in the churches: for it is not permitted unto them to speak; but they are commanded to be under obedience, as also saith the law. And if they will learn anything, let them ask their husbands at home: for it is a shame for women to speak in the church' (1 Cor.14:34-35). This sounded so categorical that she could hardly believe it was written by the same person. Whatever could he mean? Did this second statement cancel out the first? Had he gone away and thought about it, then changed his mind but forgotten in his haste to alter the first passage before sending the letter off? Was he in two minds? Was he speaking in the first passage as a liberated Christian and in the second suddenly remembering his past as a rabbi? He certainly sounded just like one here, calling in 'the law' to back up his argument. Did he mean that women were, after all, the same under the new covenant as they had been under the old? If so, what on earth had Peter meant when he said Joel's prophecy was fulfilled?

In this state of perplexity she noticed a cross-reference in the margin of her Bible and frantically turned it up, hoping it might solve the problem. It didn't; it made matters worse. The reference was to 1 Timothy 2:11-15, where she read: 'Let the woman learn in silence with all subjection. But I suffer not a woman to teach, nor to usurp authority over the man, but to be in silence. For Adam was first formed, then Eve. And Adam was not deceived, but the woman being deceived was in the transgression. Notwithstanding she shall be saved in childbearing, if they continue in faith and love and holiness with sobriety.' That capped it all. It was back to the law and the synagogue where the women took a back seat and no part. They must do as they were told and concentrate on having children. After all, they were second on the scene and should take second place. And if they think this is unfair, let them remember who was to blame for letting sin and evil into the world – a woman. If Eve had kept her mouth shut the world wouldn't be in such a mess. So the least she can do now is to keep quiet, go home and look after her babies. Teaching and preaching is man's work. So it seemed, was praying, according to verse 8: 'I desire that *the* men' (the Revised Version carefully pointed out that the Greek word carries the definite article!) 'pray everywhere, lifting up holy hands.' And what about the women? Well, they must take care they don't overdress or overdo their hairstyles and jewellery, as the passage went on. Let them take care they behave themselves – she supposed that was what 'good works' meant – 'Do as you're told.'

As she read and thought about all this, Eve began to feel indignant. The feminist blood, which had cooled over the past year or so, started to boil up again and course through her veins. She felt disheartened and depressed. It seemed that these ladies she had pitied for their bondage and had ever so slightly despised might be right after all. She seemed to be right back where she was in her teens, and some of her old thoughts, together with conversations and arguments from those years, flashed before her mind's eye again. Had she been making a terrible mistake? Did she belong in the church? Did she still want to be a Christian? What a terrible thought! Then she began to pull herself together. She recalled her own studies on the position of women in the Bible and how everything had pointed to a great change brought about by Christ – the welcome he gave to women, the example he set his apostles, who followed it by giving women a place in the church alongside men. She couldn't really have been wrong about all this, could she? And Peter and Grace were at one with her, as was the pastor. Surely they must have thought about these passages? There must be something she had misunderstood somewhere.

'I know what I'll do,' she suddenly said to herself, 'I'll

raise it at a members' meeting. Then we can all face the
problem, and hopefully come to a solution.' There had only
been two members' meetings since Eve joined the church,
but she was already clear on how the system operated and
felt it would be in no way precocious of her to raise a matter
such as this. Eve mentioned her problem to the pastor, who
agreed it was an important and appropriate subject and duly
announced it would be the main matter for discussion at
their next meeting. Meanwhile everyone was to do some
homework on the passages at issue, so that, whether or not
they contributed, they would at least be able to follow the
discussion.

The evening of the meeting arrived, and the pastor opened
by putting the problem in very much the same way as Eve
had put it to him: two passages seeming to come down on one
side and two on the other. He proposed that the discussion be
conducted around two questions: What did the first two
passages permit? What did the other two forbid? It should
then be possible to see whether there was any contradiction
between them or whether they were referring to different
things. He then put the first question as to what the two
passages, Acts 2:17-18 (along with Acts 21:9) and 1
Corinthians 11:5, permitted. These were clearly related since
they each referred to women exercising the gift of prophecy.

The first contributor took the view that there were special
charismatic gifts which accompanied the outpouring of the
Spirit at Pentecost, such as the speaking in tongues practised
by some of those who had been present in Jerusalem on that
occasion. This was a phenomenon and not the normal thing;
the norm was for women not to participate. However, when
the Spirit came in unusual power, the rules were laid on one
side lest the Spirit's authority be resisted and his influence
quenched. This was evidently what was happening in
Corinth. Special things were done through the Spirit and
even women were prophesying. Paul was a great believer in
the work of the Spirit and would do nothing that might
interfere with his ministry. But this did not mean he thought

it was all right for any women to join in at any time and in any place. One could not generalize from an abnormal situation.

Someone else raised an objection to this, pointing out that Paul mentioned not only prophesying but also 'praying'. Surely he was distinguishing the abnormal gift (prophesying) from the normal exercise of the spirit of prayer. His words, therefore, could not be limited to special manifestations, but applied to the life of the church generally. The promise of Joel and its fulfilment opened up worship to all members of the church irrespective of sex, age or class. Even if the special manifestations like prophesying and tongue-speaking did not continue in every age and place, they established the principle of female participation. If women could prophesy and use a very unusual gift, surely it followed that they could pray in the more normal fashion?

But another answered this by saying he thought this was reading too much into these passages. Paul was not specifically dealing with female participation in 1 Corinthians 11, but with dress, particularly head-dress. It was putting too much weight on a few words to regard this as a *carte blanche* for women taking part in public worship and prayer. We should judge this passage by one where he was dealing specifically with the issue of female participation. Was this not a sound principle of interpreting Scripture, to explain obscure passages in the light of clearer ones? Surely Paul was just summarizing in the interests of conciseness when he talked about 'praying and prophesying'. He was speaking generally about a gathering of a fairly informal nature in which prayers and prophecies were the chief features. All he meant was that women were present when these things were being done, not that they were personally doing them. What he was concerned about here was how they dressed, and he would have been horrified to know that he was being interpreted as granting permission for women to participate vocally in these gatherings.

That might be so, replied another, if Peter's quotation from Joel had not been made. The discussion was beginning to forget about that passage, but was it not the crucial one? Did it not lay down the guide-lines for the new age, the age following Christ's appearance on earth as Redeemer, and his return to glory? Wasn't Peter saying that Jesus was celebrating his return to heaven in triumph by distributing gifts all round, without any distinction or discrimination? Nor should they forget the climax of the passage: 'Whosoever shall call on the name of the Lord shall be saved' (Acts 2:21). This was the message of the new kingdom: there were no natural barriers now, it was open to all who believed in Jesus. This was what the apostles consistently practised, and Paul was specially strong on it. He opposed those who wanted to make Gentiles into Jews before they could become Christians. There was no question of this being a temporary or limited arrangement. Must not the promise of the gift of the Spirit to women be seen in the same light? What authority had we for saying that Paul was suddenly hedging it about with restrictions, that it could only be exercised on special occasions, or in private or at women's meetings? Where was the proof that there were to be conditions about practising it? If there were to be conditions for that part of the prophecy, why were there no conditions about the way of salvation, limiting the 'Whosoever shall call on the name of the Lord'?

Then someone else came up with yet another view. He went along with what the previous speaker had said in general, but thought that the problem in Corinth was that some women were taking this new situation too far. He had done some very careful homework on the background of Corinthian life and on the exact words and phrases used. He thought the words should read, 'Any woman who prays or prophesies *by* uncovering her head.' What this meant was that some Corinthian Christian women were becoming too liberated. They took the gospel to mean that women were now totally equal to men. They were not under their authority and could do just as they did. To demonstrate this even more explicitly they were throwing off their veils and appearing uncovered just like males. They thought that if they did this it put them on a par with men, so that they could also pray and prophesy like men. They were claiming the right to pray and prophesy *by* uncovering their heads and looking like men. This was why Paul reprimanded them for uncovering their heads, and this included a reprimand for praying and prophesying.

This was a clever argument and everyone was reduced to silence while they thought about it. Up to this time none of the elders had expressed a point of view. The hiatus in the discussion afforded an opportunity, and one of them now spoke. He pointed out that Joel's prophecy was rooted in the Old Testament, where certain women were given the gift of prophecy and exercised it. What Joel foretold was the day when this would be a general, not a special gift. So Peter's quotation of Joel's words must be the definitive statement about women's freedom to participate in worship. Paul did not therefore need to reiterate it. What he did was simply to assume it, which was why it came out the way it did – not 'a woman *may* pray and prophesy *if* she covers her head', but 'a woman *who* prays and prophesies . . .' indicating it was the practice and that he didn't disapprove of it. The last speaker's argument had been very ingenious, he said, but there was a flaw in it. If these Corinthian women were trying to assert their equality, why didn't they set themselves up as preachers and teachers? Surely that would have been the way to make their point, if that was what they were trying to do. But they clearly didn't do this, or Paul would certainly have had something to say!

At this point someone intervened to say that he thought prophesying *was* preaching. 'I was just coming to that,' replied the elder. 'In fact prophesying does not always mean preaching; the majority of the Old Testament prophets were not preachers. Of course, the prophets named in the Old Testament, the ones who have become famous, are the preaching ones. But there were many more whose main occupation was praising rather than preaching. The context

in which Peter quoted Joel at Pentecost indicates that the
way the prophecy was being fulfilled was with an outburst of
praise. Those to whom the Spirit gave the gift of tongues were
"declaring the wonderful works of God", that is, engaging in
an act of worship. What the prophecy means is that this
would no longer be the prerogative of priests and Levites,
along with official "prophets", but that the people generally
would take part. Thus what the women in Corinth were
probably doing was praying and praising God under the
direct influence of the Holy Spirit, rather than announcing
special messages to the church, although this is not
necessarily ruled out. It is possible that Philip's daughters
received messages from God, for his people, just as the Old
Testament prophetesses did. But it is interesting that in Acts
21, in spite of the presence of these four prophesying women,
the prophet Agabus made a special journey from Judea to
Caesarea to warn Paul of what was in store for him in
Jerusalem. However, as far as the subject of our discussion is
concerned, it seems impossible to avoid the conclusion that
women were permitted to participate vocally in worship, and
did so. We don't know in any detail how they conducted their
meetings, but obviously open prayer was included and in this
the women took part.'

While the members were considering what had just been
said, the pastor stepped in to say he thought this would be a
good point to move on to the other question. Several had
advanced arguments for saying that what the passage
permitted was for women to take part in gatherings for
prayer and praise, although others took a different view. He
said that for himself he was surprised no one had raised the
question of authority, since this seemed to be very much in
the forefront of Paul's mind in 1 Corinthians 11. 'He starts
with a run-down of who is head over whom in verse 3, and
goes on from there. He is very particular that this headship
be maintained on earth between man and woman, as it is in
heaven between Christ and God. If women taking part in
prayer and praise infringed this, he would certainly have said

so. But he doesn't appear to say that. However, this point cannot finally be established without going into the other two passages and trying to decide what they forbid. They certainly forbid something. The question is what? Let's take the 1 Corinthians 14 passage first, verses 34 and 35. Any offers?'

Eve remembered it had been she herself who had first spoken to this question, but only to say this passage had been her big problem. She could go along with what had been said on the other passages, but this seemed a categorical denial of women so much as opening their mouths in a church gathering. She was even afraid she might be breaking the rules by what she was saying at that very moment! Someone else followed this up by saying that surely this passage proved that the interpretation some had given of 1 Corinthians 11 must be wrong, since Paul would scarcely have contradicted himself or changed his mind. Another argued that there was no need to be as drastic as that; perhaps Paul was referring to something else here. After all, he didn't say, 'It is not permitted to them to *pray*' but '*to speak*'. 'Does that word have something to do with teaching or preaching?' this member asked. Someone else got up to say he knew what the word meant: it was a word used of conversation, and what Paul was complaining about was women chattering to each other and disturbing the proceedings. This was why he told them to wait until they got home and to ask their husbands.

None of these contributions really seemed to solve the problem, and eventually the pastor came to the rescue. He asked them to look back over the chapter to see what it was about, and that was prophesying, the same as chapter 11. After making a number of points, the apostle eventually came to the matter of 'judging' the prophets (verse 29), that is, assessing whether they and their messages were truly of God. This would be done partly by asking them questions and partly by making statements. It was when he came to this part of his argument that he made his prohibition on

women participating. For women, whatever their gifts, to
evaluate male prophets, would be a breach of the authority
structure of the church which he had already laid down in
chapter 11, verse 3. So when he referred to 'silence' he did not
mean total silence on every occasion. In verses 28 and 30 he
used that same word 'silence' of the prophets themselves,
obviously meaning that in these circumstances (where
another was given a message) the prophet should remain
silent. He must be silent while the other prophet spoke, but
he was not being told never to open his mouth in the
assembly again! The same applied to the women. When
prophets and their messages were being examined and
evaluated, the women were to keep silent. But this did not
mean they were never to speak again under any
circumstances. If a question occurred to them about
something a prophet had said, this was all right, but they
should not raise it there and then, but wait until they got
home and discuss it with their husbands. What Paul said
about God being a God of order, not of confusion, was much
to the point here, and in fact seemed to spark off his warning
to the women. Verse 33, 'God is not the author of confusion,
but of peace', was the immediate context of the prohibition
on women in verse 34. For women to have joined in at this
point in the proceedings would have meant they were taking
authority on themselves and this would have been
disorderly. 'So,' concluded the pastor, 'it looks rather as
though the position we are arriving at is that women may
take part in worship, but only so long as the authority
structure established by God is not broken. The reason Paul
gives for this warning to women is that they are
"commanded to be under obedience, as also saith the law".
In other words the old structure of the relationship between
man and woman is carried on in the New Testament and
combined with the greater freedom given to women in
worship. But this interpretation needs checking against the
passage in 1 Timothy 2: 11-15.'

All that had been said up to now was giving the people much light and they were beginning to see what it was Paul was arguing for in this passage. What was coming out loud and clear was that women were not to teach in the church, or do what would reverse the pattern of authority established by God from creation. The pastor felt it right to point out that the word translated 'silence' here in 1 Timothy 2: 11-12 was a different word from that used in 1 Corinthians 14: 34 and meant simply 'quietness' rather than total silence. This meant that what Paul was against was loud-mouthed and domineering women who tried to lord it over everyone. Of course, he was against men doing this too, but there were other reasons for forbidding it in women. Thus the passage did not mean that women could not pray in the church. The reason why he said in verse 8, 'I will that men pray' was because he was thinking in terms of more formal gatherings, where one person led the whole church in prayer, rather than the type of gathering which was open to contributions and not dominated by one person. It would be inappropriate for a woman to be the one to do this since it implied leadership and authority. But joining in open prayer and praise or contributing to a discussion did not involve arrogating authority and therefore was to be allowed and even encouraged.

Most people in the meeting were thus coming to see there was no incongruity between the various passages on women in the church. For Eve herself it was all a great relief. No wonder she had found difficulty with these passages a few months before! Left to herself she would never have seen them in this light. This was the value of being able to share things openly and to have some gifted and learned men to tackle difficult problems. Unfortunately, the meeting had solved one problem only to create another. What was all this in 1 Corinthians 11 about women being 'covered'? Indeed this seemed to be the main theme of the first part of that chapter. Whereas women praying and praising was only

mentioned in passing, this other matter was treated with
explicitness, thoroughness and even dogmatism. She had not
been the only one to notice this. In fact someone had tried to
raise it, but the chairman had ruled that it would only
complicate matters, and that it was best to stick to the one
issue: 'Sufficient unto the day is the evil thereof.'

Eve was not the type of person who could shelve problems
for very long. If something puzzled her she had to get to the
bottom of it. In any case it was not just an intellectual
problem. If the New Testament said that women should not
appear at gatherings for worship 'uncovered', then they all
ought to do something about it. She wondered if she should
go out and buy a hat or at least put on a headscarf when she
went to church. She suddenly began to notice what the other
women were wearing. Up to this time she had been only
vaguely conscious that some of them wore hats and others
did not. She had not given this serious thought, assuming it
was just a matter of personal preference and taste. Women's
fashions in dress were changing, so you would expect the
older to preserve the pre-war styles and the younger to begin
changing them. If the designers said that hats were out, then
it would be the younger women who would discard them
first. However, when she thought more seriously and began
to observe more closely, she realized it was not entirely a
matter of the generation difference. Some of the girls wore
hats – usually members of the same family. But there were
middle-aged women who came bareheaded. Others seemed
to have no set way of dressing. Come to think of it, the men
were not so uniformly attired as they had been at one time.
Not everyone wore a suit. Blazers and sports jackets were a
not unfamiliar sight, and even ties were not a universal
article of clothing. 'Sunday best', it seemed, was becoming a
thing of the past.

So what about it? Were there any rules about dress for
Christians? Did it matter what was worn or not worn in
church? She must find the answer to these questions. But
how to go about it? She did not feel she could propose a

church meeting on it, so soon after the previous one for which she had suggested the topic. As a comparative novice she did not want to gain a reputation for stirring up mud and provoking and dividing people. She thought she would revert to the quieter and less official approach. She would do as much private reading and research as possible. But she did not see why she should not approach people privately and ask them for their views. If she did this with selected representatives of the different styles of dress, she might be able to gather together the various interpretations, and compare them with her own researches.

There was one family where it was 'hats all round', from the oldest teenager to the little six-year-old. The husband and wife were Christians of long standing, with decided views, who played an active part in the life of the church. They had contributed to the discussion on women praying, and not surprisingly had supported the practice, since the wife freely took part in the church prayer meetings and other gatherings. They were obviously not bigoted traditionalists and their point of view should be interesting, Eve thought. So she asked them one day if she could come and pick their brains on this matter and the response was to invite her to Sunday lunch. She would have preferred the late evening when the children would be out of the way, but when the time came Mr Goldney said immediately, 'You can talk quite freely in front of the children. They know our views on these things and have no objections to them. They quite happily put their hats on when we go to church.' So Eve waded straight in and asked them how they had come to be so clear on the matter.

'It's all quite plain to me, ' came the answer. 'Paul says quite definitely in 1 Corinthians 11 that the man must not come to public worship covered, because he would dishonour Christ. But the woman must be covered or she dishonours the man. He says it would be so dishonourable that she might just as well have all her hair cut off. I understand that was the punishment for prostitutes and

adulteresses in order to expose their shame. They had
brought disgrace on themselves, their family and society,
and should be shown up for what they were.'

'But surely,' Eve said, 'a woman going to church without a
hat can't be compared to a prostitute, can she? Isn't that a bit
extreme?'

"They are not being compared from the moral point of
view, of course, but rather from the standpoint of
disorderliness. Paul says that the head-covering is a sign of
authority, showing she is under the authority of her husband.
If she discards the covering she is flouting that authority and
upsetting the order God has established, which makes the
man head of the woman. As someone pointed out at our
church meeting, this was what the Christian women in
Corinth were doing. They thought that the gospel meant that
since women were equally acceptable to God and equally
welcome in the church, there was no difference now. So why
need they wear something to mark that difference? Some of
the members appealed to Paul and he ruled that there was a
spiritual equality which allowed women to take part in the
worship and contribute to it, but they were still under the
authority of men in the home and the church. Since the veil
was a symbol of authority, they must still wear it. If they did
so, it was quite in order for them to pray.'

Eve glanced round the table. No one batted an eyelid.
They had had all this explained to them and could see it as
clearly as their father. Eve felt herself beginning to bend
before this plain logic. But she was not completely satisfied.

'You said it was a veil. So is a hat really good enough?'

'Ah, well, you have to allow for changes of style. The veil
gradually evolved into the hat, but it's still a covering. That's
the main thing.'

'That's the main thing,' echoed the ten-year-old boy, as he
put his serviette on his head and pulled it tight at the corners
so that it almost came down over his eyes. 'That's the main
thing!' This brought giggles from the other children and
smiles from the grown-ups. When order had been restored,

Eve raised another point. 'If the veil is the sign of authority, why does Paul talk about the woman needing to have long hair? If she's wearing a veil, her hair won't be visible, will it?'

'No, but it will be when she takes the veil off. She will have that all the time as the symbol of her womanhood. Then on formal occasions or when appearing in public she wears the veil as a further sign. I can't really see there is any problem.'

Eve had not come to raise problems or create doubts, especially in the minds of the children, only to get information. She had been given this in no uncertain terms. Since she had come to the end of her questions, it was agreed they should wash up and go out for a walk to use up some of the children's surplus energy. Having heard the argument on this side of the question, she was anxious now to discover how others justified *not* wearing a hat, so she looked around the congregation that evening to try to decide who would be the best person to approach on this. Her eye fell on a nurse from the local hospital, unmarried and living alone. She rarely if ever appeared in a hat, and so Eve thought she might have good reasons for this. So she invited her back to her own flat after the service in order to raise the matter.

'I was not brought up in a Christian home,' she said, 'and was not taught any specific Christian standards of dress, if there are any. I was already nursing when I became a Christian and just carried on dressing as before. I saw no reason for changing my ways. I just feel more free being bareheaded, especially after wearing the nurse's cap for hours on end most days.'

'But have you never been convicted about it from 1 Corinthians 11? Doesn't Paul say there that women should appear in church with their heads covered?'

'That passage was discussed once by the church, a good while before you came. It wasn't such a full-scale debate as the one we had recently on women praying, but it was aired. It is true that some took the line that head-coverings were the rule for women in church for all time, but not everyone agreed. There were quite a few who thought that Paul was simply following the custom of the day, by which women were expected to appear in public veiled, as Moslem women do today. But fashions have changed down the ages. Hardly any Christian women wear veils. And hats don't really symbolize anything, if they ever did. The main point of 1 Corinthians 11 is that women accept their place in the hierarchy. I'm quite happy about that. I don't think women should be leaders and preachers in the church. But I can't see any need for them to wear a special article of clothing as a kind of badge. That's a matter of custom, just an outward thing. The customs change but the principle continues. Doesn't Peter say that Christian women should not worry about clothes and hairstyles, but attend to their spirits and cultivate meekness and quietness? Because a woman wears a hat on her head doesn't mean she behaves in a docile manner. I know some ... well, perhaps I'd better not go on, or I shall be infringing against the rule of meekness and quietness for women!'

So Eve had heard two virtually opposite points of view within the same fellowship of people. At least it did not disturb the fellowship, she thought, or if it did this was not apparent. However, she decided to go back to Mr Goldney and ask him what he thought about those who did not adopt his line on the head-covering question. He replied that he didn't think it was something on which Christians should judge each other. Since it was an external, a sign, it came under the heading of things which were a matter of individual conscience, like the distinctions of foods and the observance of days that some Christians in New Testament times maintained because of their past life as Jews. It occurred to Eve that Paul said it was the people who kept to these externals who were classed as the weaker brethren, and she wondered if that was how Mr Goldney regarded himself. She doubted it. She said nothing, however, and he added that there were those in the church who took a stronger line than his own. Some time before, there had been a proposal put forward to have a notice at the entrance to the church

asking that women attending services should have their
heads covered. But the elders refused this because they could
not see the New Testament gave authority to the church to
force people to conform to any particular rule about dress.
They held that on a matter of this kind, which did not involve
doctrine, it was for everyone to be persuaded in their own
minds, and not to be compelled. This would be an
infringement of Christian liberty. 'I agreed with that,' he
added, 'and I think most other people did, however strong
their views.'

Eve was glad to hear that at least she had not stirred up a
hornet's nest in the church. However, as far as she was
concerned, the matter was still far from settled. She felt there
were one or two loopholes in Mr Goldney's case. For one
thing, she couldn't see the connection between the hair and
the veil in 1 Corinthians 11, and was not satisfied with his
explanation that the hair was a kind of permanent symbol,
whereas the veil was added for public appearances,
especially at worship. In any case it seemed a long way from
the general ethos of Paul and the New Testament to make
sartorial matters such an issue. The man who risked his life
to save the Gentiles from compulsory circumcision was
hardly likely to be so sticky over women's headgear. It
somehow did not fit. On the other hand, she felt Nurse
Duncan had dismissed it all rather too sweepingly as just an
obsolete custom. Again this did not ring true for the New
Testament, in which every word was precious and
meaningful. There must be more to it than that. But how to
find it? That was the problem. Her own researches had not
really got to the bottom of it. Modern translations and
paraphrases helped a little, but the Bible commentaries she
had managed to lay hands on were disappointing. They
discussed things she did not want to know about or made
points which were obvious anyway. But they just evaded the
questions she wanted answering, especially the question:
what did Paul require women to wear on their heads? Why
was this important enough to include in a letter in which

space and time were in such short supply? What had all this
to do with Christians today? The last question was the vital
one, but she knew it could not be answered honestly until the
first one was cleared up. What was the actual situation in
Corinth that Paul was trying to rectify?

Eve had hoped to be able to handle the whole thing on her
own without calling in outside help. But she was beginning to
despair of this. It looked like a field which called for some
original research, and she had neither the time, the ability
nor the equipment for such a task. A good subject for
someone to do for a Ph.D., she thought. Having swallowed
her pride and consulted Peter, she expressed this opinion to
him. 'Funny you should say that,' he remarked, 'somebody
has.' Seeing Eve's face light up, he added, 'Don't get too
excited. I don't have a copy. In fact, it isn't even published.'
Then, seeing her face fall again, he went on, 'But what I have
got are some articles by the same man in a magazine which
came my way when we were discussing it in the church. In
fact, I think these may be of more use to you than the thesis,
unless you know Hebrew, Greek and a few other ancient
languages! I'll see if I can find them for you.'

When the articles eventually came into Eve's hands, the
first thing she did was to glance right through to see what the
headings were. The sections were entitled: 'The situation in
Corinth'; 'Head-coverings and authority in 1 Corinthians
11'; and under this various sub-headings: 'The meaning of
"uncovered" '; 'Woman as the glory of man'; 'Because of the
angels'; 'Long hair'. Then there was a section on 'Relevance
today' and in smaller print at the end an appendix, 'Veiling
customs and hairstyles'. 'That's the bit I want,' she said,
'that section at the end. I think I'll begin there. The last shall
be first!'

So she waded through quotations from the Mishnah and
the Talmud, from Greek and Roman writers, descriptions of
inscriptions, paintings and sculptures depicting women from
the ancient world. What did it all add up to? Well, evidently
veils were not the order of the day, as many had seemed to

think. The Old Testament did not require them, and even the Talmud only regarded them as signs of exceptional piety rather than the general rule. Women were often depicted wearing a shawl – a large square cloth which could either be draped over the shoulders or else pulled up to cover the head. But men wore these too and it seemed their main function was protection against the sun. There was nothing symbolic about them. The Greek and Roman practice at the time of Christ seemed to be similar, so that the Corinthian women would not have seen any garment they wore over their heads as having any particular significance for their status as women. None of these nations veiled their faces as a general practice, although they might have done so on occasions. This custom was instituted by Islam many centuries later, to be copied by others.

Moreover, she gathered that hairstyles were of more significance than head-coverings. Here there *was* a distinction between the sexes. According to the Old Testament women wore their hair long, but men normally cut theirs. Hence the Nazarite, to show he was set apart, had to let his hair grow. But to shave it off altogether was a sign of shame, something a leper, for instance, had to do. Also the women, although they wore their hair long, did not let it hang loose, but tied or pinned it up. Loose hair was a sign of special sorrow, which might accompany mourning, or repentance over something like adultery, at least the accusation of that sin. Greeks and Romans at the time of Christ had a similar practice. Although the earlier Greek men had worn their hair long, the later ones were beginning to copy the Romans, who cut theirs short. Women's hair was long but pinned up. The richer and more worldly women often did this with elaborate coiffures and even decorated the curls with gold and jewels. For them too, to let the hair down was a sign of grief or shame; it was something unusual, setting a person apart.

Eve was glad she had read this section first as it gave her a picture of what women in the Corinthian church would have been like. But the introduction to the first article warned her of the great difficulty of reconstructing the situation too exactly. Paul had received a letter from the Corinthians of which we can only guess the contents. Since it was this he was answering in his first letter to them, we have to try to work out what was in it and thus what he meant. With this caveat coming on top of the smallness of her own efforts, Eve was not looking for too much from the articles and would have settled for just a little more light. In fact the appendix had already taken her a few steps forward and she was hopeful that the main part of the articles would further enlighten her. She felt as if she knew and trusted the writer. He was obviously a scholar who had done his work thoroughly. He did not give the impression he had decided on the outcome before he had started and was going to produce only those points which would support his own case. It was more of an investigation into a problem, which was exactly what it was for Eve; hence she felt a sympathy with the writer, and also that he had sympathy with his readers and was trying to help them understand a difficult part of Scripture. So she worked on through it, checking it with her Bible and making notes, so as to be sure she understood what she was reading.

The first point she noted down concerned the first two verses of 1 Corinthians 11: that Paul was writing with the authority of Christ himself. He had taught in Corinth with that authority and expected them to practise what he had laid down. In other words, we were not to regard what Paul said here as personal opinion; it came as if from the mouth of Christ himself. Next came the big theological point of verse 3: that God had established a kind of hierarchy, in which he was head of Christ, Christ was head of man and man head of woman. The fact that Paul spoke of God as head of Christ indicated that he was not specifying a spiritual inequality between the man and the woman; he was talking about order in the church. At the same time, because there was spiritual equality did not mean that order was now abolished. It seemed from the words, 'I would have you know', that the

Corinthian Christians were not observing this order, or at least querying it. It might have been that the women were over-asserting their liberty in the gospel, especially in the church. 1 Corinthians 14 showed how they had to be restrained from participating in the evaluation of prophets and their messages. But this was not the point under discussion in chapter 11, which had to do with the appearance of their heads.

This formed the next section of the chapter, that is to say, verses 4 - 7. One thing at least was clear: there was to be a difference between men and women as regarded their appearance, as there was regarding their place in the hierarchy of God. The man must not 'have his head covered' and the woman must not 'have her head uncovered'. This was evidently all tied up with their place in God's hierarchy. A man who 'covered his head' dishonoured his head, which meant not only himself and his position of authority and dignity, but also Christ, who was his immediate head. Likewise a woman who left her head 'uncovered' brought dishonour on herself (she might as well be 'shaven and shorn'), that is, on her own womanly dignity and on the man who was her immediate head. But the big question was what this 'covering' and 'uncovering' actually meant. Verse 4 *appeared* to say that a man must not wear a head-covering at worship. However, the author of the article pointed out objections to this interpretation. For one thing, literally translated the words read, 'having upon his head', without saying what he was not to have on his head. But even more serious was the fact that the Jewish men at worship wore a tallith, a long rectangular garment. This had over the ages gradually become reduced to a skull cap, but even in the twentieth century Jewish men did not appear in the synagogue uncovered. If Paul had been attacking this practice he would never have been allowed inside a synagogue, let alone been asked to preach in one. And worst of all, the law required the high priest to cover his head with a turban or mitre when he led the worship (Exod. 36:35-37).

The idea that verse 4 referred to a head- covering therefore seemed to be ruled out.

The position of verse 5 turned out to be similar. Superficially it appeared to refer to some kind of garment, but certain facts went against this. One was that the word used for 'uncovered' meant in the Old Testament 'letting the hair loose', rather than leaving off a veil. Having read the appendix first, Eve now understood the significance of this: it was a sign of grief and shame, something done to a woman suspected of adultery. This made sense of the reference to being 'shaven and shorn', for this was what was done to women convicted of adultery now that the Jews no longer had the power to inflict the death penalty. Paul was saying that if a woman appeared at public worship with loosed hair as if she were an adulteress, she might as well go all the way and have it cut short or shaved off. Another objection to regarding this verse as referring to veiling was that it would not be consistent with what both Paul and Peter said elsewhere about the hair-styles of Christian women. In 1 Timothy 2:9 Paul spoke against 'braided hair with gold and pearls' and in 1 Peter 3:3 Peter opposed women 'plaiting the hair and wearing jewels of gold'. They were not here speaking of the wearing of bracelets, necklaces and earrings, but those elaborate coiffures which introduced gold bangles and jewels into the braids and plaits every inch or so, making the whole head glitter. The apostolic opposition to this was not merely because it was expensive and showy but because it was practised by courtesans, and therefore a disgrace to Christian women. But the point here was that if the head were veiled, the hair-style would not be visible and these exhortations would be pointless. Whatever the details, the very fact that in the same sentence where he had spoken of women being 'uncovered', he went on to speak of hair, indicated it was hair rather than veils which he had in mind.

Verse 6 confirmed this. Where would be the sense in saying, 'If a woman is not *veiled* let her be shorn; but if it is a shame for a woman to be shaved or shorn, let her be *veiled?*'

Cutting off the hair is hardly an appropriate punishment for appearing at worship unveiled. It made far more sense to read it, 'If a woman does not wear her hair pinned up (that is, she lets it hang loose), let her cut it off . . .' Verses 7 - 9 then reverted to the hierarchy principle of verse 3 and developed it. Paul was bringing out the religious importance of the matter, showing it was all part of the difference between the two sexes, and especially their distinctive places in the created order. The man, said verse 7, by the appearance of his head, reflected the glory of God who made him directly from the earth, unlike the woman, who was made out of the man (v. 8). The woman was to reflect the glory of the man and therefore to look different, being made from him (v. 8) and to be his companion (v. 9). Verse 10 explained where the head's appearance came into the matter, although the explanation was a bit obscure with its reference to 'the angels'. What was clear was that the appearance of her head was 'a sign of authority', that is, she was under the authority of the man. Perhaps it was necessary for Paul to point this out because the Corinthian women thought that the gospel had broken the old marriage structure. But what was this about 'the angels'? What had they to do with it? The writer thought that Paul had added this lest he discourage his readers by making them think women had received no advantage from their position under the gospel, but must for ever remain at the bottom of the pile. He hastened to reassure them that although below man during the present age they were above all other orders of creation. He had already referred to this in chapter 6, verse 3: 'Know ye not that we shall judge angels?' In other words, at the end of the world our superiority to them would be demonstrated. Now women were included in this. Let them reflect this dignity and authority by the very way they wore their hair in public. This tied up with the next two verses which spoke of the interdependence of man and woman. The fact that one was over the other did not mean they did not need each other. So let not the Corinthian 'feminists' think they were so liberated that they did not need their menfolk, nor that the men did not need them!

Having said that to restore the equilibrium, as it were, Paul then returned to his theme of the place of man and woman in the created order, and how this was reflected in the hair-style. What he meant by 'comely' or 'decent' in verse 13 was explained in verse 14. He did not mean 'acceptable to society', since many things were this which were not the will of God for his church. He meant something more basic – 'nature', that is, the created order as established by God. It had been God's intention from the beginning to keep the sexes distinct. He abhorred transvestism (Deut.22:5). Also he laid down certain rules about hair, to which he attached significance. There was a sex distinction in this: men were not to have long hair but to cut it. The only exception to this was the Nazarite vow. On the other hand, women were to wear their hair long and to fasten it up, not let it flow loose. The exception to this was an occasion when great sorrow was being expressed, such as mourning over a bereavement, shame over a leprous condition, or a moral disgrace like adultery. Then the hair was left to flow free and even become dishevelled. Paul said that this distinction should be maintained in the church. In verse 14 he related this to men: they were not to wear long hair because it expressed 'shame' or 'dishonour'. This explained what he meant in verse 4 by having the head 'covered'. He meant 'covered with long hair'. From our standpoint it would have been helpful if he had told us he meant hair in the first place, but, of course, the Corinthians to whom he wrote would have well understood this. Similarly, the woman's distinctive nature and place were reflected in her long hair. If she wore it in the right way, pinned up, it indicated her 'glory' – her high place in the order of things, second only to the man. But if she left it loose or cut it short it indicated dishonour. This was what he had meant by 'uncovered' in verse 5 – cut hair or loose hair. If she did either of these she despised her natural covering that God had given her. 'Her hair is given her *instead* of a covering (or veil).' Now everything had been made clear. The woman's

head-covering was not a veil or shawl but her hair. If she
wore this properly she needed no other covering. So Paul
seemed to be going so far as to say that wearing a veil or
shawl *as a religious rule* was dishonouring to God, and this was
probably the meaning of verse 16: the churches established
by Paul had no fixed customs about head-dress and therefore
such customs were not to be imposed on Christians. Of
course, this did not prohibit the wearing of head-coverings
for utilitarian purposes, only the insistence on them for
religious reasons. It was the hair difference that was
important, since this was created by God, and intended by
him to mark the distinction between the sexes.

What then of the relevance of all this so many centuries
later? Clearly it could not be written off as just a cultural
thing long passed away. Paul said it was something written
into 'nature' by God himself. It was connected with the order
of things, the relation between man and God, man and
woman. This order continued under the gospel. At home the
husband was head of the wife, and in the church authority
was in the hands of apostles and elders, who were invariably
men. Thus the two sexes had to look different, especially as
regards their heads, because 'headship' was the issue. It
seemed impossible to avoid the conclusion that this must still
apply. But this did not mean the precise styles of the first
century had to remain in operation. It was accepted then
that loose hair meant sorrow or shame. This was not so now.
What mattered was that hair was worn in such a way that a
man did not look like a woman or a woman like a man. This
might involve Christians in taking care where they drew the
line in following contemporary styles, but since it was only a
relative, not an absolute distinction of length or style that
was required, that should not prove too difficult.

Eve went and looked at herself in the mirror. 'I think I
look more like a woman than a man,' she said, 'even since my
haircut the other day! So perhaps I should pass! At any rate I
am clear that I don't have to wear a hat, although I can if I
wish. And since the apostles did not make head-coverings a

rule, the church has no authority to do so either. That's what I wanted to know, and that's what I've found out. But I haven't quite finished. There are one or two other questions about dress.'

These proved nothing like so difficult. Her study of 1 Corinthians 11 had already referred her to 1 Timothy 2:9 and 1 Peter 3:1-6. Those passages laid it down that women were not to be showy or immodest in their hair-styles or dress. What this meant had been made clear to her. Christian women must be careful not to resemble luxurious or immoral women who spent vast amounts of money and time having their hair piled up with elaborate curls, then having gold droplets and pearls fastened into them. Thus it was not a blanket prohibition on rings and jewellery, or on hair-styling. It did not stop a woman wearing bracelets or visiting the hairdresser. But they must be careful not to do these things in such a way as to draw attention to their own wealth and thus the poverty of others in the church. Above all, their appearance must never be sexually provocative, for this would bring disgrace on the whole church.

It would appear these were the only rules for dress among Christians and churches. There was certainly nothing about formality or Sunday best. These came under the heading of 'things indifferent', which were not to be made rules for the church. Freedom should apply in this realm: what members wore or did not wear was their own business. It should not even be suggested to them indirectly that there was a style to which they should conform. A subtle form of discipline consisting of hints or disapproving looks was not even to be applied. But the New Testament warnings on how freedom was to be used must also be heeded. While Christians were free to dress as they wished, they must avoid allowing their freedom to cause others to stumble. If there were those among them who regarded formal dress as part of a reverent approach to God and therefore a matter of worship, their consciences, although weak and in bondage, should be respected. Some way of meeting these people should be found, short of anyone's actually being forced into some kind of uniform. Non-conformist churches did not have a tradition of clerical attire for their ministers, but the latter usually thought it wise to dress in a way that did not give offence and hinder the unity of worship or the hearing of the message. Individual members could follow this example without bringing themselves into bondage or feeling they had to wear clothes they regarded as old-fashioned or constricting. There was a happy medium in the matter.

It had been a busy few weeks for Eve, but it had been worthwhile, not just intellectually but to her faith. 'Whatever is not of faith is sin,' she read. She had been dogged by guilt feelings that she might have been doing the wrong thing in participating in prayer meetings and discussions. She had become conscious of matters of dress, which were distracting her worship and fellowship. Now that these things were cleared up, she felt free again. And, yet, in clearing these things up she had run headlong into this teaching about 'authority' – the man as 'head' of the woman! This went against the grain a little. Some work would have to be done here now!

6.
Under authority

Among the papers and booklets Eve had brought to light
along with her old diary on the day after Sarah's visit to her,
was a copy of the Church Members' Manual she had been
given on making her request for membership. The paper had
gone somewhat yellow and the pages were rather loose, but it
was all there. As she flicked through the pages her eye fell on
the section entitled 'The Government of the Church'. Then it
came back to her how she had gone about tackling the
problem she had been left with after settling questions
concerning the silence and head-coverings of women in
church. This was the problem of authority. The dispute over
whether women should speak or keep silent and over
whether they should or should not wear anything on their
heads centred around this question. The reason women were
to be silent in certain circumstances was because they were
under authority. 'Let your women keep silence in the
churches: for it is not permitted unto them to speak; but they
are commanded to be under obedience, as also saith the law'
(1 Cor.14:34). In the same way Paul introduced the subject
of the appearance of women's heads at worship with the
statement that 'The head of the woman is the man' and if she
prayed and prophesied with her head uncovered she
dishonoured her head (1 Cor.11:3,5).

Now Eve had come to the conclusion that the silence
imposed on women was not total and did not forbid
participation in prayer meetings and discussions. But the
principle which justified this practice seemed to be that this
participation did not impinge on the authority of the men.
This implied that women in the church were under male
authority just as they had been under the old covenant. Was
not this what Paul meant by 'as also saith the law'? The same

applied to the head-covering question. She had been led to the view that the covering referred to was not a garment – neither veil, nor shawl nor hat – but the hair given her by God 'instead of a covering'. This was because her hair symbolized her place in God's hierarchy as a woman, having authority over all other ranks of creation, angels included, but being herself under the authority of the man. This was why a distinction in the woman's appearance had to be maintained. Paul had been checking the tendency of women to underline their new-found spiritual equality with men by literally 'letting their hair down'. This was tantamount to a rejection of their subordinate position. The situation seemed to be that Christian women were under the authority of men in two areas - marriage and the church. Thus although she was a single woman again, as a member of the church it appeared that Eve still had to accept male authority. Once again she had resolved one problem only to create another. But it was no good ignoring it; she must solve this one too.

With the members' manual in front of her, she remembered now that this was where she had begun, with its statement on church government, in the course of which the basis of authority was stated thus: 'The sole governor of the universal church and of each particular church is Jesus Christ its Head (Isa. 9:6-7; Eph. 1:22-23). His instrument of government is his Word, which he has entrusted to the ministers of his churches, termed in the New Testament "elders, bishops, pastors and teachers" (Eph. 4:8-12). The authority of Christ is thus vested in these officers and exercised through teaching the Word and overseeing the members according to the Word. The members of the church, of both sexes, are to honour and submit themselves to the teaching and decisions of the elders so long as these are in agreement with the Word of God.'

That as it stood was all well and good. In itself it did not seem to place women on a lower plane than men, since 'members . . . of *both sexes*' were required to accept the authority of the elders. But there remained the question of

whether the eldership was open to women. Turning to the
section on 'Qualifications for Eldership' she read, 'Only men
displaying the qualities set down in the New Testament are
eligible for the office of elder.' Then followed a list of these
qualities drawn from 1 Timothy 3:1-7 and Titus 1:5-9. So
here was the crunch. Was this really what Christ required for
all time – a 'men only' ministry? If this were so, why was it
so? What was it about men that qualified them and about
women that disqualified them?

Eve had sought to check this out by referring back to the
researches she had done into the position of women a year or
so before. Her study of Old Testament women had shown
that, although the structure of authority in Israel was
male-orientated, there had been prophetesses such as
Miriam and Huldah, and one female judge, Deborah, who
was recorded as having actually given orders to the military
leader, Barak. Apart from the usurper queen, Athaliah,
Deborah seemed to be the only woman who exercised
authority over men in the Old Testament. When Moses
appointed seventy elders to assist him in governing the
people, they were all men, 'heads of families'. The priesthood
also was open only to males, and a very limited number of
them – unblemished ones of the line of Aaron. What was to
be made of all this? The case of Deborah showed that a
woman was not constitutionally incapable of exercising
authority. Nor was it morally wrong to do so, or this would
have been made clear. But why just this one instance? Was it
that when times were disordered, as they were in the days of
the judges, then this would be reflected in the reversing of the
usual order of the sexes? Or was it that Deborah was to be
seen as a purely civil leader and that therefore it was
permissible for women to wield authority in the civil sphere
but not the religious – the eldership and priesthood?

This, if it were the answer, would certainly tie up with the
New Testament position regarding the church. She had
noted many times how Jesus had welcomed women into his
band of disciples and had come to lean heavily on their

support. However, when it came to selecting the leaders of his future church, he passed them over and chose twelve men. Then when these apostles founded churches and looked about for suitable people to oversee these churches while they themselves moved on, the 'elders' they appointed were invariably male. But was this because they had probably been elders in the synagogue before becoming Christians, and therefore of necessity male? Or was there more to it than that? She looked again at the qualifications set down in 1 Timothy 3 and Titus 1. Although the majority of these were within the capabilities of a woman, it was also stipulated that an elder was to be 'the husband of one wife' and 'one that ruleth well his own household, having his children in subjection'. The reason given for this was revealing: 'If a man know not how to rule his own house, how shall he take care of the church of God?' Here was the connection between the human family and the family of God so noticeable in the Old Testament. Right from the earliest days, the father of the family was regarded as head, not just of his own wife and children, but of the families of his children and his children's children, and so on. He thus became a patriarch, and it was a patriarch, Abraham, whom God had chosen with his family to constitute his people, his church. This principle remained through the Old Testament, especially in the eldership as set up by Moses. This then was carried over, it seemed, into the New Testament, which retained the headship of the husband and father in the home: 'Wives, submit yourselves unto your own husbands, as unto the Lord. For the husband is the head of the wife even as Christ is the head of the church' – there again was the connection between family and church. 'Therefore, as the church is subject unto Christ, so let the wives be to their own husbands in everything' – there it was again. That was from Ephesians 5, but there were other passages to the same effect: 'Wives, submit yourselves unto your own husbands as it is fit in the Lord' (Col. 3:18); 'Likewise, ye wives, be in subjection to your own husbands . . .' (1 Peter 3:1).

There seemed no way round this, then – authority remained vested in the male, both in the home and the church. But for someone like Eve, this was not enough. The fact that the Bible said it was enough for her to accept and obey it, but not enough to enable her to understand it. She felt it was very important to understand God's teachings and commands. He was a wise God who always had good reasons for what he said and did, including what he required from his people. To understand these reasons, she felt, enabled one not only to obey him and believe him, but to do so gladly, with the whole heart. We are to praise him with our understanding as well as with our will. Also, understanding helps in our witness and instruction of others. We are not just to confess our faith but to 'give a reason for it'. Eve did not favour that despising of the intellect which some Christians seemed to indulge in, perhaps as a cover for their own mental laziness. So she had proceeded to carry out an investigation into the reasons God may have revealed for this arrangement of the sexes.

She approached the matter by asking herself, first of all, what reasons there might conceivably be, and also what reasons were popularly thought to lie behind it. With her background of struggling to lift women on to the same level as men, it was not difficult to bring these reasons to mind. The basic overall ground was that there were things in the constitutional make-up of the female which rendered her unsuitable for leadership and authority. Physically she was smaller and weaker, she needed protection and therefore could hardly set herself up as a protector of others. Intellectually she was less advanced and therefore not equipped for decision-making, tending to act on intuition rather than reason. She was the childbearer and childrearer; her talents lay in the direction of serving rather than leading. Because of this, many said, women actually preferred to leave the leadership to men. They felt inadequate to assume roles which involved making decisions and exercising authority. They felt the life of serving and playing second

fiddle came more naturally to them. Women who did not feel
like this were the exception which only served to prove the
rule. There was usually something odd and unfeminine
about such women, who drew on themselves uncomplimen-
tary names such as 'virago' and 'Amazon', or even
'battleaxe'!

In addition to these arguments from the natural realm
there were certain allegedly biblical and Christian reasons
for denying her this authority. Both Old and New
Testaments pointed out that she was created out of Adam
and therefore after him, and specifically to be his companion
and helper. This meant taking second place to him. Also
there was the fact that it was she who first succumbed to
temptation and sinned against God. Clearly there was some
moral as well as physical and intellectual weakness in her.
God himself confirmed this by the punishment he inflicted on
her, which was specifically to subject her to her husband.
That seemed a powerful case! But was it right?

Clearly this view of woman was one that must be taken
seriously and checked out carefully. It had a long pedigree
and a wide following and could not just be discarded out of
hand or cancelled out by an appeal to some slick slogan.
There were two main arguments to examine – the
constitutional and the biblical. As regards the first, there
were three main areas to look at. The first was the physical.
Of course, there could be no denying that on average women
were smaller and lighter then men, and also less muscular.
The shape of their bodies was also a handicap to many
physical actions. This was proved by the fact that in the vast
majority of sports and games women never competed against
men, and even where they did, such as in golf, the men were
given handicaps. All this suggested that women were more
vulnerable and in need of protection. But the question at
issue was authority – leadership quality. When had this had
anything to do with physique? The answer in practice, she
was forced to admit, was – all too often! History showed how
often men had risen to power by sheer brute force. As

civilization progressed, however, this became less the case.
In primitive societies, the tallest, heaviest and toughest man
became chief of the tribe. But as time went by, and they
began to use their minds more, they came to realize that it
was more important to control those who had the power,
than to have it themselves. It was not physique but
personality that mattered here. Napoleon Bonaparte had
been a small man, but one of the great leaders of all time. And
on the question of personality men had no natural advantage
over women, whose sex could produce personalities as strong
as the male sex could, provided they were given room to
develop. The Bible itself showed this in the case of Deborah,
who was stronger in personality than the army general,
Barak. Because he failed to recognize this and disregarded
her counsel he was brought to shame by being denied the
honour of slaying Israel's enemy, Sisera, and this honour fell
to another woman, Jael. Secular history bore this out,
particularly recent history, which had seen some remarkable
women come to the fore as statesmen. Even in preceding
centuries, when women were generally kept out of political
life, some outstanding ones had still emerged. She considered
how the whole of Britain was dominated in the sixteenth
century by Queen Elizabeth 1 and in the nineteenth by
Queen Victoria. If authority were connected with
personality rather than physique, then in and of itself this
would be no barrier against a woman assuming it.

Then what of the so-called 'intellectual' argument – the
idea that the female brain was inferior to the male? It so
happened that a radio programme had recently investigated
this matter. It pointed out that for centuries intellectual
activities had been dominated by men – science,
mathematics, philosophy, literature and so on. Women were
hardly represented in any of these fields. When they began to
challenge this male monopoly, the reply from the male side
was that women were mentally unsuited to these disciplines.
One German psychologist went as far as to state, 'The
average female mind is capricious, over-suggestible, often

inclined to exaggeration and therefore disinclined to abstract thought, unfit for mathematical reasoning, impulsive, over-emotional.' Moreover, it was thought possible to prove this by a medical examination of the brain. The male brain was larger and heavier, therefore it was superior, Q.E.D. However, since men were larger over all, this was hardly surprising. But what of small men with correspondingly small brains? Napoleon, being a small man, had a small brain, but plenty of mental ability. This showed there was no relation between brain size and intellect.

Next they had turned their attention to the lobes – frontal, parietal and temporal. But no deficiency could be discovered in the female lobes. Perhaps the answer lay then in a discrepancy between the two hemispheres of the brain? Since women were reputed to shine in language facility (associated with the left hemisphere) rather more than in mechanical skill (associated with the right hemisphere) perhaps the latter side was less developed in the female brain? Once again experiments drew a blank. So why did this myth continue to receive credit? The answer, according to the programme presenter, was that anything that explored sex difference and sex conflict was 'good copy'. It was in the interest of the media to maintain the myth of female intellectual inferiority. This, thought Eve, must be one reason why sexism was so hard to break down – without it life would be that much duller. But the facts were against it, and when a woman had sufficient determination and a certain amount of luck (or perhaps she should say 'providence'!) on her side, the myth was exploded. To say that such women were 'freaks' was hardly complimentary to the Marie Curies of this world.

Then what of the third argument – the one from function? Did childbearing, nursing and home-management militate against exercising leadership? Probably they did in the case of those women who devoted themselves to such a life; or at least they confined the exercise of that leadership to a smaller sphere. Within that sphere, however, considerable qualities of leadership were required if a home was to be organized, children brought up and troublesomeness quelled. The fifth commandment recognized this, for the mother was given authority over the children equal to that of the father. It was therefore largely a matter of degree – a woman's ability to lead applied in a smaller sphere than a man's. But these abilities were no less real. How many dozen decisions did a woman with a home and family have to make during the course of a single day? In any case, this argument only applied to those women who took up domestic life. What of those who did not? Surely the qualities women were required to employ in the home could be used in other walks of life? There was nothing then in the functional argument. And the idea that women preferred the back seat was inconclusive, since many did not and, given opportunity, would take up positions of leadership in the world. There was no obligation on a woman to marry and bear children. Why should it always be assumed that if a woman remained single it was invariably because she had not managed to catch the eye of an eligible man? This attitude belonged to the gossip and humour of sexist folk lore but it was not necessarily true to fact. It might only apply to a small minority, and some of these only felt frustrated because it was continually suggested to them that unless they married they were in some way inferior to other women. The pressure of custom and opinion was very strong and could create preferences which were not really there at all. If this pressure could be lifted it might transpire that many women would choose an active and prominent role in preference to a domestic and more secluded one. Because the latter came naturally to most women, did not mean it was unnatural not to prefer it.

There still remained the biblical reasons for denying authority to women. Here she was more hopeful of finding the answer to her question. Since it was the Bible itself that put forward this view, it could be expected that the Bible would explain, justify and make it acceptable. The most categorical statement in the Bible denying women the right to authority in the church was to be found in 1 Timothy 2:11-15. It was interesting that this was also the passage which gave the most explicit reasons for this 'subjection'. It read, 'For Adam was first formed, then Eve. And Adam was not deceived, but the woman being deceived was in the transgression. Notwithstanding she shall be saved in childbearing, if they continue in faith and love and holiness with sobriety.' There was no getting away from the fact that this was the reason given by Paul. But how were his words to be interpreted? The usual way was to say that man had the authority because he was created first. The woman then proved she was unfit for leadership by her behaviour in relation to the serpent. Also she was punished by being forced into submission to her husband, whose rule over her would become more tyrannical (Gen. 3:16). Her role of childbearing would also become more painful, nevertheless God would support her through it if she respected his Word and submitted to his instructions. This was the usual interpretation, but was it the correct one?

Although in general the commentaries had not been helpful, one of them had explained verse 13 in terms of the right of the firstborn, something which ran through the Old Testament. The firstborn son always had the superior position over the other members of the family. It was nowhere suggested that he was superior in constitution, personality, intelligence or any other way. The Bible showed that in fact on occasions the firstborn son was weaker than a subsequent child and behaved far worse. There were cases such as Cain, as compared to Abel, Esau to Jacob, and Reuben to Joseph. But this did not affect the right of the firstborn to the superior place in the family. So the fact that the man was created first did not mean he was necessarily superior. It simply meant God had given him the right to hold the leading position in the home and church. The reference to Christ himself as 'the firstborn of every creature' in Colossians 1: 15 bore this out, for the subject under discussion in that passage was the place of supremacy God

had given him over all his creatures. It was not his
divine nature and perfections that were under discussion,
hence Paul had no qualms about placing him *under* the
Father, as in 1 Corinthians 11:3: 'The head of Christ is God',
and 1 Corinthians 15:27-28, where everything was to be put
in subjection to Christ except the Father himself. Then,
when everything has been put under the Son, 'shall the Son
also himself be subject to him that put all things under him,
that God may be all in all'. Jesus himself had referred to his
subordinate position in the Godhead: 'My Father is greater
than I.' But this took nothing away from the equality of his
divine nature with that of the Father. Now it was interesting
that Paul used the relationship of Father and Son as an
analogy of the relationship between man and woman in 1
Corinthians 11: 'The head of every man is Christ; and the
head of the woman is the man; and the head of Christ is God'
(v. 3). This showed that the subordination of woman to man
had nothing to do with any spiritual inequality or
constitutional inferiority. It was purely a matter of order.
God was a God of order, and therefore had laid it down
clearly in his Word who was to exercise authority in home
and church. But authority carried with it responsibility. It
meant the man was responsible to God for the state of his
whole household, for which he was to provide, and which he
was to keep in order and cherish. The same applied in the
church: 'ruling' meant taking responsibility, undertaking the
care of the people's souls. Elders were 'overseers' or
'shepherds', who were there to take care of the flock. But for
this to function satisfactorily those 'under' the authority of
the man must accept his leadership and co-operate with it.
This was the meaning of subjection, and applied to both wife
and children in the home, and also to members, male and
female, in the church.

Now it was almost certainly this thought that had
prompted Paul, in 1 Timothy 2:14, to add what he did about
Eve being the first 'in the transgression'. It was not that she
was to blame for the Fall and was being singled out for

punishment. It was to show the consequence of not following
the divinely created order. It was Adam who was chiefly to
blame, if anyone, for following the lead of his wife instead of
leading her. Eve never forgot a book she had read in her
Women's Lib. days by a nineteenth-century feminist from
the U.S.A., Elizabeth Stanton, called *The Woman's Bible*. It
sought to bring out how badly Adam had behaved, making
no attempt to intervene in the parley between the serpent
and Eve, then just capitulating when she offered him the
forbidden fruit and finally, and worst of all, hiding behind
her skirts when God came to conduct his enquiry. The
account was of course slanted, but Eve could not deny the
large element of truth in it. It seemed to her that Paul was not
blaming Eve so much as excusing her by saying she was
'deceived' while Adam was left with no excuse at all. His
action (or lack of it!) stood on record as a warning that God's
order was no mere formality, but of great importance.

This then was the Bible's reason for giving authority in
home and church to the man. It was for the sake of order and
therefore in everyone's interest. When things got out of order
they went wrong, as at the beginning. So there was no
question of its being invented to punish women or prove their
inferiority. It was to be a good and helpful arrangement. And
the fact that it dated back to the beginning of the world put
beyond any doubt that it was God's appointment and not
invented by men to keep them at the top.

It was through this process of study and reasoning that
Eve had become clear about her position as a woman in the
church. Although not under the authority of a husband at
home, she was under the authority of men in the church. This
evidently was the will of Christ for the remainder of time. Of
course, this equally affected those men who were not called to
the office of elder, for they were also required to 'obey those
who have the rule over them'. But as a woman she had an
additional restriction – the office of elder was not open to her,
because it involved exercising authority over men. This was
something God in his wisdom had forbidden, at any rate in

the home and the church. The same did not necessarily apply
in society, for there could never be any guarantee that
non-Christians would abide by divine rules, even if they were
made aware of them. But this knowledge was given to those
who set up Christian homes or formed churches. They could
be expected to follow this order. It was a demonstration of
their obedience to God and of their confidence in his wisdom.
It was not a matter of women being inferior or unsuitable for
eldership in some way, but purely that this was how God
would have it. It simplified the situation if everyone knew
their place and accepted it. It served to curb any intersex
rivalry, such as went on in the world outside, and to restrain
ambition.

Eve had now become sufficiently well acquainted with the
workings of her church to be able to see that this
arrangement worked well. Far from making the women of
the church passive and idle, it had the opposite effect. For
one thing they involved themselves very much in the
children's work, teaching Bible classes and running leisure
activities. The majority of these teachers were single ladies
who, having no children of their own, had a certain amount
of time and a good deal of affection to bestow on the children
of others, especially those who lacked the benefit of a
Christian home. The older children and teenagers were
placed in a separate group in the hands of married couples,
since they were deemed to need more balanced leadership,
including the male touch.

But the place where the principle was having the biggest
effect was the women's organization which bore the name
'Tabitha', after a Christian woman in Joppa mentioned in
Acts 9:36-42, who had been a leader of Christian women in
the church there and devoted her time, talents, means and
energy to 'good works and almsdeeds'. Grace was involved in
this and from her Eve had learned something of its history.
Evidently when the present pastor and his wife had been
called to the church, there had been a more traditional type
of women's meeting, consisting of a devotional hour followed

by cups of tea. To this various women simply came and went, and little seemed to be achieved. In fact it became such an exclusive clique that women who came fresh into the church found it difficult to be accepted and tended to keep away. The pastor and his wife came to the conclusion that it did more harm than good and increasingly thought in terms of bringing it to an end. However, they discussed it with some of the members who felt that something was needed to enable the women to meet together, and that it would be better to try to steer it in a different direction. The devotional meetings with visiting speakers were cut down to one a month, and the main emphasis was placed on practical activities. The leadership was strengthened and the whole group took over responsibility for the cleanliness and general appearance of the church building – supplying flowers, plants, pictures, curtains and whatever else they felt necessary. They also saw to all catering requirements at regular or special occasions. They were given a completely free hand, so that these matters ceased to appear at deacons' or church meetings, except for giving reports of anything extra or special. Furthermore, they tried to acquaint themselves with some of the personal and domestic needs of members and their families, with a view to offering help with services such as baby-sitting, assistance during sickness by taking in washing, or doing cleaning or shopping. At that particular time they were investigating the possibility of some kind of service in the local community, such as a playgroup for pre-school children or a gathering for the elderly, lonely or handicapped.

Some had said this would never work and would gradually fizzle out, but in fact support had steadily increased, and attracted those to whom the old-fashioned type of women's meeting had little appeal, but who felt an urge to do something more practical in the service of Christ. After a time it became so successful that it moved the men of the church to set up a similar body to perform other tasks. The women could not be expected to undertake everything

that required attention, so the men came together to tackle
things such as repairs and decorations in the church
buildings, and occasional heavier jobs required in the homes
of those among them with limited means.

All this activity began to make Eve think. Here was
everyone else involved in some work or other, while she
seemed to do nothing except come and go. She began to
wonder where she fitted in to all this. It was not enough to
come to the conclusion that the eldership was closed to
women and settle for a passive role. There were functions
other than those involving authority and leadership. The
other women were showing that. However, she did not see
that she could play much part in Tabitha, since it was mainly
conducted by married women and operated during working
hours. Her job and home did not leave her very free for
activities. The youth and children's work were fully staffed
and running well. What else was there? She did not feel
happy about just 'offering her services' in an open-ended
way. So she was left with only one choice – to 'go back to the
drawing board', that is, to look at the Bible again and work it
out from there. Did it have anything to say about what a
woman like her could do in the church?

The first point that became clear to her was that, whatever
had been the situation in the past, marriage and family life
were no longer the be-all and end-all of a woman's existence.
There could be no denying that in the Old Testament
marriage was central, not just for a woman but also for a
man. To remain single was disastrous, and there were very
few unmarried persons in the Old Testament. As for women,
the high points of their lives centred around their marriage
and the birth of their children. A childless woman was an
object of pity or even scorn. The wives of Abraham and Jacob
had even offered their slave girls to their husbands when they
themselves had been unable to conceive. Nevertheless even
in the Old Testament they were not totally confined to
bearing and raising children and serving their husbands. It
was interesting that the model wife of Proverbs 31 was active

in business not only in the home but outside it, undertaking matters to do with agriculture and real estate, surely traditional male preserves? She was represented as the object of her husband's confidence, rather than the subject of his rule. If married women were capable of such achievements, how much more could a single one do, if only she could be released from the stigma of the unmarried and childless state!

It was to this problem that the Lord Jesus Christ had addressed himself. As so often in his teaching, Jesus managed to bring in new ideas without destroying what was good in the old. This was nowhere more so than in his teaching on marriage. He actually succeeded in exalting it above the contemporary view and at one and the same time raising the status of the single person. For in spite of retaining the Old Testament esteem for marriage and childbearing as central to life, the contemporaries of Jesus had debased it by the way they made divorce easy, although only for the husband. In his debate with the Pharisees in Matthew 19 he had said that divorce was never God's original intention, but only a concession he permitted Moses to introduce to save rejected wives from ill-treatment. But they had turned Moses' concession into a right and almost made it a virtue. This did not honour marriage and Jesus called for a return to the original institution of permanent monogamous marriage, although he did allow divorce in cases of adultery. Yet in the very same statement he also managed to bring out the honour of the permanent single state when he added, 'There are some eunuchs which were so born from their mother's womb: and there are some eunuchs which were made eunuchs of men; and there be eunuchs, which have made themselves eunuchs for the kingdom of heaven's sake. He that is able to receive it, let him receive it' (Matt.19:12). The term 'eunuch' was an abomination in the ears of a Jew; eunuchs were debarred from public worship, according to the law. In any case they were furthest of all from what Jews regarded as almost obligatory – marriage and child-rearing.

But Jesus here declared that voluntary eunuchs had an important place in the service of his kingdom. He was not, of course, recommending self-mutilation any more than he was in the Sermon on the Mount when he spoke of cutting off the right hand or plucking out the right eye. He was speaking of the exercise of self-control, of so subduing the desires of the flesh that marriage was not sought for – not because it was seen as unholy, but in order to leave a person free to serve the kingdom of heaven. These ideas were to be developed by Paul in 1 Corinthians 7, but they originated in Christ's preaching of the kingdom of heaven. He was to go even further later on in reply to the Sadducees in Matthew 22. They had asked a question about a much-married woman: whose wife should she be 'in heaven'? To which Jesus replied that there was no married state in heaven, but those who reached it were 'as the angels'. Thus marriage was not to be thought of as virtually indispensable, with the single state relegated to a very third-rate position. Those whose aim in life was to serve the King of kings and be a citizen of heaven could do so either married or single.

To Eve such teaching meant that there must be ways in which she could serve God in his church without remarrying. So she set about discovering from the New Testament what these might be. She found that she had already done the donkey work in her researches into women in the Bible the previous year. What was needed now was to work through this material and select those points that related to the service of women in the church of God. It was clear that throughout the Bible women played a large part in the worship and work of the church. This was so even in the Old Testament, and did not only apply to the occasional outstanding woman such as Miriam, Deborah and Huldah. Miriam, for example, was but the leader of a vast number of women who participated in the worship that celebrated the crossing of the Red Sea: 'All the women went out after her with timbrels and dances' (Exod. 15:20). Even though 'all' might not be an absolute term, it at least meant 'a lot'. Nor was this the only occasion in which they were prominent in worship. When David set up the tabernacle on Mount Zion and organized the worship under three leaders – Asaph, Heman and Jeduthun – the daughters of Heman as well as his sons were involved, and in fact received special training for the task (1 Chron.25:5-7). This practice continued during subsequent generations: there were 'singing women' who took part in the mourning over King Josiah (2 Chron.35:25); and no change was made after the return from exile, for there were 'two hundred singing women' in the second temple (Ezra 2:65). The activities of all these women were not confined to music, but were also of a more general nature, for they 'served at the entrance to the Tent of Meeting' (Exod.38:8), although there was no record of precisely what services they performed.

The age of the rabbis had been a severe setback for the status of women, who were segregated from men in temple and synagogue, and were regarded as too stupid even to understand the teaching, let alone to take any active part in religious life. But Jesus had restored them to their rightful place and even extended their privileges. He accepted them into his band of disciples, capable of both learning and following his teaching for, 'looking around on his *disciples*, he said, "Whosoever shall do the will of my Father which is in heaven, the same is my brother, and *sister, and mother*" (Matt.12:50). Moreover he needed their assistance in his ministry, and collected a group of women who 'ministered unto him of their substance' (Luke 8:1-3), which must have meant more than giving money, since they accompanied him in his travels, along 'with the twelve'. It probably covered attending to all their material needs, which would be considerable, involving not only money, but constant labour. This was done not just by the three named (Mary Magdalene, Joanna and Susanna) but 'many others' unnamed. This same group was still with him at Golgotha (Mark 15:40-41) and after his death took charge of the funeral arrangements with the help of Joseph of Arimathea

(Matt. 27:55-61). It was they too who first learned of his resurrection and reported it to the apostles (Matt. 28:1-7).

This same group of women was to be found among the foundation members of the church who gathered in Jerusalem to wait for the coming of the Spirit (Acts 1:14-15). The gift and gifts of the Spirit were bestowed on them too, as Peter's quoting of Joel's prophecy indicated: 'Your sons and *your daughters* shall prophesy . . . and on my servants and on my *handmaidens* will I pour out in those days of my Spirit and they shall prophesy' (Acts 2:17-18). This was further fulfilled in the exercise of prophetic gifts by the four daughters of Philip the evangelist (Acts 21:9) and more generally by a number of believing women in Corinth (1 Cor.11:5). In this way the tradition of female vocal participation, which dated back to the Red Sea, was continued and extended. But there were many other ways in which women were involved in the work of the church. Sapphira was an equal participant with her husband Ananias both in the sale of their property and the donation of the proceeds to the church, not to mention the decision secretly to withhold part of them (Acts 5:1-11). Thus when Saul of Tarsus launched his campaign against the church he imprisoned the women along with the men as equally dangerous (Acts 8:3). Those who escaped this by fleeing the city 'preached (literally, 'gossipped') the word everywhere' they went (Acts 8:4), and in view of the previous verses there is no need to restrict this activity to men. For this was by no means a precedent. Right at the beginning of his ministry, Jesus had gone out of his way to speak to an immoral Samaritan woman who, as a result, had returned to her town to issue her clients with an invitation very different from her usual one – to come and meet the Messiah (John 4:28-42). These and many others flocked out to Jesus at the well and claimed that they accepted him as the world's Saviour. Jesus did not reject their faith on the grounds that it had come about through a woman's testimony, but pointed it out to his disciples as part of the harvest of souls he had come to gather.

As the church spread into the Gentile world, women became even more prominent in it. Custom and Jewish prejudice might have served to make them somewhat reticent to come forward in Jerusalem and Judea (although Mary, the mother of Mark, was active even there, Acts 12:12) but there were no such inhibitions in Europe. Hence in Philippi a church was founded around a prominent business woman, Lydia, and her household, in fact at first the church was based in her house. Later two other women, Euodias and Syntyche, came to the fore in the church in Philippi (Phil. 4:1-3). Evidently they had worked closely with Paul in his evangelistic activity, and his earnest appeal to them to heal their quarrel showed how they must have been leading figures, whose influence and example would affect many. Lydia was not the only woman to play hostess to a church. In Colosse (according to the Revised Version margin) Nympha had 'the church in her house' (Col.4:15) as did Apphia (Philem. 2). So did Priscilla and Aquila, who were probably at one time in Ephesus (1 Cor. 16:19) and later in Rome (Rom. 16:3-5). Women were clearly active in other ways, and several were mentioned as having assisted Paul and given him much help – Phoebe, Priscilla, Mary, Tryphena and Tryphosa, Rufus' mother, Julia and Nereus' sister (Rom. 16:1,3,6,7,12,13,15).

Women seemed to have been more involved in spiritual work under Paul than they had been in our Lord's ministry, as was indicated in the case of Euodias and Syntyche who, he said, 'laboured with me *in the gospel*'. What exactly this meant was not clear, but since the church in Philippi had commenced with a group of women, there would have been considerable scope for them. Perhaps they were used to help those who had been mixed up in the occult, such as the slave girl with the 'Python' demon (Acts 16:16-18). The ministry of Priscilla did not even seem to have been confined to females, since, along with her husband, she instructed Apollos in 'the way of God', putting him right where his thinking was deficient (Acts 18:24-26). Nor was the women's contribution limited to giving occasional assistance to the apostles and their travelling companions. They were also employed in the regular work of settled churches. Phoebe was a 'servant' (literally 'deacon') of the church in Cenchrea, near Corinth (Rom. 16:1) and was in fact chosen to represent it in some kind of mission to the church in Rome (Rom. 16:2). The use of the word 'deacon' of Phoebe might be more than just a description of her usefulness and could indicate some kind of calling or office. If this were so, she would not have been alone. In 1 Timothy 3, where Paul listed the qualifications required of those to be appointed to offices in the church, he spoke not only of 'bishops' and 'deacons' but also of 'women' (1 Tim. 3:11), as the Revised Version translated the phrase which the AV rendered 'wives'. Although he did not term them 'deacons' he associated them with deacons and listed qualifications which corresponded exactly with those required of deacons. Whatever they were called, whether 'deacons', 'deaconesses', or just 'the women', they were obviously a recognized group who had to be tested with respect to specific qualities, and then set apart for duties in the church. Older widows also had a special place and function: in return for their material support they seemed to have undertaken works of hospitality, and if they were too old and infirm for this, gave themselves to prayer (1 Tim. 5:3-10).

What a wealth of material on the subject Eve had unearthed! It only needed bringing out of obscurity and taking notice of. True, the New Testament was not very specific about the precise functions which women performed or were allowed to perform. But why should it be specific? After all, it was to cover all ages, all nations and all cultures. A variety of tasks would arise during the course of the spread of the gospel through the world in the ensuing centuries. How could all these be envisaged in the first few decades? Surely the lessons of all this material were that the contribution of women to the work of the gospel and the church was greatly needed, that there was a variety of tasks they could perform, short of actually assuming leadership in a church, and that apart from eldership there was no such thing in the church as 'men's work' and 'women's work'. Had not God when he created the race in two kinds conceived of them as a partnership and commissioned them to go and be fruitful, multiply and replenish the earth? Did not the same principle apply in the spiritual realm? Christ had brought into being a 'new creation', 'the kingdom of heaven', and wanted it peopled with spiritual children, 'born of God' through the seed of the gospel sown by those he himself called. How much more should he use the partnership of men and women in this great task?

This made sense and there was scriptural evidence that it happened. There was a train of events – the witness of the women to the resurrection, their share in the 'gossipping of the Word', Euodias' and Syntyche's 'labouring with' Paul 'in the gospel'. It was not beyond the bounds of possibility that a woman, Junia, was numbered among those named 'apostles' (Rom. 16:7). It was not certain that the name was feminine, since some manuscripts rendered it 'Junias'. This person and Andronicus were Paul's 'kinsmen and fellow-prisoners' and 'of note among the apostles'. The term 'apostle' in the New Testament was used not only in the technical sense of the twelve who had seen the risen Christ, plus Paul who had seen him in his vision on the Damascus Road, but also in the more general sense of 'messenger' – one who went forth from the churches to spread the gospel. Although a woman would not have been commissioned to go and preach publicly in a synagogue or market-place, she might be part of a team which did this. Hence she might be referred to as an 'apostle', just as a woman who served in a missionary team today was called a 'missionary'. Paul tended to work in a team; he was not happy working on his own, as the accounts of his stay in Athens and his first days in Corinth showed. Possibly Euodias and Syntyche had been members of one of these teams. If Junia was a female she, too, could have played a similar role, getting herself imprisoned along with Paul in the

process. As a close relative he would know her well enough to
be able to take her on a journey with him. There would be
nothing in such an arrangement to infringe the principle of
male leadership.

Eve made all this a matter of much prayer. As she did so, it
was the thought of the Samaritan woman which was
uppermost in her mind. This woman had met the Lord Jesus
and her past life had suddenly been placed before her eyes as
God saw it. She could no longer excuse or justify it. Nor did
she wish to, for here was one who offered her something
better – 'living water'. The way she had lived in the past had
been by seeking pleasures of which she quickly tired, so that
she was always looking for something new. In this way she
had acquired five husbands (or was it now six?). But Jesus
offered her something she could keep in her soul which could
not continually run out and need renewing. How similar to
Eve's own experience! She too had gone from one thing to
another to find satisfaction, only to discover the novelty wore
off. Her experience of Christ was something that remained
fresh, in fact seemed to grow newer and newer as she delved
more deeply in it. Truly she had within her a well of water
springing up into eternal life. But there was one way in which
she differed from the Samaritan woman: she had not gone
back to her fellow sinners and told them of the change
wrought in her by Christ. She had rather cut herself off from
them, as they had from her. Of course, the break-up with
Frank had made it difficult to maintain friendly relations
with them, but she had to admit she had not even tried to get
round the problem. Consequently, she had not had the joy of
seeing what the woman of Samaria saw – a number of her
friends going to Christ and believing in him, not just because
of what she had said, but because they had seen for
themselves and come to 'know that this is indeed the Christ,
the Saviour of the world'.

Eve now knew she had received the answer to her question
as to what was her role in the work and ministry of the
church, at least for the time being. What right had she even

to think about offices, positions and acts of service when she had not fulfilled the basic obligation of every new convert – to go home and tell how great things the Lord had done for her? Somehow she must put this right at once. But how could she pick up the traces after all this time? She couldn't just call on people she had not seen for a couple of years and blurt out her experience. It might be casting pearls before swine. So what was she to do? Next time she found herself in conversation with the pastor she explained her difficulty. He could not, he said, give her specific advice; that was entirely a matter of the guidance of God. The important thing was that she had seen her neglected duty and was willing to perform it. It had been God himself who had taught her this and he could be trusted to finish the job and show her how to fulfil the task. In fact in his providence he would order the circumstances. Her part was to keep her spirit willing and be alert for her opportunity. This would involve much prayer, not only for herself but for her former friends. It was vital that her motive was a concern for the souls of her friends, not just the salving of her own conscience. Eve took this advice to heart and immediately began to act upon it.

7.
Fellow workers

The box from which Eve had taken her diaries was full of
mementoes from the past – letters, newspapers, magazines
and photographs. As she rummaged through it a packet of
old photos caught her eye. She looked through them. They
went a long way back – some even to her university days –
and each one revived memories. Here was one of Anne. ('I
wonder where she is now? Pity I lost touch with her.') Anne
had been a year ahead of Eve at school and was one of a small
group of girls she had come to know during the period when
she was chafing at the bit over her male-dominated home.
They had continued their friendship at university, where
Anne was also on the Economics course. By the time Eve
arrived, Anne had become active in the feminist movement
there, and she introduced Eve to the other members almost
the moment she arrived. Anne had continued doing research
after graduation, hence although she had gone up a year
earlier than Eve she was still there when Eve came down.

Eve had seen her once or twice during the period of her
marriage to Frank, but since Anne had gone to work in a
different part of the country their paths did not cross after the
marriage had broken up. Then one day, at about the time
when Eve was feeling concerned about her contribution to
the church's witness, a notice came round the various
departments of her firm announcing recent new appoint-
ments. Among them was the name of Anne Longley, who
was to take a fairly high position on the personnel
management side of the firm. At first Eve was inclined to
doubt whether it could be the same person (she seemed
young for such a post) but then remembered that Anne had
attained high honours in Economics, after which she had
proceeded to a course in personnel management. Anne

combined intellectual brilliance with personal ambition and a fervent desire to promote the status of women. It was in keeping with this that she should have succeeded in invading this very male preserve. Nevertheless it was a considerable achievement and Eve felt a surge of envy rise up in her. Perhaps if she had been more determined and stuck to her guns she would have risen higher in the profession and struck a blow for the cause of women's freedom.

These thoughts preyed on her mind for several days and disturbed her times of prayer. Then one morning she was reading in the eighth chapter of Romans and came to the words: 'All things work together for good to them that love God.' She reproached herself for her negative attitude to herself and her circumstances, for had not losing interest in the women's movement created the vacuum now filled by faith in Christ? Did not the first have to go to make room for the second? Moreover, was she not able to do far more for her fellow women as a Christian than as a feminist? Although she still accepted the justice of many of their complaints and aspirations, she also knew that even if they succeeded in putting their part of the world to rights they would still feel unfulfilled. The sense of triumph would soon wear off and they would find that their brave new world was still very much like their cowardly old one. There was only one thing and one Person who could 'make all things new'. She had found this thing and this Person, or it and he had found her, and her ambitions and crusading zeal henceforth must be devoted to the campaign for real liberty – the liberty of the human spirit, male and female. Had she not recently been convicted in her heart by the example of the woman of Samaria? Could she forget this so soon? Here was one of her former friends and fellow sinners coming back into her life and all she could do was to envy her! It should be the other way round. Anne should be envying *her* for the much higher position to which she had attained.

Having got her thinking straightened out, Eve began to direct her prayers to the time when she and Anne would meet

again. Her appointment was due to commence at the
beginning of the following month, in just under two weeks'
time. 'O Lord,' Eve prayed, 'make me like the woman of
Samaria! I'm not asking for *all* my old friends to come
running to Jesus – just this one. Give me that sense of wonder
and amazement she had at having met the one who knows
everything I ever did and thought, all I was and am, who has
all my sins on record, and yet wants me to be contented and
happy. Fill me with living water and let it flow out so that
Anne can see, and taste of it herself!' But how was she to
approach Anne? What should she say to her? It would be
difficult, even embarrassing, after the way they had worked
together for Women's Lib. She could see herself chickening
out, even trying to avoid meeting Anne. She almost hoped
they would not come into contact; after all it was a large
building and Anne would be working in a completely
different part of it. She told Peter and Grace of her struggles
with herself over this matter. They were very understanding.

'Everyone feels like that. Winning souls is not like winning
the pools – more like winning a pitched battle. We have to
fight with sin, the world and the devil to rescue someone from
their clutches.'

'I can see it will be like that when I get started with Anne,
if I ever do. But why don't I feel more enthusiastic about it
now? Why am I almost fearing it and starting to find excuses
for avoiding it?'

'Because that's where the battle begins. The devil knows
what you are thinking and is trying to stop you making your
witness. The only way to keep him back is by putting up a
barrage of prayer, and we will join you in that. We can enlist
the church too. What's a prayer meeting for, if not things like
this? But my advice would be: "Don't try to imagine how it
will be or rehearse scenarios." In my experience it always
works out differently to the way we think it's going to.'

Peter's words proved right in several ways. Firstly, in that
it was not she who sought Anne out, but the other way round.
About a week before Anne was due to start her job, Eve went

out of her office to go to lunch and there was Anne standing outside the door! 'Hallo, Eve! Coming to lunch?' she said, as if they were still at university and had never been separated. It transpired that Anne had come over to the firm a week early to make some advanced preparations. She knew that Eve worked there and enquired as to her whereabouts. No sooner had they sat down to lunch than Eve was in for another surprise. Anne immediately raised the subject of Eve's 'religious conversion'. Eve was so taken aback, she hardly knew where to begin. But it drove all her fears to the winds. She felt excited, elated. Could it be that Anne herself was actually seeking God and had come in search of Eve to find the way? Eve had never yet spoken personally of her experience to someone she had known for so long. She was surprised how naturally she was able to do so, and the fact that she had been invited to speak of it took away all the worry as to how to open the matter without forcing or contriving it. It seemed indeed as though God was answering her prayers, that he had been preparing Anne's heart for this meeting, and herself to exploit it.

In this, however, she was to be disappointed. Anne's reaction to her testimony was on the lines that 'blood is thicker than water'. Eve had been born and brought up in Christianity. Her rejection of it in her teens had been adolescent reaction. But as she matured her early influences had reasserted themselves. To Anne it all proved the unfairness of the family system. Parents had a totalitarian power over their children and exploited it to force them into their own mould. They had such a long start over all other influences that, even though these might gain some ground temporarily and even appear to overtake the others, they stood no chance in the long run. Children therefore were not really free to make up their own minds. *They* needed liberating, as well as women. As Anne got into her stride, Eve could see what was happening. Far from her drawing Anne to Christianity, Anne was trying to draw her, not only back to Women's Lib., but to her latest campaign of children's

liberation! She had been playing into Anne's hands; she had
provided her with a further piece of evidence that children
have no freedom of thought and decision, for she herself had
returned to the 'prison' she had been brought up in. Eve tried
to reply that in fact she now experienced a greater freedom
than she had ever known, that she was still interested in the
women's movement, although she would now approach it
somewhat differently. Moreover, Anne's theory did not fit
the facts, for Eve could introduce her to people who had no
religious upbringing but had undergone an experience
similar to her own. But Anne made light of this. Such people
usually went back sooner or later, and *she* could introduce
Eve to plenty of people who had been Christians for a time,
but had eventually returned to their former ways.

Eve could see now why Anne had taken the initiative in
seeking her out. She had wanted to have an argument in
order to strengthen her own case. Anne went away obviously
feeling she had had the better of the exchange and Eve could
not help agreeing with this. What meant so much to her – her
personal experience of God – had been brushed aside as
merely a stage in her psychological development, and an
inevitable one at that. How hard were such people as Anne!
Whatever chance did she have of doing what the woman of
Samaria had done, and leading a whole bunch of her former
unbelieving friends to meet Christ and proclaim him
'Saviour of the world'? She took her disappointment to her
friends and received sympathy and encouragement. They
told her she must not place too much emphasis on the
Samaritan woman. She seemed to have sowed and reaped on
the same day, but Christ had pointed out to his disciples
afterwards that 'Others have laboured and you have entered
into their labours.' So it was not the full story. There is never
a birth that is not preceded by long gestation and many
pangs, and there is never reaping without preparatory
ploughing, sowing, weeding and watering. So she must not
think that all was lost because she had failed at the first
attempt. In time Anne's experience would teach her that her

theory was far from watertight and this might make her more open to alternatives, perhaps even to the gospel. Meanwhile Eve should not try to force anything on her, or she might be in danger of casting her pearls before swine. Let her leave the running to Anne and be content to 'give a reason for the hope that is in her', if and when challenged. Above all, she should get on with living her life as a Christian, for this could not help speaking volumes, not only to Anne, but to everyone else. She should act naturally and unselfconsciously, and as she herself grew in grace, the blossom would be smelt and the fruit seen and tasted.

Eve tried to put this into practice and to take every opportunity to mix with Anne socially. Anne, although so sure of herself, was not proud or above seeking help where she needed it. In the early days of her work with the firm she was frequently having to consult people in various departments to get to know her way around the company's workings. As Eve had now worked there for several years Anne frequently came in to see her, or called her up on the phone. However busy Eve was, she made a special effort to be co-operative by not only giving the information or advice asked of her, but by watching her manner and tone of voice. In this way she found herself often being consulted and frequently meeting Anne for lunch. Although they differed now on principles, they had much in common, especially as they had known each other from schooldays. After a number of attempts she succeeded in getting Anne to visit her in her flat, and in return was invited to a party Anne was holding in her own house.

When the day of the party came Eve arrived early, hoping for a few private words with Anne before the others came. However, she found she was not the first, since a young woman who appeared to come from South-east Asia was already there, sitting quietly in a corner while Anne completed the preparations. Anne introduced the girl to Eve who went and sat down with her. Her name was Jameela and she came from Burma. She was shy and her English was not

good, so Eve found it difficult to ascertain her connection
with Anne. She gathered they had not known each other
long, and that they had met at a meeting which Jameela had
wandered into. Since she did not have many friends, Anne
had invited her to the party to meet some of hers. Eve spoke
of her own friendship with Anne and by the time she had got
round to their reunion at her firm, the other guests were
beginning to arrive. Jameela seemed bewildered by so many
people, all of whom seemed to know each other, so Eve tried
to make sure she was not left on her own. Although it was still
not late, Eve sensed that Jameela wanted to go home, and to
save her from the embarrassment of being the first to leave,
went over to Anne and said she would like to be going, at
which Jameela said she would too. Eve offered to accompany
her home, but she declined so firmly that Eve thought she
was trying to hide something. So instead Eve invited her to
come and have a meal with her in her flat some time. The girl
was rather non-committal, so Eve did not press the matter,
and simply left her with her telephone number.

She went home thinking that would be the last she would
see of Jameela, yet she found it difficult to get her out of her
mind. She was sure there was some deep-seated problem and
felt more than a little concerned. To her surprise, when her
phone rang two or three days later, it was Jameela asking if
she could visit Eve and bring a friend with her. A date was
agreed on; nothing was said about the friend and Eve did not
enquire, for she felt Jameela was someone who had to be
handled gently, and could easily be frightened off. When the
evening arrived and the pair had settled themselves in Eve's
sitting-room, she realized why the friend had been brought.
Her name was Bushrah and not only was her English much
better than Jameela's, but she was as extrovert as Jameela
was timid. They were both from Burma and Bushrah
explained that they had been brought up together in an
orphanage because the parents of both of them had been
killed in the fighting that had taken place in their country
during the war. But in addition to that, Jameela had been

badly treated by a foreign soldier she had met when she left
the orphanage and started work. He had gone through a
form of marriage with her, but it came out later that he
already had a wife in his own country. He deserted her,
leaving her with a baby who was now in the same orphanage.
Bushrah was slightly the older of the two and had managed
to get a government grant to come to England and train for
nursing. She had somehow managed to scrape together the
money to bring Jameela over, in the hope that she too might
be able to start a career here and put the past behind her.
Meanwhile she was sharing Bushrah's rather small
bed-sitting room. They had not yet succeeded in finding an
opening for Jameela, and this was why she had been
wandering around going to meetings such as the one where
she had met Anne. It was the same problem that had now
brought them to Eve's door, and no doubt Bushrah had had
to use quite a lot of persuasion to get Jameela to go to the
telephone-box.

That evening proved to be one of the major turning-points
of Eve's whole life. The main things that happened to her
subsequently sprang from the story she heard from the two
Burmese girls. For Jameela was by no means the only girl in
her position. What had happened to her had happened to
many others in her country, but very few of them escaped to a
better life in a more developed land. Jameela was fortunate in
having a friend who was prepared to go to such lengths to
help her. With her limited means and small accommodation,
she could not do this for any others. And there were very few
who could even do what she was doing, so that thousands of
them just had to go on suffering. Eve saw the magnitude of
the problem, but what could she do about it? Then she
remembered the widow in the Gospels who gave her mite,
which was all she had, and of whom Christ had said, 'She has
done what she could.' Because Eve could not do everything
required did not mean she could do nothing. At least she
could give this girl a room of her own and ease the
accommodation problem for both of them or perhaps enable

Bushrah to help another girl. So when the shyness had
evaporated a little, Eve took Jameela into her flat. She
proceeded to improve her facility in the language, especially
in writing. Jameela proved so quick to learn that Eve
wondered if it might be possible for her to train as a clerk.
Her own firm often had vacancies for this type of work, but
first Jameela would have to become much more proficient.
So when Eve had taught her all she could herself, she paid for
her to take a business course at the local college. Jameela did
not lack intelligence and had a capacity for hard work, so
that within a year she had reached a good enough standard
to be able to take a job in Eve's own firm.

Jameela's spiritual life did not amount to much. From
what little Eve had been able to gather, the native religion of
her part of Burma was primitive and animistic, but Jameela
had been taken away at an early age and the orphanage in
which she had spent most of her childhood was run by
Roman Catholics, who were in fact doing most of the rescue
work in that part of the country. On coming to England, she
had lost touch with the Roman Catholic Church and seemed
happy to come along with Eve on Sundays, as did Bushrah
too when off duty. In private Eve did not try to force the
gospel on to Jameela, but let the seed sown grow secretly.
Probably it would not have been difficult to persuade her to
be baptized, but there was a danger it might have been just a
social action, like her previous baptism and confirmation in
the orphanage. Her tribespeople had a strong community
consciousness, in which the tribe was everything and the
individual came a poor second. All acted together or not at
all. Eve felt that Jameela could easily transfer this outlook to
her new environment. She was well received by the other
church members and her family feelings became directed
towards them. It would be natural for her to do what they
did, and Eve felt she needed to some extent to be set free from
this strong tribal sense, at least to the extent of realizing that
she must stand before God as an individual person and not a
member of a group. This would take time and Eve was

content to be patient. But problems arose over the Lord's Supper, as Jameela found it difficult to understand why she could not join in with the others, especially after attending mass for several years in the orphanage. Yet it was probably her exclusion from the Lord's Table that made her begin to think more deeply about the need for personal faith in Christ, although clearly she found it far from easy to see herself standing alone before God. This posed problems for the church, too. The individualistic outlook of modern Western culture meant that in Britain the hard part was not so much getting people to see themselves as distinct persons as it was to weld them into a family and a body. When someone who saw things in the opposite way came along, the question was raised as to the point at which it became evident that their faith was personal and real and not merely an accommodation to the others. Meetings and discussions centred around this question, which proved a thorny one to solve.

Meanwhile Eve, having succeeded in helping one needy person along, could not get out of her mind what she had been told right at the beginning of it all – that many girls and women in Burma were in the same boat. One person could not rescue a whole community, but if a number got together surely they could do a great deal. Wasn't the church large and powerful enough, if it acted as one, to make some impression on this problem? She discussed this with her friends in the church, also with the pastor and his wife. On making enquiries, the pastor discovered that there was a missionary society operating in the part of Burma next to the area where this trouble was at its worst. This was based mainly on a mission hospital they had established. At the present time they had neither the resources nor the personnel to expand the work, and certainly not to tackle the problem that Eve had stumbled across. Her pastor, however, was not content to leave it like that. He felt that if the situation was made known among the churches, it might be possible to get together a team to go out there. If the interested churches,

whether or not they were supplying a member of the team,
would undertake to share the cost of financing the project,
then the limited resources of the mission would not need to be
called upon. The directors of the mission liked this idea and
put their machinery into operation to make it known among
the churches with which they had contact. They put articles
in their magazine, circulated prayer sheets, sent deputation
speakers around and held central meetings. The project was
soon   arousing   interest   and   offers   from   prospective
candidates began to come in.

One evening, after a prayer meeting at which the
missionary secretary of the church had reported on
developments in the project, the pastor called Eve aside and
asked her if she had thought of offering herself as a member of
the team. She replied that she had not considered it at all,
since she felt that women were no more eligible for the
mission field than for the eldership of a home church. They
could go out as doctors or teachers, or as the wives of
missionaries, but not as evangelists in their own right. She
had none of these qualifications and was therefore not
eligible. She had been thinking along the lines of getting
another girl like Jameela over here and helping her in the
same way, but actually going abroad was out of the question.
The pastor, however, was not satisfied with this point of view
and they arranged that she should come and have a fuller
discussion with him. When this took place, he began by
saying he was glad that she understood the principle of
authority in the church and how this affected the mission
field.

'This is very important,' he said, 'because it affects the
whole concept of missionary work. Many have the idea that
the word "missionary" means someone – man or woman –
who feels a call to go out to some remote place, learn the
language, convert people to Christianity, build a hospital
and school and found a missionary society so that the work
can be established and extended. This is not to question the
devotion and courage of these people, nor the value of their

work, which God has often blessed. But in terms of the New Testament, this was not the way the apostles worked. They concentrated on one thing above all others – the founding of churches. This did not mean they ignored material needs, but their priority was to set up a church similar to the one they themselves had come from, so that in time these new churches would send out other workers to plant more churches. To plant a church requires the same qualifications as to lead and oversee a church, and therefore they had to be men. Eventually they chose others to take over the leadership so that they could move on. Paul left Timothy in Ephesus and Titus in Crete while he went elsewhere. He gave them instructions as to how to lead the churches, and how to appoint leaders who could take over from them so that they themselves could also move on. So basically there is no difference between a missionary and an elder or pastor.'

'That's exactly the conclusion I came to,' said Eve, 'and that's why I thought I should confine myself to trying to help individuals – girls and women, that is. I take my cue from the Samaritan woman, Mary Magdalene and the people who left Jerusalem in Acts 8 and "went everywhere speaking the word". They witnessed to others, but they didn't start churches. That's why I can't become a missionary.'

'Just a moment. There's a little more to it than that. Remember what you read about Jesus and the women. You told me yourself how you discovered he had several women who travelled around with him. They didn't do the preaching, but enabled him and the apostles to do it by keeping them free from too many material worries. And then there's Paul and all those references to women as his "fellow-workers" and to one, Junia, whom he calls "apostle". These women must have been in some way involved in his founding of churches. In other words, they formed part of a team. They were not leaders of the team nor preachers, nor did they take over the churches, but they did as much as they could, short of this. The New Testament doesn't tell us in detail what tasks they performed, but they

must have been significant ones, since Paul so often makes
special mention of these women in his letters. In a way it may
be good that he does not specify their contribution, otherwise
the English legalistic mind would probably lay down that
women can only do those things and no others, even if they
were right out of date! The position as I see it is that women
should do anything that needs to be done and of which they
are capable, short of actual leadership, preaching and
pastoring. How else can God's original commission be
fulfilled? He created man and woman to work together to fill
the earth with creatures like themselves. Doesn't the same
apply to the church family? He wants his church to be fruitful
and multiply, to spread across the earth. Women have their
place in this along with men; it is a combined operation,
team-work. Is there anything to stop you being part of a team
in carrying out this task we are working on? After all, it has
all arisen out of your meeting Jameela and seeking to help
her. Who has a better claim to a place than you? You
obviously have a concern for these people. You have the
personality and the gifts to win their confidence. You are
willing to give yourself, your time, your money, even your
home, to help them. What more is needed? I would think you
were ideally suited!'

'I must admit I hadn't thought of it like that. I suppose if
there are all these girls and women who are derelict, women
are better placed to help them than men. After all, to a great
extent men have been the cause of their problems. And I
suppose what I've tried to do for one girl here can be
multiplied, if everything else was set aside to deal with the
problem. There's only one thing though ...'

'What's that?'

'I am a divorced woman, don't forget. Did you ever hear of
a missionary society accepting a divorced person as a
candidate?'

'No, I don't think I did, but there has to be a first time for
everything. The question is not whether it would be a
precedent, but whether it would be right. Now we've been

into all this and your case fits Christ's teaching like a glove. Your marriage was dead – murdered in fact – and all the divorce did was to bury it publicly. It was because of this that we received you into the church like anyone else; we made no special conditions and we did not give you second-class status. If you are acceptable in a church in England you are acceptable in one abroad. Why should there be any difference? A society is only a branch of the work of the church. It doesn't have different standards or principles. We have the same New Testament to guide us.'

'On the other hand, would it not cause offence? Not everyone accepts our view of divorce, not yet at least. You have often said we are not to insist on our rights and liberties if it upsets another person's conscience.'

'Until it is done we don't know how it will go down. We thought here that it might create problems, but these melted away. And we wouldn't have to publicize the fact. The society would have to know, but they aren't obliged to placard it in their literature. And there's another way of looking at it. It was through that experience that you came to Christ in the first place. It was that more than anything that made you realize that all you are as a Christian is entirely of the grace of God. It was also that which enabled you to help Jameela in the first place. You wouldn't have been free to do all you have done if you'd remained married. Your experience has given you an understanding of something of what these girls go through. You can deal sympathetically with them and they sense this and give you their confidence. I would think it was a qualification rather than a drawback?'

Eve laughed. 'As usual, you've answered all my objections. I don't seem to have any reason for refusing.'

'We mustn't press you into a snap decision. It's too big a matter for that. Give it a little time while you think and pray more. The idea is very new to you. Then if you feel positively about it in a few weeks' time, I think the society is going to get the interested parties together to meet each other, along with representatives of the churches involved and the society's directors. After that they hope to decide on the team. If you really are interested, I could arrange for you to go to the conference.'

And so it came about that Eve found herself applying to join a team of missionaries. The conference itself she found rather overwhelming, although she was by no means the youngest present. There were two male students just finishing their Bible College courses and a nurse who had recently completed her training. The project had created considerable interest and caught the imagination of a number of churches. Enough finance had been promised to enable five people to be sent. A couple in their late thirties, Alec and Rachel Gilbert, had recently returned from a spell of service with the mission in the Far East, and it seemed likely the society would invite them to lead the team. In addition they were planning to have a doctor or nursing sister, a teacher and then another woman to work with Rachel Gilbert among the women and girls. It was this latter post in which Eve was interested. In fact, it had been this that had given rise to the whole enterprise, although it was now to be extended in order to get to the root of the problem and not merely to try to clear up some of the mess it was causing. The thinking behind the project was that there was no point in attempting rescue work among women and girls unless a church was set up to receive them. In time, given the blessing of God, the influence of the gospel and the church would begin to alter the whole way of thinking and living among these people. There were no Protestant missions in that area, so it would be virgin soil.

Although Eve enjoyed the conference in every way, she felt very much a novice and thought it likely the society would try to find a more experienced person. However, at the interview she was given before coming away, it seemed to be assumed that she was going. The directors appeared to know everything they wanted to know about her, and spent most of the time discussing practical matters: what would she do with her present accommodation while abroad? What length of time was she thinking of working on the field? Would she be prepared to start learning the language now? What about home ties – parents, for example? On the question of the language she had in fact already picked up a good deal of it from Jameela, and was sure she could have a good working knowledge of it by the time the team was ready to go. She came away feeling the matter was out of her hands, and in a way she was glad she did not have to agonize over coming to a decision.

No date had been fixed for the commencement of the work, since there was a good deal to be done by way of obtaining premises, equipping them, negotiating with officials for entry permits, and dozens of other matters. But at least things were under way. And the intervening time could be spent usefully. Not the least important part of the preparatory work was to plan the strategy. The country had been devastated by war and the problems this left in its wake had mounted rather than decreased. There was still a dearth of male workers and a surplus of orphaned and homeless children. There were undernourishment and disease, very little education and next to no religion. The old superstitions had suffered a blow, but not much had come in to take their place. The Roman Catholics seemed to be the only people doing anything that remotely resembled Christian work. There was no point in the team clashing with them, whatever was felt about the validity of their type of Christianity. To enter into controversy at this stage would only complicate things. They therefore chose a town well away from the one in which the Roman Catholic orphanage and its other institutions were situated. They planned to set up a clinic which would aim to treat diseases in their early stages, thus helping to relieve the strain on the government hospital, such as it was. They would also establish a school geared particularly to those in their mid-teens, which was the age when they emerged from such institutions as existed, usually with insufficient training to obtain any regular work, so that they were left at the mercy of the criminal element. Girls were particularly vulnerable in this respect. The building or room used for school classes would also double up for worship services, preaching and teaching of Scripture.

Everyone in the team was given basic training in all branches of the work, so that all could help each other. They would begin by devoting the mornings to school classes and the early evening to a surgery or clinic. The rest of the time was to be used by the individual members at their own discretion to pursue their own specialities. Eve and Rachel were to concentrate on deserted wives, unmarried mothers and other girls in difficulty or moral danger. How they would go about this they could not envisage until they arrived out there. No doubt much would turn out differently from what any of them could expect. 'How true that feeling proved!' thought Eve, who still held Anne's photo in her hand. She looked up from it to the framed picture on top of the bureau, which was of Alec, whom she had married on her return to England, some six years or so after going out there. 'Who could have thought that would be the outcome of attending Anne's party?'

The way it had come about was the last she would have wished or expected. At first they had all acclimatized well and there seemed to be no problems with health. Because of the desperate need they worked at full strength. Opportunities were unlimited, the school expanded, the church grew, with conversions and baptisms. They were just beginning to involve some of the more able and willing Burmese in aspects of the work and were in the process of starting training classes, when sickness struck. How it happened after so long was difficult to explain. Perhaps their initial strength and resistance to disease gradually ran down because the food available was not sufficiently nourishing to sustain it; perhaps the water became contaminated; perhaps they had been in contact with a patient with an unusually virulent disease. Whatever it was, they went down one after the other. A doctor and medicines had to be brought over a thousand miles. Eve and Prudence, the nursing sister, had to be moved to higher ground away from the heat and humidity. But Rachel was the worst affected. A helicopter was brought in to fly her to hospital, but she worsened on the journey and died soon after arriving.

The others recovered only slowly, and as soon as replacements could be found, they all returned to England for six months. Alec had the additional grief over the loss of his wife as well as having to contend with the effects of his own sickness. He spent most of his time near his two children, who were at school in England. However, the team met together once a month to hear reports of the work, to pray and generally keep in touch with each other.

When they were all pronounced fit they returned to take up the work again. One good result of all this was that three of the replacements remained and this, with three Burmese who were now sufficiently skilled to be trusted with responsibility, meant the team was now more than double its original strength. This was all to the good since the four who had first gone out did not feel strong enough now to cope with the volume of work they had done before their illness. Indeed they wondered how long they would be able to continue at all.

But this was by no means the only result of this episode! Since the death of Rachel Eve had taken over responsibility for the work among the women and girls, helped by an English girl and a Burmese woman. This meant she worked much more closely now with Alec than she had when his wife had been alive. He also looked to her increasingly for something of the friendship he had lost with the death of Rachel. Eve had been there from the beginning and understood the running of things better than most. They were able to talk together about the various situations that arose and the individuals involved. Also, Alec was not very proficient in the business side of the mission, and Eve with her training and experience was able to help out here. For her part, she had few books, all of which she had read more than once, and borrowed freely from Alec's portable library. He

let her read letters from his children and consulted her
sometimes over how to reply, saying he felt a bit out of touch
with the younger generation. All this threw them together a
great deal, and as they liked each other and got on well
together the friendship deepened. Probably the fact that
neither had fully regained health and strength increased the
need for sympathy and love. But they were anxious – too
anxious, perhaps – that the other members of the team
should not think they had a special relationship, lest jealousy
should be aroused, and so they acted more coolly towards
each other than either really felt, had they been honest with
themselves. Nothing further developed for a couple of years
or so.

Then, a few weeks after Alec had sent in his quarterly
report, he took Eve aside one day and said he had some news.
The mission had written that they were concerned about his
health and thought he should return to England. As the
secretary of the society was due to retire at the end of the
year, they would like Alec to consider replacing him. They
also wanted the other members of the original team to go to
Rangoon for a thorough medical check and to get the opinion
of doctors as to whether they were fit enough to continue out
there. Eve was not altogether surprised at this news. Alec
was ten years older than herself and must be feeling the
strain. Nevertheless it still came as something of a shock to
learn that in a very short time they might all be going their
separate ways. She had expected this to happen more
gradually. Nor had she thought her own future would so
suddenly have been placed in doubt. She told Alec she would
miss him very much if he left and that it would be difficult to
adjust to new companions and new leadership. But she also
felt relieved because she could see his health was
deteriorating, and accepted that this was the best thing for
him, especially as he would be able to use his experience in
the home base. He would also be able to have his children
with him again at an important stage in their lives. A staff
meeting was called and the news broken to everyone. It had

an unsettling effect on the whole team, which had become very close knit.

The result of the medical examination was that Eve and Sister Prudence were recommended to return to England for an extended furlough, while Andrew, the teacher, was pronounced fit to continue for at least another year. It was arranged that Eve and Sister Prudence should come back as soon as replacements could be found for their posts, but that Alec should stay on a few more months to give sufficient time to find a leader to replace him and take over from him. Eve's departure might therefore occur at only a week or two's notice. While she could look forward to the possibility of returning if her health were up to it, she knew that her days of working with Alec were now numbered. The prospect of separation drew them closer, and they spoke of meeting up again in England as something to look forward to. Eve could see he had something on his mind, but assumed it was to do with all the decisions that had to be made and the changes which were going to occur over the next few months. She herself felt far from clear about the future, especially if, after the extended furlough, she was not able to return. What then? Would she just go back to her former job? What an anticlimax that would be after all these years so full of purpose and achievement, of Christian fellowship in God's work, and above all of experiencing God's blessing so richly! She sought to trust God over the matter and put it to the back of her mind so that she could concentrate on the job in hand. With her imminent departure there was much to do to prepare for those who would be taking over from her.

Then one morning she went into the office as usual to see if there were any special matters to attend to that day. Alec handed her a letter. 'I'm afraid it came yesterday,' he said, 'and I apologize for keeping it from you for a whole day. There is a reason,' he added mysteriously.

Eve looked at him for a second and then bent her head to read the letter. It said that two women would be arriving in a week's time to take over from her and Sister Prudence, and that arrangements had been made for them to fly back to England a week later, allowing a few days in which to make the change-over. 'So this is it,' she thought to herself, and looking up said out loud, 'This is it, then.'

Immediately Alec spoke: 'I couldn't sleep at all last night – not for the first time since all this arose, I might say. But I've come to a decision now and feel much calmer. But it would help me to sleep tonight if you were to answer the question I'm going to ask you – in the affirmative,' he added, looking deeply into her eyes.

Eve realized what was coming and before he could say any more she had thrown her arms round his neck and tears were streaming from her eyes. Words were no longer necessary, and they remained thus for some time, when Alec said, 'You haven't even heard my question yet! I was going to ask you if, while you are in England and I'm still out here, you would consider something seriously, and then give me the answer when I see you again. But I think you know what the "something" is that I've got in mind!'

'Yes, I do, and I think you know what the answer is, so I don't need "time to consider seriously". There's nothing to consider. I know what my feelings are – I suppose I've known for a long time, it's just that there hasn't been much leisure to think about such things.'

'You must know too what my feelings are, although I've tried to hide and even suppress them, probably not very successfully.'

'I don't know. I think you've done quite well. I knew you liked me, but never thought it went any further. In any case,' she dropped her voice and a wistful note came in, 'even if I had thought it possible, I would have ruled it out because of my being divorced, and it isn't done for Christians to marry divorcees, let alone for missionaries to do so.'

'I've heard all about that, and it doesn't make a scrap of difference. I don't take the Anglican and Roman Catholic view that divorce is always wrong. I did at one time because it seemed the position of Christians generally, and no one came up with any other view. As a matter of fact, it was when the mission directors told me about you that I started to go into the subject more. I'd begun to wonder about it since studying books on Christian ethics at college, where some of the books put forward the view that the innocent party in a case of adultery could divorce and remarry. But other things put it out of my mind, and I never had to face up to it until the mission directors told me about you, saying that if on grounds of conscience I couldn't accept you, then they wouldn't invite you on to the team. I looked at the whole matter again and Rachel and I discussed it. She was taken with you in any case and didn't want anything to prevent your coming on the team! She must have been far-sighted! However, I needed something more convincing than feminine intuition, and read up on the matter. The books I'd read at college had not all been evangelical, so I needed to satisfy myself it was according to Scripture. As a result I came to see there was no problem. To explain away Jesus' words in Matthew 19 involves going through mental contortions!'

'I never knew anything about all that! No one ever told me! In fact the mission asked no questions at all about my marriage and divorce. I began to wonder if I ought to say something in case I went out under false pretences.'

'I can explain that,' said Alec. 'It had all been included in a report from your church, and your pastor had represented your case so well that the directors really had no objections or problems to raise. In the end it was down to me. And I've never regretted the decision – least of all now!'

'But there's still a problem,' said Eve. 'Not everyone may look at it like that. Some evangelical churches and Christians are quite sticky about divorce. They think that to allow it in this one instance is the thin end of the wedge, and soon all sorts of other grounds will be allowed. They think Christians must make a stand, because of the escalating divorce rate since the war. We might be denounced for setting a bad example to the younger generation and acting irresponsibly.'

'Yes,' replied Alec, 'that is a difficult one, and we must respect their consciences. That thought has held me back, and has been one reason why I delayed speaking to you for so long. In fact it is one of the things that has cost me my sleep recently. It's not easy to do something which may turn good Christian people against you. Then last night something came to me about this question of conscience. In Paul's letters the things he includes under this heading are secondary matters, some of them quite trivial – things like food and drink, the observance of days and so on. I suppose today they would correspond to things like smoking and drinking, theatre-going and cinema-going. If any of these caused offence to brethren you would stop doing them. After all, you can easily live without them; none of them is that important. Marriage on the other hand is quite different; it's something very big. If we allow people with weak consciences to dictate to us about whom we marry then we shall become like a Jewish sect. This was the kind of thing Paul was strongly opposed to. I'm quite sure that if he had decided to marry he would not have consulted the consciences of the Christians and the churches. It was when I realized this that the clouds of doubt blew away and I came into the light of day.'

'You have no idea what a comfort those words are to me,' Eve responded. 'This has always been the thing that's worried me most. It's one thing to get your own ideas clear, another to persuade others. But do you have to wait until everyone else sorts themselves out before acting? I can see now what the answer is to that question. But we may have difficulties to face. You realize that, don't you?'

'Of course. But the difficulties which would result from *not* marrying you would be far greater! No I'm sure it's right with the Lord, and therefore it's a matter of faith as well as love. I believe God is with us in it and will see us through.'

'That's all right then – if you're quite sure you don't mind a second-hand wife!'

'In exchange for a second-hand husband it seems a fair

swop! But I've just remembered something – Pru doesn't know about the letter yet!'

Later in the day they discussed when they should break the news to the others. At first they were inclined to postpone any announcement until after Alec's return to England. But on reflection they felt this would be too big a strain; nor was it really necessary since, with Eve having only two weeks left out there, no one was likely to be put out. In any case the members of the team were not really like that. So Alec called the staff together, told them the news and everyone was delighted, except at the prospect that they would be losing both of them permanently. Mission work is like that, they agreed. You work so closely that deep relationships are formed, only to be broken after what seems a very short time. But life generally was something like that.

'Yes, it certainly is,' Eve thought, as she looked over her photographs. They were all there – the team, the Burmese Christians, and Jameela and Bushrah, the two who had been the original cause of it all. 'And now I scarcely see any of them,' she said sadly to herself. 'But I have no regrets about any of it, least of all about marrying Alec.'

8.
The head of the wife

Along with the photos in Eve's archives was a bundle of
letters which she and Alec had written to each other after her
return to England while he remained in Burma. The rubber
band around them broke as she touched it and the letters
ceased to be a bundle. Each one represented a stage in the
development of their relationship, and she relived those
stages as she unfolded and read through them one by one.
Being methodical she had arranged them in the order in
which they had been written, which meant that normally one
of hers alternated with one of his. On top of the pile was the
one she had written on arriving back in Britain.

'Thank God we are safely back in England,' it read. 'I
can't complain about the journey, which was comfortable,
but I never lost the sense of being torn away from you the
whole time. It's still there now and I long to be with you
again. Peter met me as promised and took me to their home,
where Grace had prepared a lavish welcome. It is so kind of
them to take me in until I get something sorted out. Pru was
met by her brother and has gone to stay with him. I'm afraid
I wept a little when we said goodbye! It all seems so strange
at the moment, although it's only just over two years since I
was last here. But then we were all together and knew we
were going back. Now there's a new life to prepare for. It's
going to take some time to settle down, I think. You'll be
getting the details as they happen, but I wanted you to know
as soon as possible that I had arrived safely, as I know you
will be waiting to hear. Now I shall be looking forward to
hearing from you. I'm longing to know what you've been
doing over the last few days and whether there have been any
developments.'

Alec's reply to this consisted mainly of a diary of the

events of the days since Eve's departure, during which
nothing of great moment had occurred. Eve's next letter,
however, revealed that much was happening with her.

'The day after arriving I felt too tired to do much. But I did
speak to Jameela on the phone. As you know she is married
and doesn't live here now. Her husband is a fine Christian
man and they have two children. I hope to see them all when
we can arrange for me to go and visit them. But the
immediate question is where I am going to live. I can't stay
here until you get back! In any case it would be good if we
could get a place and I could start making it livable before
you arrive. I went to see the pastor the other day and we
discussed this. The church is willing to help. By the way, they
laid on a special welcome on Saturday, which was very nice.
But I've got to sing for my supper by giving full reports at the
prayer meeting over the next month. I'm also going to the
mission to talk the situation over with them. And I've got an
interview with my old firm to see what the prospects are
there. You see, it's all happening here! What about you?
How are you coping with your new workers? How is the new
lady superintendent?'

'It was good to hear so much news of you,' Alec's next
letter ran. 'I feel as if I'm leading two lives at the moment and
don't quite know where I actually belong! I can't say I'm
getting on so well as when you were here, but am making the
best of it. Sheila is settling in well but finds it difficult
superintending the Burmese women when they know so
much more about the work than she does. I am having to
help a good deal, and also do more of the secretarial work, as
it doesn't seem fair on Sheila to expect her to do it, at least
until she has got on top of her own job. However, to
compensate, I am excused teaching duties and only help in
the surgery when there's an emergency on. Dorothy, the new
sister, is capable, although she hasn't had too much time to
get hold of the language yet. It's easy for me to forget that we
had so much more time to prepare before we started than the
present staff have had. I've not heard much from the

mission lately, so I am looking forward to hearing what they have had to say to you.'

Eve's next letter took up this last point. 'I had a happy and profitable time with the mission directors. They are pleased about our engagement, as they had been very concerned about you since you lost Rachel. For a time they couldn't see much future for you, but after a good deal of prayer and discussion they thought they should offer you the secretaryship of the mission when it falls vacant. They feel that our plans to marry confirm that this was the right decision, and they can see the providence of God operating. They think that having a wife will make all the difference when you come back and start the work. They even think I might be quite a good person for you to marry!

'Anyway, what they propose is that, instead of making me an allowance, they will start paying your salary as secretary right away. Evidently my church and yours are contributing to make this possible. This money will be available to make payments on a house. Then if I can get work with my firm I shall be able to live on my wages and even start buying things for the house. The question to be answered first is location. Obviously you will want to be near the mission office. This will mean I shall have to try to get a transfer to the office in the same town, so that I can move in as soon as possible. It's all a bit complicated and it will mean both of us leaving our churches. However, I suppose in some ways it's a good thing to make a fresh start. Now I've got to start surveying the housing market – that is, if you approve of the woman taking the initiative in these things!'

Although Eve had intended the last comment to be taken semi-humorously (hence the exclamation mark) Alec sensed there was a little more to it, or it would never have come into her mind at all, as is the case with most humorous remarks. He was well aware of her former connections with feminism, and that even now her views on women were not altogether those traditionally held by Bible Christians, although she herself was sure they were biblically based. He also realized that at some time they would have to discuss the matter of husband-wife relationship, and the questions of authority and submission. He therefore took it seriously and did not pass over it in his next letter. After responding to the various news items Eve had reported he went on, 'I don't see that the Bible's view of the husband as head of the wife is incompatible with the woman taking the initiative in all sorts of ways. I've always taken very seriously the so-called "virtuous woman" of Proverbs 31. Her "virtues" are not in the moral and spiritual realm (although no doubt she had those too) so much as in the practical. The things that woman got up to! She did all the shopping, although it took her a long way from home. But she still found time to do the cooking and make clothes, not just for the family but also the servants. And they were good strong clothes that would not wear out quickly and were proof against the cold weather. Not content with this, she made carpets and curtains. She even made clothes to sell to merchants. She was a good business woman and transacted the purchase of land in order to plant a vineyard on it. No wonder she was up first in the morning and in bed last at night! I don't know when that woman slept! Yet she didn't neglect her health and seems to have done physical exercises to keep herself strong. Nor was she just a workaholic, because she could speak wisely and kindly, which meant she was a good thinker. And she wasn't houseproud or just out for her own family – she helped provide for the poor. Most important, she did not "wear the trousers", even if it does sound like that, for "her husband trusted her", which means he had confidence in her ability to cope with all these demands. He, it seems, had a place in the government of the country and was able to devote himself to this with the knowledge that his household affairs were in good hands.

'Now perhaps I've frightened you and made you think I expect you to be just like her! Actually I'm sure there never was such a woman as this one, nor intended to be. She is obviously an "ideal", not a human figure. That's why she's introduced with a cryptic question, "Who can find a virtuous woman?" There's no such animal! The point as I see it is to indicate there is plenty of scope for a woman to exercise her talents without trespassing on the sphere of her husband's authority. The thing is for both of them to be clear about what she's capable of and enjoys doing, and allow her plenty of scope, not insisting on the idea that there is "man's work" and "woman's work". Some of the things this woman did were traditional male preserves, like purchasing real estate and participating in agriculture. Remember that in the Old Testament land was inherited and always left to the sons, except where there were none. The exception is important because it showed that this law did not mean the daughters were necessarily incapable of estate management. The reason was that they usually married and were given dowries in lieu of property. Also if they had inherited the land, the family estate would have been joined to their husband's estate and ceased to remain in the original family, which was against Old Testament law. But the Bible has plenty of examples of women carrying responsibility, even in legal matters.

'I must bring this letter to a close or I shall be charged double postage, or, even worse, it will go by surface mail, in which case I shall get home before it! The answer to your question in brief is that if the "virtuous woman" can purchase a field you can purchase a house! That is, provided you feel able to do so without putting yourself under too much stress and strain. Don't feel on the one hand that you've got to do it, nor on the other that it would offend me. I want you to feel quite free in these things. Rachel and I always worked on that basis, at least ever since our attention was drawn to the "virtuous woman". In some things she was much more able than I, so I usually left them to her. You yourself know what I'm like in business matters. I probably would not make a very good job of house purchase, so perhaps God is keeping me out of the way while it goes on! Now I sound as if I'm trying to opt out of my responsibilities!

I hope you won't misunderstand what I'm saying, but you did ask me!'

Eve hastened to reply lest Alec should be torturing himself with anxiety in case she had misunderstood. 'It took me quite a while to marry up your points about the "virtuous woman" with the actual verses in Proverbs 31, since you didn't arrange them in order and translated them into present-day situations. However, I think I've found them all now, and it's been quite an eye-opener. Funny I never really went into that passage when I was doing my studies on women in the Bible after I first became a Christian. Perhaps it was just as well. I might have drawn up some sort of woman's charter on the basis of it, and put the cat among the pigeons! But it does show that the nineteenth-century idea of a virtuous woman is not precisely the same as the Bible's. Pity that idea is so long dying out!

'Anyway, let me hasten to assure my future husband that I shall not try to model myself on her in every detail. Certainly not as regards the needlework, which has never been my strong point! But I hope I shall do enough for him to say "she doeth him good and not evil all the days of her life". By the way, you didn't comment on the piece at the end about the fear of the Lord being more important than beauty! I hope you'll always remember that! But to be serious, the scope given to the woman in Proverbs 31 seems so great as to leave hardly any place for the husband's authority. Yet the New Testament lays as much stress on the husband being the head of the wife as does the Old Testament. So has this headship any teeth or is it just nominal? I'm not quite clear what it involves. Perhaps you could let me have your thoughts on it. Meanwhile I'll try to do some research on it myself – that is, with what time there is left after house-hunting!

'That reminds me, darling, the mission have kindly said I can use their lawyers. I went to see them and they put me on to a Mr Richards who was very helpful and said I could consult him at any time and it would not go down on the bill;

174 *Eve's Story*

they would only charge for the actual documents. At the
moment I'm a bit uncertain what size of house to look for.
I'm thinking about Jennifer and Brian. I know they're at
school most of the time, but once you're back, won't they be
staying with us a good deal? Perhaps you'd let me have your
thoughts on this.'

The reply that came to this letter read as follows: 'I'm glad
you're not going to let the "virtuous woman" be a burden to
you. She's meant to be an encouragement, to satisfy those
deep-seated feminist inclinations! You seem to be doing
quite well in this direction so far, and it's a relief to know you
have expert advice you can turn to. Our years in these
primitive parts have not really fitted us for the complicated
financial and legal processes of purchasing property in a
sophisticated society. You must find it quite bewildering
after bamboo huts! Still, I suppose we should try to raise our
standards to those we shall be living among, just as we
lowered them when we came out here! One thing the mission
field does is to make the lowest way of life in Britain seem like
luxury! However, in view of the uncertainty hanging over
Jenny's and Brian's futures, it would be good if we can give
them a home and be together when possible. A four-bedroom
house will be ideal if we can afford it. The extra room can
then double up as an office. But how do *you* feel about taking
on a couple of stepchildren you haven't even met? Do you
find it daunting, my darling? You've not said anything about
this. And another thing you haven't mentioned is how you
are yourself. You went home not in the best of health, so how
are you now? And weren't you supposed to be having a
medical check-up and some treatment? Don't go charging
round hunting houses and getting back to work until you're
fit for it. It's good to have these discussions on theology and
Christian behaviour, but I'd like to hear more about *you*,
please!

'However, you asked me a question and I'm not trying to
duck it. Although what can one do in a flimsy air letter?
Someone should have written a book and then I could just

have given you the name of the author and the title! For what they're worth, here are my thoughts. You ask, "Is the headship of the husband merely nominal?" No, not "merely", although a word like "mainly" would be nearer the mark. Basically this is a matter of the order of creation, which gives to the man the right of the first-born. It has little to do with any constitutional differences between man and woman; but I think you've been into all that. This arrangement was acceptable to both parties until the Fall. Adam fluffed his responsibility and allowed Eve (am I glad my name's not Adam!) to bear the brunt of the temptation, weakly giving in when it was too late, and then turning round and blaming her. In spite of his failure as head, God confirmed his position and told Eve he would rule over her. Because sin had come in, he on his part overdid the authority and she on hers resented this. God had to give special laws to protect women against the abuse of authority by their husbands. In godly partnerships such as that of Abraham and Sarah it worked fairly well (she called him "lord"), but even here there were some unhappy scenes.

'Jesus did not alter this arangement, but he gave a new concept of "lordship" in general, not as an occasion for self-exaltation but as an opportunity for service (read Luke 22:24-27). He himself gave an example of this when he washed the disciples' feet, although he was their "lord and master", and told them to act like that towards each other, to base their idea of authority on his. When he rose and ascended he became "head of the church" or rather "head over all things *for* the church". So his headship was not something he thought of as a chance to be boss, but as a way to build up his church. He thought of himself as head, not only in the sense of "chief " but as "head of the body", to which he was joined and which he supplied with life, energy, understanding and so on.

'Now when the New Testament talks of the husband as "head" it appeals to the example of Christ. In 1 Corinthians 11:3 Paul says the man is the head of the woman, as God is head of Christ. This means it's not a matter of nature but of order. God is not *better* than Christ or *wiser* or anything like that, and neither is man better or wiser than woman. His superiority lies in his position, which is to reflect God's appointed order of creation. The important thing is how he *uses* this position. Ephesians 5:23-33 helps us here. It says nothing about commanding, ordering or suppressing. It takes its cue from Christ and therefore talks of loving and cherishing, considering and respecting, serving and building up – doing for her what he would do for his own body. Nor does it say he does everything because she is incapable of responsibility or decision-making. Once again Christ is the example. Although he is head, he delegates his authority to those he chooses as under-shepherds. They in turn delegate their authority to others and everyone in the church becomes involved in its functioning. In other words, it is like the human body. Every part and member has its function, and doesn't feel it is being manipulated by the head, but feels quite free to act. That's how Christ deals with us: we don't feel we are forced to do this or that. We *want* to obey and serve him because we enjoy it. So with husband and wife there should be no sense of domination on either side, just a quiet recognition that this is God's order. If we accept it as such it will work fine. It's only when we misunderstand or disagree with it that there is trouble or unhappiness.

'Well, that's all there's room for – no space even to send my love! I hope it directs your thinking along the right lines, if nothing more!'

To this Eve responded in the next letter: 'To show you I have taken what you said to heart, I begin by accepting your rebuke and humbly putting matters to rights by giving a narrative of my state of health. I can't deny I've been up and down somewhat, which is one reason why I've not said anything. The day I write to you I might be feeling awful, but by the time you get the letter I might be O.K. and you would worry needlessly. Anyway because of this, the mission postponed my medical until things settle into a pattern. So

I've just visited the local G.P. who is fairly new (at least to me) and he's keeping me going on vitamins and tonics. But I have a date now for the medical – the week after next. After that's over I shall go and stay with father and mother, which will help the recuperation and get my strength back to return to work and tackle the housing question more seriously. But I haven't told you yet that I had an interview at the firm, and they hope to arrange a transfer so that I'll be on the spot to look out for houses. They seem quite short-staffed at present, and I think they will be glad of my previous experience. It will be funny to go back to office work again.

'All you wrote was very enlightening, but I still have questions! In fact every answer seems to lead to another question – something I've always found. Still now I have a husband (almost) to ask, and Paul did say, "If they have questions let them ask their husbands"! The question is, if all you say is right (which I'm not doubting!), how does it fit those passages where the wife is told to "submit" or "obey" or "be subject to" her husband? Terms like that suggest rather more than your description of what the relationship implies. And if the wife is to be subject to her husband "as the church is to Christ", this sounds as though she comes in ignorance to be taught, falls down in worship and asks for instructions! So what about this?

'Incidentally, while we're talking about health, what about *yours*? You reproach me for not giving an account of mine, but you were worse than me when I left and you've had to continue to struggle with the climate, disease and diet, and all the other things which brought us low. But not a word have I heard about it!'

To this Alec replied, 'I shall restrain myself from saying, "Just like a woman!", which would not be consistent with our present discussions – and between ourselves I doubt whether we can ever generalize to the extent of using such an expression! But you know what I mean! You ask me deep questions requiring lengthy answers, and when I give them you proceed to tell me off for not writing about other things!

Having got that off my chest, I can tell you the good news.
Things have settled down sufficiently well for me to be able to
take a fortnight's holiday in the mountains. I can't deny I've
been feeling low lately, but the atmosphere up there is so
different – fresh and bracing – I'm sure I shall come back
feeling a new man, or at least sufficiently renewed to last out
the remaining time here. That shouldn't be too long, as the
mission think they will have appointed my successor by the
time I come back from holiday, and the time schedule will
soon follow after that. In any case, it seems it's going to take
us all our time to sort out these questions of husband-wife
relationships!

'Now concerning those things whereof you wrote unto me,
as Paul would say, the matter of submission comes in two
main passages – Ephesians 5 and 1 Peter 3. The first one is
the one that speaks about the husband as head, which we've
already discussed. I won't take up space writing it out; you
can easily read it for yourself in your Bible. The submission
of the wife corresponds to the headship of the husband. So
obviously the first thing it means is that she (or "you" in this
case!) must accept the principle as being God's appointment.
You must be quite happy that God in his wisdom has fixed an
order in marriage which means husband and wife don't
share equal status and position. But this is not unique; the
same applies in the church: some have authority and the
others have to submit to it, men as well as women. It even
applies in the Godhead: the Father is "head" of the Son.

'The next important point is that the submission is
voluntary; the wives are to "subject *themselves*", not *be*
subjected by compulsion. Now there should be no problem
here if the first point is all right. If it is God's will that this
should be so, a wife who knows and trusts God will accept it
gladly. The other point follows from this: she does it *because* it
is his will; this is her motive, "as unto the Lord". In other
words she is not saying, "I subject myself because my
husband is superior, I bow to his wisdom," but "I recognize
this is God's way, and it glorifies and pleases him for me to be

in this subjection." This is why Peter tells the Christian wife to submit even to a non-Christian husband. Obviously in this case the wife will have more understanding of the vital issues of life than her husband. Nevertheless she is not to preach to or lecture him, but behave as she would to a Christian husband, which Peter says is the best way to win him.

'In any case many of the things married couples do are not directly spiritual, so the fact the husband is not a Christian does not mean they cannot continue to live together in a husband-wife relationship. If this is so where they are not agreed spiritually, how much more so where they are! And the fact that the arrangement doesn't imply one is superior and the other inferior means the husband does not act unilaterally, but that they confer together and agree on the best course of action. But God knows that, being in the flesh we won't always agree, with the best will in the world. Even a Christian husband and wife will not always see eye to eye. When everything possible has been done to come to an agreement, and a course of action has to be taken, the only way to resolve the situation is for God's order to be accepted and the husband to take the decision. But he must not do it in the spirit that because he is head of the relationship what he says is necessarily identical with God's will, but in a humble way, realizing he may be wrong. However, because God has placed him in that position he must accept the responsibility that goes with it. In the same way the wife must accept it as God's ordinance. Even if she thinks the decision is wrong, it's more important to fulfil God's will and command about marriage than to get a particular issue right; although it may not seem that way in the heat of the moment! Doing it this way may mean mistakes are made, but this is not so bad as creating disharmony in the marriage and, above all, displeasing God. This is always the main thing to keep in view – that God's way is wisest and best at the end of the day, even if in the short term mistakes are made.

'So there it all is, at least as I see it. But how do *you* see it?

That's just as important to me. Are there any more questions to go into, or can we say, "This correspondence is now closed"? Perhaps over the next fortnight with nothing much else to think about I might have a few more thoughts on the matter. If so, I'll put them down and send them from there. By the way, you know the address to write to, don't you? Don't send letters to the mission. I can't go two whole weeks without hearing from you!'

Eve bundled up the letters again with a smile. 'We should have published this correspondence,' she said to herself, 'the first marriage preparation course ever conducted by air mail!' But how good it had been to get those issues clarified before embarking on marriage! 'We might just have drifted into it, unconsciously following the way everyone else thought and behaved, or, worse, determining everything according to our own personalities and probably clashing frequently. Not that we didn't clash on occasion – I suppose everyone does – but it was only when we forgot the way God had taught us. Then, when we came to ourselves and remembered, things could be put right. What a wonderful guide the Bible is on everything! How fair and beautifully balanced, not taking sides in a sex war. What a pity men and women so often have to be presented as in conflict, scoring points off each other, making jokes at each other's expense! No doubt there are humorous aspects, and we mustn't take ourselves too seriously. But surely we should look on our differences as like the treble and bass on the piano – harmonizing to give the music greater richness. Instead of which it's so often presented as if we were playing two completely different pieces of music. Worse, that's how it's often lived, so that either there's continual clashing, or the partners go their separate ways, even when they stay under the same roof. That Ephesians 5 passage is the cure for all this – the Christian couple's charter, and the woman has as much place in it as the man.'

At their wedding, which had taken place in Eve's church, they had requested that Ephesians 5 be read and the pastor should make a few comments on it. Alec and Eve wanted as many as possible to share what they had discovered and make it the basis of their own married life. After the wedding and honeymoon, they had gone to live in the house Eve had chosen on the outskirts of the town in which the missionary society was situated. Alec's two children, Jennifer and Brian, were frequent visitors, although they never lived there permanently. It was thought best they should complete their education at their boarding schools, after which they went on to university. Jennifer then proceeded to a career in the legal profession and Brian became a teacher, both living and working in other parts of the country.

Eve had two children of her own, James and Mary, and so the house was in full use for over twenty years, by which time Alec had retired from the mission and they moved to a bungalow. During that period, with Alec away a good deal and her children growing up, Eve had not been able to take what is usually called 'an active part' in the life of her local church. She was fairly housebound and could not undertake much that took her out of the house on a regular basis. Some of the other Christian wives and mothers compensated for this by clothes-making and other handicrafts, but this had never been in Eve's line. She did help Alec with a certain amount of the secretarial work for a while, but as staffing at the mission improved this became unnecessary.

Although she saw little of Jameela now that the girl was married and raising a family, Bushrah was a not infrequent visitor and would spend a few days with them when she was off duty from her hospital. She still had a gift for collecting lame ducks around her and never lost touch with her home town in Burma. Eve felt remorseful at not doing more about her former work abroad, other than receiving news in order to pray for the workers and write to them. Then it suddenly occurred to her that she was in an ideal position to do for someone else what she had done for Jameela years ago. She and Alec discussed this and prayed, and felt they could and should give their extra room to some overseas girl who was struggling to make a start in life. The mission and Bushrah would know of plenty who were in need of this.

And so it came about that for something like fifteen years they had one or more Burmese girls living with them. Knowing the language herself, Eve was able to teach them English. During this language training their talents would begin to surface so that she could go on to guide them into some career. When fully fledged they either returned to Burma more equipped to make their way, or took up work in this country, so that Eve was free to take on someone else. In this way she was able to help a number of girls on to their feet who might otherwise have led a life of poverty, misery and shame. Most of them attended the church and became Christians, at least in name and profession. Thus Eve felt that the work she had been called to was not brought to an end after all by ill-health and marriage, but was going on. And she could do it all almost without stepping outside her door. She was thankful to God for enabling her to perform this service, and was sorry it had to come to an end with Alec's retirement and their removal to smaller premises. 'But *I* haven't come to an end yet!' she added to herself.

9.
Teach the young women

Eve put everything back into the boxes – diary, notes, pamphlets, photos and letters – and put them away. 'It's time I stopped reminiscing and did something useful. It's nearly midday and I've done nothing.' She took a duster out of the cupboard and set to work to clean her bungalow. She worked through the kitchen, the dining room and her own bedroom, but by the time she reached the lounge she was ready for a breather. As she looked around the room more thoughts came flowing back. In the chair opposite to the one where she was sitting there appeared to her imagination one after another women and girls who had sat there pouring their problems into her ears. The occasional one still came, as her own niece Sarah had only yesterday, but not as many as in the first years she and Alec had lived there.

By the time Alec had come to retire from the secretaryship of the mission, all four of the children had left home and a large house was no longer necessary. Nor did they need to live in a town the size of the one in which the mission was situated. Eve's younger brother (Sarah's father) lived in a small country town where some development was taking place, and they managed to find a two-bedroomed bungalow there. Since Alec was ten years Eve's senior, they were looking to the future, trying to ensure they would not take on something they could not manage as they grew older, especially if Eve should be left on her own.

This move meant that her work with the Burmese girls was brought to an end. However, it also left her more free to participate in the life and work of the local evangelical church. This was less flourishing than the previous churches to which she had belonged. In fact it was struggling somewhat, being short of men with any leadership ability.

The pastor's time was limited, as he was having to do part-time work. He and the church were very glad of Alec's and Eve's support, and after a period of time Alec was made an elder and undertook a substantial amount of pastoral work, functioning almost as a co-pastor.

But at this point housing development around the old town began to gather pace. In the area new industries were being opened and more and more people were looking for accommodation. New estates began to spring up and the population increased rapidly. Some of these people found their way to the evangelical church, which not only meant numerical growth but brought in a much younger element. Several families joined, some with small children and one or two with teenagers. The new surge of life was welcome to those who had struggled there for years, and eventually the pastor was able to give up his job and live on his increased stipend. But it also brought a number of problems with it and in some of them Eve herself became involved.

Mary Blake was a single lady in her forties who had taught in the Sunday School for many years. During most of that time this had consisted almost entirely of children whose parents had no other connection with the church or the gospel. Now all this was changing and the majority of the children belonged to the families that had recently moved in and joined the church. After their classes they would rejoin their parents, along with their brothers and sisters, sitting together as families during the service that followed. Eve had always got along well with Mary, until her attitude began to change. Eve's attention was first drawn to this on one occasion when the pastor had been speaking about the Philippian gaoler and had become rather dramatic in describing how the man, thinking all the prisoners had escaped, took out his sword and was about to fall on it and kill himself. At this point one of the younger children, who had a very vivid imagination, forgetting he was listening to a sermon and thinking he was watching a Western film, called, 'Don't do it! they're all still there!' making everyone laugh.

Everyone, that is, except Mary Blake, who was sitting next to Eve, so that Eve could not help noticing. She soon forgot about it, however, until at the end of the service Mary got straight up out of her seat and left without a word. Eve presumed she was upset about something and, although this was not usually like Mary, she thought no more of it. But when Mary did not appear at the evening service the incident came back to Eve's mind and on returning home she telephoned her and asked if anything was wrong. Mary replied that she had a headache but otherwise everything was all right. Eve accepted the explanation at the time, but her concern was revived when Mary continued to behave in an unusual manner. She ceased to make her usual helpful contribution to the prayer meeting, sometimes missing it altogether, left quickly at the end of meetings and services and kept herself somewhat aloof generally.

After this had gone on for two or three weeks, Eve turned to her one evening when they were sitting together in church, and said, 'How's the headache?' at which Mary, being caught unexpectedly off her guard, bit her lip and her eyes filled with tears. Then collecting herself she said, 'It comes and goes.'

'You should see a doctor if it goes on,' said Eve.

'Oh I don't know,' replied Mary, 'it's probably the humid weather, or something like that.'

'No,' said Eve, 'it's more than that, isn't it? You've got some problem.' Mary made no reply. 'Why don't you come round and have a chat with us? It may help.' Eventually Mary did agree, somewhat reluctantly, to come and have a meal with them one day that week.

As Eve prayed during the next few days, she felt more and more convinced that Mary's problem was one not uncommon among single ladies in their thirties and forties – frustration over being unmarried and childless. She was also sure she knew the answer to this, having had to face it herself long before. But what she was not so sure about was how she could broach it to Mary in her present mood. So it was this

that she made the main subject of her prayers, sharing it with
Alec, who would, of course, be present at the meal. In the
event Mary seemed much more relaxed than she had been at
church recently, although still not really her old self. This
convinced Eve that her problem was connected with recent
changes in the composition of the congregation. So she began
by talking enthusiastically about the improvement in the
situation.

'*We* find it encouraging, and we're comparative
newcomers, so you must be really thrilled after bearing the
burden and heat of the day all this time.' Mary made no
comment, so Eve went on to ask her, 'How do you like your
enlarged Sunday School class?'

'Well,' replied Mary, 'naturally I'm glad to have more
children, and to see more people in the church, but what
I'm afraid of is that these new families are beginning to take
over. In my class, for instance, the children of the Christian
families now dominate it, and the others don't get much of a
look in, because they don't know as many of the answers.
But they're the ones who need most attention.'

Alec made a suggestion: 'Why don't you change your
approach slightly and put your questions to them
individually? Then you could ask the Christians' children
things they won't be able to answer, and this will make them
realize they don't know everything after all.'

Mary sighed. 'That will only make the job so much
harder. Anyway, how can I know if a particular child knows
the answer to a question or not? No, I don't think that would
really work.' The conversation continued very much on these
lines, with Mary constantly raising objections to the positive
points or suggestions put forward by Alec and Eve,
convincing the latter that Mary was covering up a deeper
problem.

At the end of the meal Alec asked whether they would
mind if he took his coffee to his study as he had an article to
write for the mission's magazine. (He still helped in the
society's work in a voluntary capacity, especially in the

production of their publications.) Eve and Mary took their coffee through to the lounge and sat down there with it. Eve decided to take the bull by the horns – there seemed nothing to lose, and the only alternative was to go on rallying for the rest of the evening. She looked across at Mary and asked her a question.

'Have you ever considered, Mary, what Jesus said about single people in Matthew 19, verse 12?' Mary looked puzzled for a moment and then said, 'Oh yes! That's the passage about divorce, isn't it? And it ends up by saying there are different types of eunuch – some born that way, some made eunuchs by men, and some who have made themselves eunuchs. What about it?'

'What I mean is, have you ever thought about it in relation to yourself?'

Mary coloured slightly. 'What on earth do you mean? Isn't it about men who can't face the demands of marriage and deliberately renounce it? Perhaps they get themselves doctored to make it easier. I don't know whether that's what monks do, but I suppose it would help!'

Mary was being a little evasive, but Eve pressed on patiently. 'I don't think that's quite what Jesus was saying. I'm not trying to instruct you, Mary, but I went into all this years ago when my first marriage broke up. It seems to me Jesus is responding to what the disciples had just said: "It's better not to marry." That is, if divorce is forbidden except in extreme cases then it would be better to keep out of marriage altogether. Jesus' reply was that they should think the whole thing out again from a fresh standpoint. The current view was that a man should be able to divorce his wife if he saw anything in her he didn't like. But Jesus taught that they should go back to creation and see that God intended marriage to be permanent. Its bond was only to be broken in extreme cases, that is, adultery, and this applied just as much to the man as the woman: the man could be a guilty party and the woman could divorce him. He adopted the same radical approach to the question of being a eunuch or celibate. The Jews thought that even to be unmarried and childless was a cause of great shame, but a eunuch was absolutely anathema, whether he was born that way or underwent an operation. But Jesus spoke of a third type of eunuch – one who is so voluntarily for the sake of his kingdom. Obviously he didn't mean a eunuch in the literal sense of someone mutilating himself, any more than his words in the Sermon on the Mount about cutting off the right hand or plucking out the right eye are to be taken literally. He meant someone who deliberately renounces marriage in order to devote himself to Christ's service. Now do you see what I'm getting at?'

'I don't really see what it has to do with me. A eunuch is a man, and it's the man who has the initiative – he can decide whether or not to marry. The woman doesn't have quite the same choice – she's not in the driving seat.'

'And yet Paul talks about the unmarried woman in just the same way.' Eve opened her Bible. ' "There is a difference between a wife and a virgin. The unmarried woman careth for the things of the Lord, that she may be holy both in body and spirit; but she that is married careth for the things of the world, how she may please her husband." So it's exactly the same for a woman as a man. The single state is always good in God's eyes and shouldn't be despised.'

'I still say it's different for the woman,' Mary replied. 'Not every woman is single because she has chosen to be. She might have wanted to marry, but has never had the opportunity. What Jesus and Paul both said surely applies to those who are voluntarily single, not to unclaimed treasures like me.'

'Are you referring to yourself there, Mary?' asked Eve. Mary did not reply, so Eve continued. 'May I ask you a very personal question?' She paused, but there was still no answer. Since Mary had not exactly said 'No', Eve put her question. 'Is it just marriage in general, or was there someone in particular?' There was silence for a few moments before Eve spoke again. 'I may be wrong, Mary, although I don't think I am, but I have the feeling that you are envious of family people because you would like to have been married yourself. What I'm not quite so sure about is whether this is just a general wish, or if there was some particular person you wanted to marry.'

Eve waited. Mary stirred her empty coffee cup for a full minute. Then Eve asked, 'Shall I relieve you of that?' Mary gave a nervous laugh as she passed the cup over, but it broke the tension. She cleared her throat.

'As you know,' she began, 'I've lived here most of my life and been in the church since I was quite young. There was always a shortage of males, which is why there are several of us old maids in the congregation today.' She paused and cleared her throat again. Eve could see that her mouth was dry and poured her some more coffee. She took a mouthful. 'Thank you. That's better. I've never told anyone this, or not for a long time. When I was about twenty-seven or twenty-eight I became very friendly with someone a year or two younger who worked at our place. I went out with him a few times, although I never asked him home. You see, he wasn't a Christian, or remotely interested in the gospel, although when I told him what I did on Sundays he did start attending his parish church for a while. He wouldn't come to our church, which I suppose was a bit of a relief to me as it might have been embarrassing. I felt after a time we were getting too close, and it was affecting my spiritual life and my relationship with the other Christians. I'd not long become a member when it happened. There seemed no likelihood of him becoming converted, so I stopped seeing him. He tried two or three times to take it up again, but I refused, and a year or so later he moved on. That's all.'

'This is exactly what I'm talking about,' said Eve. 'You fit the picture like a glove. From what you say it seems very likely he would have married you if you'd kept up the friendship. You were obviously very fond of him, but you deliberately chose to remain single for the Lord's sake, in case you were drawn away from him. This is what Jesus

meant by becoming a eunuch for the kingdom of heaven's
sake – renouncing marriage on a spiritual principle. This is
what Paul means when he talks about remaining a virgin in
order to care for the things of the Lord.'

'I suppose that's true when you put it like that. I've never
really thought about it in quite that way. I did see it as a kind
of sacrifice and for a while I felt quite good about it, which
helped to mend the broken heart. But I don't think I ever
quite realized there were actual texts of Scripture dealing
with it. Not that I really understand 1 Corinthians 7 anyway!
Even now I'm not quite sure that I fit these passages. I can't
honestly say I ever actually renounced marriage altogether. I
always felt open to it, but it just didn't happen.'

'No, but you must have been prepared for it not to
happen. You must have realized it might not come your way
again, when you reached thirty and there was no one in the
offing.'

'Possibly I did. I don't really remember very clearly now.
I just know that in my mind I've never really closed the door,
and that may be putting it too mildly.'

'Yes, I think it is, and I think there's a reason. It's this
social pressure that is put on unmarried people, which I've
long felt is unfair. And Christians are as bad as others. They
drop hints and make comments, they match-make and they
leg-pull. They say it's only in sport, but it's a cruel one. The
League against Cruel Sports ought to campaign against it in
my opinion. They have no idea what a person feels like
inside. It never happened to me very much because I'd been
married and divorced and no one quite knew what to make of
me. Most were surprised when I remarried. But since all that
happened a long way from here they didn't have much say in
it!'

'Lucky old you! Perhaps I shouldn't say that. I'm afraid I
say a lot of things I shouldn't – and think them even more.
But what to do about it I don't know. I wish I did.'

'Well, the first thing is to learn to think rightly about it,
and get out of your system this attitude we've been talking

about which looks on single people as peculiar, the butt for
jokes and so on. It's a kind of hangover from the Old
Testament, when to be unmarried was a reproach and meant
there must be something wrong with a person and to be
childless was virtually a curse from God. Look what poor old
Hannah suffered! But Christ changed all that, as he did so
many things – in fact everything really. He didn't just save
our souls, but completely renewed us. He was a true radical,
and the things he said astonished people so that they cried
out, "How can this be?" Even the chief rabbi, Nicodemus,
said that. And his behaviour, too, raised many eyebrows. But
he didn't hide his intentions: he had brought new wine, and it
needed new wineskins to contain it. Included in this were
relationships and roles; these must be looked at in a fresh
way. In marriage, the man was never intended to have
everything his own way and treat the woman like a chattel.
This was not what God had said at creation. He had put up
with easy divorce for a long time, but he wasn't going to do so
any more. And for the unmarried too, there's a positive role
for them now. It's a calling, a gift, requiring special grace.
That's the first thing, Mary – get the thinking right.'

'I suppose I'm as much to blame as the others. If I had my
ideas straight I wouldn't take so much notice of what they
say, in fact I would have told them what you've told me,
instead of being on the defensive all the time. But when you
said it was "the first thing", does that mean there's more to
come?'

'Much more. The thing to be clear about is that this
phrase "for the kingdom of heaven's sake" is vital, or Paul's
equivalent, "caring for the things of the Lord", which is the
same. That's what must come first and it's the only way to
develop a positive attitude. "I'm single not because it's
Hobson's choice, but because it's God's choice, and mine. If
I have to choose between him and a human husband I choose
him." That's what you did, Mary, and I think a great many
Christian women are in the same position because they so
outnumber Christian men, but they could have married if

they'd gone outside the church. Quite a few men who aren't
Christians themselves are attracted to Christian women
because they can trust their loyalty, they're moderate in their
tastes, lovers of home and family and so on. It appeals to a
man who wants to settle down. And it can be quite difficult to
resist. You need real divine grace to do it. Who says being
single is not a special gift? But we mustn't go to the other
extreme as some do and make out that it's morally superior –
the idea that the celibate life is specially holy. That may be so
for monks and nuns, but we can't claim to have renounced
marriage for ever, as they do. You *could* still marry, Mary,
you're not too old and worn! It's a question of accepting it as
his will for the present and being content.'

'That's the big problem. Accept it mentally, yes. But to be
content with it and look at it positively as an opportunity for
service, that's quite hard.'

'Yes, and God knows that. That's why he's given us the
Bible. There's plenty more in it yet about this! Think of the
opportunities of the single state. If your first aim is really to
serve Christ's kingdom, you are much more free to do so than
the married woman with her hands full of chores and
children. You may think when you see them all together on
Sunday morning that there's something idyllic about family
life. That's because you don't know what has gone into
getting that family turned out on a Sunday morning. It's like
any public appearance – a concert, a play, a tennis match.
We just see the spectacle, the finished article, and it
impresses us. But we don't see all the tedious routine training
and rehearsing that goes to make it possible. It's that that
makes these people wish they'd never started or causes them
to give up. It's the same in the family. When all the long
preparations are going on the wife and mother sometimes
wonders whether it's worth the effort. She can't lie in bed and
have a leisurely breakfast, or spend extra time on her
devotions or do some reading. Nor can she respond to calls
and challenges that come in connection with God's work, as
you can, Mary. You are free to follow the Lord. If the Spirit

comes on you when you're reading or praying you can go on until the blessing fades. If there's a work requiring help and support you are free to undertake it. If you really want to serve Christ you will tell him you're glad to be free to do so.'

'It's a wonderful thought, if only I could get myself into that frame of mind.'

'It's not the only thought, either. There's the future, too. Do you remember how Jesus said that although the kingdom had arrived when he came, it would not fully come until his return at the end of the world? And do you remember what he said about the position of married people then, after the resurrection – that conversation he had with the Sadducees who were trying to trip him up? He said that in heaven no one is married; we are all like the angels. This is another thing Christians don't seem to be able to grasp. They talk of seeing their loved ones again as if everything is going to be the same as it is here. Now it may be true that we shall recognize one another – no one knows for certain – but what is certain is that we won't be in the same relationship. Everyone ultimately will be celibate. Marriage is only a very temporary arrangement!'

Mary opened her mouth to say something, but Eve hadn't finished. 'There's something else Jesus said that's relevant. He said that those who forsake their houses, their relations and so on now for his sake and his kingdom's will have them a hundredfold now in this present life. He said all who do God's will are his brothers, sisters and mother. The same is true for us. If we are Christians we are not alone. We have brothers and sisters, the young ones are like our children and the older like our parents. We are all one family.'

Mary said nothing, but the expression on her face was eloquent. The eyes had lightened and the tightness round the mouth relaxed. Sounds were coming from the other room showing that Alec had finished his work. His head appeared round the door. 'You ladies must be thirsty after all that talking. I know I am, and I've only been writing! I've put the kettle on.'

Later, when Mary had left, Alec asked Eve how the
discussion had gone and Eve gave him a summary of the
conversation. 'We shall have to wait and see, of course,' Alec
commented, 'but it seems to me you did pretty well. And you
took the right approach in giving her the texts and passages
relating to the question. She can't very well argue against the
Bible and the Lord, can she?'

As Eve did not respond, Alec looked across at her.
'Anything troubling you, Eve?'

'It's true I gave her the right passages for her case, but
was *I* right to do it? Are there any passages to justify what I
did? I mean, isn't this the pastor's work, or an elder's – yours
rather than mine?'

'If you'd been counselling a bachelor, or someone's
husband there might have been some objection, in fact I
probably wouldn't have allowed it! But to counsel women,
especially those much younger than you is good, and
scriptural too, I would say.'

'I can't think of any Scriptures authorizing it. Are you
quite sure?'

'Yes,' said Alec, reaching for his Bible and opening it
towards the end. 'Here, Titus chapter 2. Titus is being told to
explain to the older members of the congregation what their
duties are towards the younger ones – first the men, then the
women. So we take it up at chapter 2, verse 3: "The aged
women . . .",' he broke off, catching sight of Eve's face out of
the corner of his eye, 'I know you're not aged, dear, by
today's standards, but I'm afraid you would have been in
those days, and I would have been positively senile, if I'd
been around at all! Let's translate it "older" or, even better,
"mature" – would that be acceptable?'

Eve relaxed her expression. 'Let's get on with it,' she said.

Alec laughed and went on reading: ' "The – hm! mature –
women likewise, that they be in behaviour as becometh
holiness, not false accusers, not given to much wine, teachers
of good things; that they may teach the young women to be
sober, to love their husbands, to love their children, to be

discreet, chaste, keepers at home, good, obedient to their own husbands, that the word of God be not blasphemed.'' There it is in plain language.'

'That's quite a programme, isn't it? Perhaps what I should be asking is not "Was I right to tackle Mary?" but "Why am I not doing more?"'

'No, I don't think you should worry about that. I wouldn't understand this verse to say that every mature woman has got to rush around sorting out all the younger women's problems. A church like that could quickly become chaotic. I think it's a matter of being available when the need arises, being alert to what's going on, and stepping in when you can help without causing trouble. We have to remember we live in a very different kind of society, one in which people are more self-sufficient and less dependent, and many may resent what they would call interference.'

'Not only that,' added Eve, 'but there are so many experts and professional counsellors around that we unconsciously feel we need some training or qualification before we can embark on anything like this.'

'Yes, and yet the idea of training is here in the passage,' said Alec, 'where Paul tells Titus to "speak the things which become sound doctrine", meaning it was Titus' job to instruct the people in how to minister to each other. In that case, I suppose pastors of churches ought to include this in their pulpit ministry. Rather hard to imagine how they would go about it.'

'Let me have a look at that passage,' said Eve, holding out her hand for the Bible, which Alec duly passed over to her. Looking at it, she said, 'We are to teach the young women to love their husbands and children, etcetera, and to be keepers at home and be in subjection to their husbands. "Keepers at home",' she mused. 'What does that mean? That they mustn't go out to work, but stay in and do the housework? It's a rather old-fashioned picture, isn't it? And a bit difficult to practise today when millions of them have jobs.'

'So much the worse – it's time something was said about

it, especially among Christians. Is it surprising that children get into trouble when the mother isn't around when they get home? No wonder homes break up!'

'I don't think it's fair to blame all that on the woman who goes out to work. If a family can't make ends meet on the husband's income, then if she doesn't get a job the children will be neglected and deprived. Really she's protecting them, and her husband from the shame of not being able to provide for his family.'

'I wonder how often it really is necessity that drives them out to work, or if it's more a desire for all the gadgets and luxuries that are coming on to the market. Or even boredom with the drudgery of housework and a desire for more social life. Still, it's really Christians we're talking about, who are more aware of the importance of these family relationships and responsibilities, and know they are given by God and not merely natural. I can't really see that Scripture anywhere encourages wives and mothers to go out to work. Whereas this verse does say quite specifically that they should work at home. And so does 1 Timothy 5:14 where he says they are to manage the household.'

'That's not how I see it,' Eve replied. 'It doesn't actually forbid them doing other jobs. It seems to me to be simply saying that they must see their homes and families are catered for, not that they mustn't do anything else except housework. It is possible to combine these things, especially if the husband helps out! Getting out of the house and among other people can actually help a woman to be a more balanced person and thus a better wife and mother. Don't you remember, dear, all those years ago, writing to me from a certain place about a certain "virtuous woman" of Proverbs 31, who did quite a few things outside the home?'

'Point taken,' Alec conceded laughingly. 'And I suppose you're ready to back that up with Priscilla and her tent-making, and Lydia and her cloth-dyeing trade. Perhaps I am being a bit Victorian. I'll have to give it some more thought. Still there is a problem, you must admit. If both parents are out working all day, the children can be put at risk, which can hardly be right in God's sight, can it?'

'No, but it's not an insuperable problem. One alternative is part-time work, to fit in with the children's hours, or the husband's. If this isn't possible, then can't the church do something? The early church took responsibility for needy women and supported them, I believe. Well, we know that's not really possible now. It can hardly support its pastor, so it couldn't take on a load of women or their families. So the best thing would be for husbands and wives to sort out what they need in terms of employment to maintain their homes, and for the rest of us to come in to help with the children. We could have a kind of crèche to cover the period between school and the time the parent gets home, or some other suitable arrangement.'

'That would need some thinking about. We would have to be convinced it was necessity, not luxury that was driving them out to work. We should not encourage luxury by making things too easy for them.'

'I still think you're being a bit hard. If you aren't careful you'll be imposing a means test before you allow them to have their children looked after! Surely, with something the Scripture doesn't legislate about, it ought to be left to the conscience of the persons concerned. We have to adapt to our own age and culture to some extent, don't we? The ancient world was so different we cannot just copy its customs as if nothing had changed. The main thing is that the family is kept together. If the wife's work threatened it, then it would probably be wrong. Otherwise, well, I don't think I could promise to train the young women to stay at home all the time and in every case!'

Alec laughed again. 'All right, my dear, you win! I should have known better than to argue about things like that with an ex-feminist! I asked for it!'

Eve joined in the joke. 'I'd almost forgotten there was such a thing. I suppose I can't deny it has affected me, and made me think things out afresh. But I hope that doesn't govern my thinking now! I hope I'm governed by the Bible! But I've done enough talking for one night. It's time the "aged men" and "aged women" – what was that word you used? "Mature", that's it. It's time the mature went to their rest!'

In the event, Eve was not called upon to express her views on this question, much less to put them into practice. As they were in a developing area, unemployment was low and wages reasonable. While there were many openings for women, the Christian wives who had young children resisted the temptation to bring in extra cash and chose to devote themselves to their homes and families, at least until their children were older. It was an entirely different problem that Eve came up against, more in the realm of teaching the young women to love their husbands than of teaching them to work at home. This is what happened.

One of the young mothers in the church was a very outgoing girl called Brenda, who had the gift of making friends quickly. She would talk to the other young mothers as they met their children from school, and when opportunity presented itself would try to interest them in the Sunday morning children's classes. Two of these responded to the invitation almost at once, and their children began to appear regularly on Sunday mornings. Eve had noticed these women waiting outside the church when she arrived for the morning service. One wet day, she asked them to come inside and wait, which they did. As they conversed, it became obvious that one of them had much more understanding of Christianity than the other. After a week or two, Eve began arriving earlier in order to spend more time with them, thus establishing more friendly relations with them. One day, the more interested girl, whose name was Joan, asked Eve if she would do them a favour. She explained that her friend, Sheila, had a hospital appointment in about ten days' time and that she would like to go with her. Could Eve come to one of their homes and keep an eye on the children until they got back? Eve gladly obliged, and when the day came she arrived at Joan's in the early afternoon to mind the pre-school child and wait for Brenda to bring the others in on her way home.

It was almost five o'clock before Joan and Sheila returned from the hospital. Sheila took her children straight off while Joan made tea for Eve and herself. As they talked, the subject of the church came up naturally and Joan spoke of how the stories and pictures her little boy brought home reminded her of her own childhood. It became clear to Eve that she had been brought up in a Christian home of some kind and was fairly clear on the elements of the gospel. Whether she had ever truly experienced conversion Eve could not be quite so sure, but it seemed she had been involved in an evangelical church up to the time of her courtship and marriage. It was obviously the old story of marrying outside the faith and destroying whatever spiritual life was there. But Eve formed the impression that the life showed signs of reviving. She was uncertain what to do about this. To try to persuade Joan to remain for the morning service would disrupt the family's Sunday programme, which she did not feel would be right at this stage. The only thing she could do was to await developments and give herself to prayer.

One afternoon Eve happened to meet Joan in the town where she was shopping before going to meet her children from school. Eve suggested a quick cup of tea at her house, offering to drive her to the school so that she would not be late. Although the conversation was not lengthy, Eve felt that something was really happening to Joan. She had taken her Bible out again and started reading it. She had been going through the stories in the Old Testament from the beginning, missing out the large chunks of law and suchlike, and had just reached the book of Ruth. She knew the story from childhood, but some words had struck her and she could not get them out of her mind.

'I can't quote them exactly,' she told Eve, 'but it's where Ruth tells Naomi that she wants to go wherever Naomi goes, and live wherever she lives, that Naomi's God will be her God, and Naomi's people her people. That's just how I feel. I want God for my God. I need him to forgive me and stop me

sinning, to be with me to help me and to talk to, and to talk to
me. And I want you and the other Christians and the church.
I want to be among you, to have you for my friends, and join
in your meetings.'

'That's absolutely wonderful!' exclaimed Eve. 'It's the
best thing anyone's told me for a long time. But do you really
know how God can become your God?'

'Yes, I think so,' Joan replied. 'I do really believe in Jesus,
that he's God's Son and died because he loved me and
wanted to bring me back to God. I thought I believed it when
I was fifteen, and I nearly got baptized. But Bill came along
and I lost interest. It wasn't until I met Brenda, and the kids
started going to Sunday School, that I began to think about it
all again. It's different now. I really feel I need him, quite
desperately. But . . .'

She broke off, and looked down sadly. 'I know what you're
going to say, I think,' said Eve. 'It's your husband, there
might be difficulties.'

'There *would* be, that's certain, and they'd be more than
difficulties, if I know Bill. He wasn't particularly keen on
letting me bring the kids to Sunday School. It's only because
we can get back by eleven o'clock that he didn't stop me.
That way it doesn't interfere with our usual Sunday programme. But if I was to be out until twelve-thirty, then
dinner would be late or we wouldn't be able to get out, so
he'd never agree to that.'

'What about Sunday evening?' Eve asked. 'Well that
would mean leaving him with the children. Not that that
would be a problem – he looks after them sometimes to let me
go out. It's that he doesn't want me to start getting religious
and mixed up with church people. He knew I was going to
church when he first met me, and he's always had a fear I
might want to go back again. He's dead against churches.'

'I know it's going to be difficult, Joan, very difficult, but
you will have to tell him what you've told me. Jesus made it
clear that we mustn't keep our faith in him a secret. If we do
that, it means things like fear and shame are greater than

love for him. If you really want God then he must come
before anything and anyone, even your husband.'

'Yes, I know that. But I don't know how to tell him, and
I'm afraid what might happen. I'm sure he'll stop me coming
to church. It may even be the end of bringing the children on
Sunday mornings.'

'Don't think about that at the moment. Take it step by
step. The first step is to tell your husband what has happened
and see how he reacts. Don't say anything about going to
church, or things like that. Leave that till later. Then we'll
have another talk in the light of what happens, and see where
to go from there. But if you're going to get to school on time,
we'd better be off!'

As Joan got out of the car outside the school, Eve put her
hand on her arm. 'Remember I'll be praying for you.'

Joan smiled. 'Thank you, and thank you for our talk too.
It's made me feel very happy to tell someone – someone who
understands.' She opened the car door and got out.

'And Joan, God *will* be what you want him to be, with you
any time and everywhere.'

As she drove off round the corner, she saw Brenda and her
children. Eve stopped and opened the car door for them to
get in.

'What on earth brings you to these parts?' asked Brenda.

So Eve told her all about her conversation with Joan.
'That all resulted from you getting to know her and inviting
her to bring the children. But she needs much prayer now,
and so does her husband.'

The following morning Eve's phone rang and she was
surprised to hear Joan's voice. But she was even more
surprised to hear her say, 'I've told him – Bill, I mean.'

'Already?' exclaimed Eve, afraid lest Joan should have
been too hasty, and wondering whether she herself should
have cautioned her to think and pray for a day or two in order
to prepare the way.

'I couldn't get to sleep last night for thinking about it, so
about twelve I asked Bill if he was still awake and when he

said he was I told him what God is doing for me.' She paused.

'And?' Eve asked.

'He said he didn't understand what I was talking about. He said he believed in God and didn't do anyone any harm, and he couldn't see anything more was needed. The rest was just imagination. How can you talk to someone you can't see? And what's the point of church services? And how can anyone believe all those stories in the Bible? They're just legends like St George and the Dragon. I told him *I* believed them, and that God is real to me. He said I needn't think I'm going to start spending Sunday in church because he won't have it. I didn't say anything to that, and he said I must have been dreaming and would have forgotten all about it in the morning.'

'But you haven't,' said Eve.

'No, and I told him so. He said I'd got to forget all about it. We shall go on spending Sunday the way we always have. Well, I don't want to give up family outings. We have nice times and we don't have much other chance to go out together. I'm afraid of us getting split up. That's the last thing I want to happen. So I don't know where to go from here.'

'You come round and have another talk with me and we'll go into the whole thing,' said Eve. 'Now when can you get away for an hour or so?'

'Thursday is quite a good day, when the shops are closed and I can't do any shopping even if I need to.'

'Come on here as soon as you've taken the children back to school and that will give us a good hour and a half before you need set off back. And, Joan, read 1 Peter chapter 3 between now and then, will you?'

'I will. 1 Peter 3. Thursday, then. Goodbye for now, and thanks, Mrs Gilbert.'

When Thursday came Joan was on Eve's doorstep shortly before two o'clock. Eve ushered her into the lounge and sat her in the chair Mary Blake had occupied a few weeks before. After the preliminary niceties Eve asked Joan if she had read

the chapter in 1 Peter. 'I read the whole book, three times,'
replied Joan. 'I can't get enough of the Bible at the moment.'

Eve smiled. 'I'm glad about that, because it will help you
get your problem into perspective. You see, I believe that
whatever situation a Christian finds himself in, there is at
least one portion of the Bible that can guide him. Your
situation is to be married to a man who at present is not a
Christian. That is what 1 Peter 3 is about, as you probably
gathered. Peter wrote it because some of his readers were in
that position. Others had other difficulties. Some were slaves
whose masters were pagans, and cruel and unjust with it.
Others were in trouble with the authorities. You see in those
days the whole of society was hostile to Christianity, and
Christians had to fight opposition on many fronts – their
homes, places of work, their city or state. But Peter's advice is
very interesting. It is not to rebel or overthrow the system,
but the opposite – submit to it! "Submit . . . to every
ordinance of man" – kings, governors, or whatever.
"Servants, be subject to your masters with all fear; not only
to the good and gentle, but also to the froward", or perverse.
And then he goes on to *your* problem – "Likewise, you wives
be in subjection to your own husbands." And he's speaking
about unconverted husbands who don't obey the Word
themselves. But I expect you gathered that yourself, did
you?'

'Yes, more or less. Does that mean I've got to try to win
Bill without preaching or even trying to get him to come to
church, just by my behaviour?'

'That's it exactly.'

'Well in that case I wonder if I did the wrong thing in
speaking to him the other night the way I did. Perhaps I
should have kept quiet and just carried on as if nothing had
happened.'

'Not at all. You weren't preaching to him. You were
confessing your faith to him. This is what Christ tells us all to
do, and do to everyone, whatever our relationship is with
them, and however they take it. It's a condition of our

salvation. But now you've done that you must concentrate on
living in a way that is consistent with your faith in Christ.
That means trying to live as Christ himself lived when he was
here. Did you notice what Peter said at the end of chapter 2,
how Christ was willing to endure anything they did against
him? Now that he has gone we have to do that. It's a way of
preaching the cross, especially to those who won't listen to
the actual preaching. This is the way to win them. And this is
the way for you to win Bill.'

'Could that really happen, do you think? But I don't know
if I can really behave in the way it says here – "meek and
quiet". That's the last thing I am, as you've probably
noticed! I react sharply if someone tries to bully me.'

'Peter was the same himself – hasty, impetuous, flaring
up. But Jesus changed him. Remember, Joan, you've only
just started; you're a new-born baby. Did you read that in 1
Peter? You've got a long way to go. The thing is to start right.
So at the moment try to keep everything as normal as
possible. Of course, it won't be quite normal because you are
different and Bill will notice that. At present we don't know
how he will react; we shall have to see. But you must make
sure you behave as a wife should to her husband – I should
say a Christian wife, because the Bible gives us a different
outlook from the world on this matter.' Eve then went on to
speak to Joan about the relation of man and woman in terms
of headship. She pointed out that although Bill was not a
Christian she must still respect him as a true husband.

Joan asked, 'Does this mean I've got to let him stop me
coming to church services? How far have I got to take this
submitting business?'

'Ultimately, no, you shouldn't let him stop you. But you
must give him time. This is only fair. It's so new to him –
newer even than to you. He's got to have time to adjust. He
may not be willing to do so, but he must have the chance. He
must see that you are really in earnest. He probably thinks
it's just a passing fancy and will wear off. You must show him
you've given your whole life to Christ, and it belongs to

Christ even more than it does to Bill. But at present try to avoid a show-down.'

'But I really want to come to your services.'

'It's lovely to hear someone talk like that! Some people almost have to be dragged there! Of course, that shows that God is really in your life. I'll tell you what I've got in mind for the present. That hour on Sunday morning while the children are in their classes, instead of going home, we could get together and have our own little service. Your friend Sheila could come and there may be others interested. I'll speak to my husband and the pastor and we'll see if we can arrange something. I'm sure your husband won't object to that, will he?'

'Won't he? You don't know Bill. Although he says he believes in God he's quite hostile to churches. But I can tell him that's what I'm going to do. I've often thought there isn't much point going home for that short time. I get up and come out again almost straight away. Sometimes I go into Sheila's as she's a bit nearer.'

'That's fine, then. We'll start like that, and take it from there.'

Eve duly reported all this to Alec, who consulted with the pastor. He had in fact already been turning something like this over in his mind. Alec and Eve, along with the pastor's wife, none of whom was involved in children's classes, undertook to contact all parents from outside the church and to take charge of the meeting. The result was a group of about seven, including two fathers, along with Joan and Sheila. Joan did not seem to be having much difficulty in remaining for the meeting and a month passed without much personal conversation between her and Eve. Eve therefore decided to invite her home again on the next Thursday afternoon.

Eve began their talk by saying, 'It's more than a month since we last spoke, and I'm very concerned to know how things have been going with you at home.'

'I'm trying to do what you said, or rather what the Bible says – concentrating on my behaviour. But it's awfully hard.

Sometimes I forget I'm a Christian and say things I shouldn't, which gives Bill the chance to call me a hypocrite. Then sometimes he just misunderstands or puts a different construction on some innocent remark, and I feel I'm getting nowhere. There certainly isn't any sign of winning him, as that verse said would happen.'

'Ah, just a minute! These are still early days for such a big thing as this. You will have to try to trust God and be very patient.'

'I'm trying to do that and I pray a lot about it. But it only seems to get worse. There are all sorts of things I used to enjoy doing – things we did together – which I don't want to do now; in fact I feel guilty about them.'

'Such as . . .?' Eve asked.

Joan seemed a little reluctant to go into details, but eventually she said, 'Well, I hardly like mentioning this, but before we were married we used to go to pubs in the evening quite often. After we got married we didn't go so often because we had a home we could be together in, but we still went once or twice a week. When the children came it was more difficult, but we developed an arrangement with my friend Sheila and her husband. We go out one evening while one of them baby-sits for us, and vice versa. But I don't enjoy it now, and Bill notices this and it niggles him.'

'In one way that should encourage you. If your tastes are changing, that's a sure sign God is with you. And if someone else notices, well, that's what we're aiming for, isn't it? But I don't think you need feel guilty about going to the pub. You don't have to drink beer or whisky, although God isn't going to damn you even if you do have the odd glass. Even if you don't enjoy it, that's one of the sacrifices you have to make for Christ.'

'It's not so much the drinking I mind – I must admit I still enjoy a glass or two – it's more the conversation that goes on – suggestive remarks, double meanings, you know the kind of thing I mean. It's the same with films and TV. We used to go to the pictures quite a lot, then after we married we watched

films on TV instead. I used to think they were great —
romantic and funny. Some of them make me feel sick now.
And when they keep saying, "God!" and "Christ!", I never
used to notice — I did it myself — but now it feels as if someone
has stuck a knife in me, and I want to rush out of the room.'

'That's wonderful!' said Eve.

'Not to me it isn't,' replied Joan.

'No, I don't mean the things that go on, but the way you
feel about them. It's the Lord's doing and it's marvellous in
our eyes. But you must remember that: it's not *your* doing,
but God's. He hasn't done it in these other people, at least
not yet. So you have to be patient. Remember how long you
were in that state yourself until God opened your eyes.'

'But how long is it going to go on? The more God teaches
me, the more hostile Bill seems to get. I like coming to our
Sunday morning meetings, but what I don't like is going
away while the other families are arriving, with husbands
and wives and children all there together. They don't have
these problems. Why can't we be like them?'

'What I'm going to say, Joan, may sound very hard, but
we have to face it. You see, God does not guarantee that,
because you behave as his Word says, Bill is bound to be
converted.'

'He doesn't? Then what's the point of all the striving and
suffering? It seems just a waste. I might as well go my own
way now and have done with it.'

'No, that isn't true. Let's look at that passage again.' Eve
opened her Bible at 1 Peter 3 and read through the verses
again until she came to the words 'a meek and quiet spirit,
which is in the sight of God of great price'. 'That means that
even if your husband doesn't set any value on what you are
doing, God does. He is pleased. And if something pleases
God it's worthwhile, whatever the cost; it hasn't failed, even
if the person you do it for takes no notice of it, even hates you
for it. That's what happened to Jesus. Everything he did was
to please God. So even when people hated him and ill-treated
him he just went on doing it because it pleased God. That's

the way we must try to live – keeping our eyes on God and doing what pleases him, whatever anyone thinks or does about it. If you can learn that now, Joan, right at the beginning, with Bill, it's the best thing you can do. Some Christians don't learn it for a long time, perhaps never.'

'It sounds a very big thing. I don't know if I've got enough faith for it.'

'Yes you have. You've already shown that. It's just a question of looking at it in the right way. And don't think it's all give and no getting in return. This part that follows here, about Sarah and Abraham . . .'

'I was going to ask you about that. What does it mean "calling him lord"? Have I got to say "my lord" to Bill, as if he were a duke?'

'No,' laughed Eve. 'That was the custom then, a token of respect, just as Victorian wives called their husbands "Mr" and the children called their fathers "Sir". What it means as far as you and I are concerned is that we recognize the role God has given them to be "the head of the wife". This was what Sarah acknowledged with Abraham.'

'But Bill isn't a bit like Abraham! If he was, I might be able to do it better.'

'That doesn't matter. Your job is to follow Sarah and the other godly women. Because he is not a godly man doesn't mean he's not your husband. You can follow Sarah even if he doesn't follow Abraham. If you do that, God will bless you, as he has promised here, in verse 6, "whose daughters you are as long as you do well and are not afraid with any amazement". That means "Don't be afraid of the consequences, do your duty to God just because it's your duty and he is your God. Then you will be blessed as Sarah and the other godly women were." That doesn't mean you will be free of troubles; they all had troubles too. It means God will own you as his daughter, as he did Sarah. That's the most important thing of all. And it's for those who are determined to please him, whatever the consequences. Is that what you are resolved on, Joan?'

'Well, yes, I can't really do anything else, after all he's done for me, which I don't deserve. Nothing else comes up to that. And when I think of what Jesus suffered, I suppose I'm having it quite easy. So what do I do then, about pubs and TV and all that?'

'You just put up with it, at least for the time being. If you can be patient and tolerant, as God was with you for so long, and show love to your husband and children, then this is what God wants and this is what will work to bring them to God. If that doesn't work, nothing will. Now we've just time for prayer before you have to go.'

After this conversation things proceeded much as they had before, with Joan continuing to come to the Sunday morning class along with the others. It was about another month or so after this that one Sunday morning she did not appear – the first time Eve had known this happen. There seemed to be no reason; they weren't away, and Sheila confirmed that as far as she knew no one was ill, she herself having been at the house the previous evening to baby-sit. Sheila said she had waited as usual that morning for them, as they usually called on the way to church, but time was getting on and she decided to set off without them. She said she would try to find out if anything was wrong. Eve heard nothing more that day and could not help worrying, as it was the first time Joan had missed the Sunday morning meeting.

On Monday morning Eve decided she would wait no longer, and drove round to the school gate to see if she could catch Joan after she had left her children at school. She waited in the car a little distance away on the road Joan would take to return home. After a while she caught sight in her driving mirror of two figures turning the corner. It was Sheila who had her arm around Joan, who was looking very dejected. Eve called out to them as they came by: 'There's something wrong, isn't there? Would you like to get into the car?' They did so and Eve asked, 'Now what's it all about?' Joan was too upset to speak, so Sheila spoke for her.

'It's Bill. He says he's going to leave her or turn her out if

she doesn't give up church and all that.' Joan burst into
tears.

'Look,' said Eve, 'I think it would be best if we went back
to my house. Will you come as well, Sheila?'

'I'd better not. I left the washing machine on. Could you
drop me at the top of the road as you go?'

Eve drove off and Sheila got out at the end of her road,
while Eve and Joan continued. Joan seemed to recover a little
as Eve enquired about the children. When they reached her
house Eve sat Joan down in the usual chair and made her a
strong cup of coffee. 'Now,' she said, 'tell me all about it.'

'I've been trying to do what we talked about last time, but
things only got worse. When we get home on a Sunday
morning the children talk about their stories and show us
their work. Bill takes no interest. He's quite rude, in fact, and
they can't understand why. They ask me quite naturally
about my class, and even ask their dad why he doesn't come
too, which only makes him angry. Another thing, I've taken
to getting up a bit earlier in the morning to read the Bible
downstairs while the kettle's boiling. Bill came down the
other morning and caught me, started arguing and threw the
Bible across the room. Well, that made me angry and I said if
I wanted to read it I would do so and he wasn't going to stop
me. Then he said if I went on with "this religion business", as
he calls it, he would either leave home or throw me out; he
can't stand much more. He said it again yesterday morning.
That's why I didn't come. It was horrible. The kids didn't
understand what was going on, why I was upset and he was
angry. I don't know what to do now. I think he means what
he says. But I don't want us to break up. He's my husband,
and my children's father. But I can't see how I can give up on
God, just like that. Perhaps *I* should go, for the sake of peace.'

'No,' said Eve, 'that would be wrong. Do you remember
me saying I believe God's Word has something to say about
every situation we find ourselves in? Well, there's another
passage beside 1 Peter 3 that talks about those who have
unconverted husbands or wives.' Eve turned to 1

Corinthians 7 and placed it in front of Joan, drawing her own chair alongside. 'This sort of thing happened to people in Corinth, as it did in many places where the apostles preached. Sometimes just the wife would believe, sometimes just the husband. The Corinthian Christians in this position wondered if they ought to remain married to someone who still worshipped idols. Wouldn't such a person pass on the pollution of idolatry? Paul said "No". The marriage was still pure in God's eyes, and the believing partner should not leave. But supposing the *un*believer couldn't stand living with a Christian? This is what Paul has to say about that here in verse 15: "If the unbelieving depart, let him depart. A brother or a sister is not under bondage in such cases; but God hath called us to peace." So it *can* happen that an unbeliever leaves home because the partner has become a Christian. It may happen and sometimes does, and God knows this. It's something we have to face up to. Jesus warned us that sometimes families would split up over him. And you have to be prepared to allow him to go rather than give up the faith. I think that's what "let him depart" means. If you have to choose between him and God, you choose God and let him go. You don't make compromises in order to persuade him to stay. That would mean letting *God* depart, which would be worse.

'Now, Joan, what's your position if he does leave? It says here you "are not in bondage". That doesn't mean the marriage is over, that the legal bond is broken. Only adultery can do that. It means you are no longer expected to give him that submission you undertook when you married. You remember about Sarah calling Abraham "lord"? This word "bondage" goes with that. He would no longer be your lord, your head. He would have given up the right to your submission. You would be free. Paul says this is the only way to keep the peace. If the relationship is so bad, if there is so much hostility, then it is better to let him go. But that doesn't mean all is lost, for he says, "How do you know, O wife, whether you will save your husband?" He is still your

husband, even if he does leave. And in this way you may win
him. You did not succeed by your love and submissiveness.
So now you make a stand and refuse to compromise, even if
he deserts you. That may win him back. So there's still hope
for you, Joan! Take courage. Personally I doubt whether he
will carry out his threat. I think he still loves you and knows
you love him. He enjoys his home and children. He isn't
going to give all that up just to get away from your Christian
testimony. I think he is bluffing, trying to pressurize you to
give in and let him have his way. If you stand fast I think he
will come round to accepting it when he's got used to it. But
even if he doesn't, your course is clear. And even if he did go
off now, he may come back!'

So Eve did her best that morning to comfort and counsel
Joan, and they spent some time in prayer. She was much
moved by Joan's prayer for Bill and quietly shed a few tears
herself. She was sure God, too, must be moved and could
hardly refuse her request. This gave her a quiet assurance
that she had counselled Joan on the right lines. She doubted
whether it would really come to a break-up, but she felt
concerned and knew that things would be very difficult for
Joan, at least for a time. 'What a way to begin your Christian
life!' she thought, and indeed said later on to Alec. 'Most of
us only get problems like that when we've settled and grown
a little. Some Christians never have them at all. Poor Joan,
what she must be going through just now! I wish I could go
through it for her.'

'I think you are,' replied her husband, 'at least
emotionally and spiritually. Which is another verse you're
carrying out: "Bear one another's burdens, and so fulfil the
law of Christ." I'm quite sure that with support like that
she'll pull through fine.'

Next Sunday Eve went down to the church at 9.30, with
rather mixed feelings. Would the worst have happened? She
could have wept for joy when she heard the sound of Joan's
voice as she came in at the door. She almost embraced her as
Joan said, 'Well he hasn't gone yet, and here I am again!' Eve

was highly relieved and felt she was vindicated in taking the line she had.

'After all,' she said to Alec, 'what I was really doing was trying to fulfil that verse you quoted to me the night Mary was here: "Teach the young women to love their husbands." My aim has been to keep them together and in the process try to win Bill to the Lord. I think the worst may be over now.' This proved right, for in the weeks that followed there was something of a softening in Bill's attitude. This was followed by a period of stalemate. But Joan was not disheartened by this. 'He doesn't speak much about it now,' she said to Eve one day, 'but I believe that's because he's starting to think. I've got a feeling it won't be long before *he* starts coming to this meeting!'

At that moment Eve, who was still sitting in her chair, staring at the chair opposite, was aroused out of her reverie by the ringing of the telephone.

10.
A widow indeed

Eve picked up the telephone and heard the voice of Fred Willcox, the senior deacon, at the other end of the line. Suddenly she remembered she had promised him a report on cases of need she had recently come across. A deacons' meeting had been announced for that very evening and Fred had reminded her that he would need the usual report by the evening before. Sarah's visit had driven it completely from her mind. She apologized profusely to Fred.

'That's not like you, Eve,' he said. 'Are you all right? Not ill or anything I hope?'

'No, it's not that. I had my niece Sarah here most of yesterday evening and since then I seem to have done nothing but reminisce. I've had diaries, notes, photos, letters and I don't know what else out today. I've done nothing at all in the house. And I've even forgotten your report.'

'It sounds to me as though you're preparing to write your autobiography.'

'I could easily do that, or rather I've got plenty of material for it, although I'd rather someone else did the writing. I don't think I could discipline myself to that now.'

'Perhaps someone will put it together for you if you give them the documents and talk to them. Isn't that how cricketers and footballers write their books? Get someone to come round with a tape recorder and interview you and then go away and put it all together.'

'What an idea, Fred! As if anyone would want to buy a book about me?'

'I don't know. You've helped a good many people over the years, and the things you said to them could help others with the same problems.'

'I see what you mean. Yes, I've had to face up to a good

many questions, both for myself and for other women. But I don't suppose I'm the only one who's done that.'

'All the more reason for getting into print before anyone else does! I can see it in front of me now – a glossy coloured cover with your face on it, and the title *Eve's story*. Perhaps you'd become a best-selling author like Catherine Marshall.'

'Now you're laughing at me! I think we'd better get to the business you phoned about. Yes, there are one or two things to report. I'm glad to say Mrs Everett has got her problems sorted out with the D.H.S.S. . . . What was that? Yes, I had to go to the office with her, but they were quite helpful. She'll be getting the supplementary benefit restored, so if we just look after her gas and electricity, she should be quite comfortable and have no worries. But I think Eileen Sorrell is going to need help, for a while at least . . . Oh! Didn't I tell you about her? I *am* losing my touch, aren't I? Going senile myself, I think. She is the deserted wife that Brenda knows . . . Yes, Brenda again! If Brenda wasn't around there'd be nothing for us to do, would there? The problem is that Eileen's younger boy has a serious allergy condition, and she has to get him special food and even special clothes, which she can't afford on her maintenance money . . . Yes, I have seen her several times, but perhaps you would like to visit her, so that you can discuss it at the meeting. I haven't given you much time, have I? Both boys are very regular in the children's class, and she herself nearly always stays for the parents' meeting. Do what you can, won't you? . . . No, I think that's all for this time . . . Thank you. Goodbye . . . and my apologies again. Goodbye.'

Eve worked closely with the deacons in carrying out their office of ministering to the needy among their circle. In fact she had come within an ace of being appointed to the diaconate herself. This was not something she had sought, although there had been a time when she might have thought about invading this traditionally male preserve. What happened was that her name was put forward in all innocence by a couple who were fairly recent additions to the

church, and who had themselves belonged to a group of
churches in which women deacons were the accepted thing.
Eve had no idea that her name was to be proposed at a
meeting for the election of deacons, otherwise she would have
prevented it. As it was, she was so taken aback that at first
she did not know what to say, and while she was thinking
about it a lively discussion got under way.

Someone who had been a member there for many years
said they had never had women deacons in that church
before. 'So that settles it!' thought Eve to herself. 'The laws of
the Medes and Persians alter not!' Somebody else, however,
who had moved into the district from a different part of the
country, said that in his previous church they had had elders
who led the church, leaving the deacons simply to deal with
material needs and that there was nothing to stop a woman
being appointed. But another, who also had a background of
a church governed by elders, said it was his view that women
were not eligible for any office in the church. The chairman of
the meeting then intervened to point out that Eve herself had
not been asked whether she wished her name to go forward,
and turned to her. By this time Eve had collected her
thoughts a little, and although she had no ambition to be a
deacon, and no appetite for another pioneering project, she
still felt sufficiently alert mentally to consider it a very good
subject to discuss. She therefore replied that she thought it
would be good for the church to come together to discuss the
principle, without anyone's name being involved and that
therefore this should be done on another occasion, when no
election of deacons was taking place. This suggestion met
with general approval, and members were invited to give
some thought to various passages of Scripture bearing on the
subject, in particular 1 Timothy 3, in order to prepare
themselves for the discussion.

Eve remembered that discussion well, because it was
during that time that Alec had first shown symptoms of the
illness which was soon afterwards to kill him. They decided
that, as well as studying the matter privately, they would

anticipate the meeting by debating it between them, with one speaking for and the other arguing against the eligibility of women for the diaconate. They agreed that Eve should prepare the case for women deacons and try to convince Alec that it was scriptural. When they felt they had done enough homework they set aside an hour or so when they could expect to be free from interruption and began. Eve spoke first.

'I want to start by answering the question, "What is a deacon?" What kind of office is it? This means raising the whole matter of government in the church, because there are two offices – deacon and elder – and these are quite distinct. Now, can we first of all agree that an elder is the same as a bishop or overseer, and that he has the responsibility of teaching and leading the church? Are you with me on this?'

'Yes,' replied Alec. 'Speaking as an elder, that sounds fine. I've no quarrel with that.'

'Good. And do we also agree that wherever the apostles planted churches they appointed elders to watch over them, so as to keep the believers from false teaching and instruct them in true doctrine? And that this means that every church should have elders over it?'

'Agreed.'

'Now in Acts we are not told how they went about choosing these elders, but fortunately, (or should I say providentially?) it so happened that Paul was not present in Ephesus and Crete when this matter cropped up. Instead he had left Timothy in Ephesus and Titus in Crete to act on his behalf. When Paul realized he needed these two brethren to be with him it became essential that they should appoint elders immediately so that there would be no gap in the leadership of those churches. So Paul wrote to them, laying down the procedure for appointing elders, which we thus find in 1 Timothy 3 and Titus 1. Right so far?'

'Perfect! I couldn't have put it better myself.'

'I'll ignore that and continue. As a matter of fact, when I was going through these passages something struck me that

I'd not seen before. There is a unity of structure in 1 Timothy. It isn't a number of separate subjects strung together. And this is very important for what we are talking about. The letter starts with Paul telling Timothy to try to put the false teachers right and contend for the true faith committed to him when he was first commissioned as an evangelist. Then in chapter 2 he goes on to show him what a vital place the church has in the whole scheme of things in God's world. This is because of the power of the church's prayers. He says it is the men in the church who lead this true worship and teach the people. The women should learn, but are not to teach or have authority over the congregation. This is because the church has to follow God's pattern in creation in which the man was the senior partner. O.K.?'

'Well, I'm very glad you see it like this, but I don't quite see where it's getting us.'

'Stop sounding like a prosecuting counsel, and be patient. The thing I wanted to mention that came to me when I read it this time was how this passage in chapter 2 prepares the way for chapter 3. I went into chapter 2 thoroughly years ago when I was concerned about authority and submission, but I didn't follow the thought right through the epistle. The reason why he starts talking about bishops in chapter 3 is because of what he has just said about authority and teaching in chapter 2. To counter false teaching there must be people with authority to do it, those authorized by God through his Word. So Paul sets down how to appoint elders. Because authority is involved they must be men; because it is a highly responsible job they must have proved themselves responsible people; because it is a spiritual task they must have proved their spirituality; because it is a leadership job they must have proved they have these gifts also, which will come out in the way they run their own homes.'

'Yes, that is interesting, I must admit, when put in context, and of course it leads on to the later chapters dealing with the kind of false teaching these elders have to counteract. And then the internal constitution of the church, with its different age groups and so on, comes in. I see what you mean by looking at the book as a whole. Now I hope we are going to see how deacons fit in to all this?'

'That's right, because he goes straight from elders to deacons. But we still have to be patient because this word "deacon" is a fairly new one at this stage. I think Philippians is the only other place where it's used. This means that there were deacons in the churches as well as elders, but we are not told anything about how they were appointed until here. Now what I'm not sure about – and you may be able to help here, darling – is whether the office of deacon is derived from the seven men in Acts 6 who took over the serving of tables. What do you think?'

'Yes, there is the view that elders were successors of the apostles and deacons the successors of the seven. The apostles realized they couldn't do it all. A division of labour was needed to take some of the work off their hands, so they appointed these seven men. The same applied in the churches: the elders needed to devote themselves to teaching and leading, and so deacons were appointed to take the ministry to the needy off their hands. I think that view makes a lot of sense.'

'That's what I hoped you'd say! Because it tells us what the nature of the deacons' office is. If you remember, that was the question I set out to answer about a quarter of an hour ago. The deacon is someone who takes the job of ministering to the needy off the hands of the elders, so that they can pursue their task of teaching and leading unhindered. Since it is these two last tasks that carry the authority, there is no authority (or very little) involved in the office of the deacon. Therefore there is nothing in it to preclude women. That's my first point.'

'You cunning little vixen! You got me to play into your hands by drawing that distinction between the apostles and the seven so that you could use me as a witness in your own case! You should have gone into the legal profession!'

They both laughed and Eve said, 'No it wasn't quite like

that, although I can see it appears that way. I genuinely did need guidance about Acts 6, and what you said only went to confirm the point.'

'Not so fast. You've still forgotten one thing. The seven in Acts 6 were all men, and it was stipulated that they must be men: "Look ye out among you seven *men* of honest report." They were being given a very important and responsible task. They were acting on behalf of the apostles and representing the church. And there *was* authority involved in the job: they had to decide who got what, and they had therefore to make decisions and judgements. I can't see that it would have been right for women to have been chosen.'

'On the question of the seven I agree they had to be men. But that was a unique situation. We agreed that the seven correspond to the apostles. But the apostles were a unique band and so were the seven. I don't see we can make the later office of deacon follow the seven in every detail. After all, it says in Acts 6 that they were to be "filled with the Holy Spirit", but this is not mentioned in 1 Timothy 3. Also, they don't seem to have continued doing it for long, because they soon become involved in preaching. This was hardly what was intended for the deacons, was it?'

'All right,' Alec sighed, 'we'll concede that point. So what's next?'

'Another thing,' Eve continued as if she hadn't heard, 'is that Christians are never told to submit to deacons or obey them as they are to elders. So that even if a certain degree of authority is involved in their work, it is not the kind that commands obedience and conformity, which would preclude women from the job. What did you say, dear? . . . Oh yes! Sorry! I got carried away! Well, the second point concerns the specific statement in 1 Timothy 3:11: "Even so must their wives be grave, not slanderers, sober, faithful in all things." I understand the Authorized Version is incorrect to translate it "their wives" because for one thing the word may refer to women in general, and for another, there is no definite article in the Greek. Because of this translation, however, it has been assumed that he is speaking about the deacons' wives. But why should deacons' wives be singled out rather than elders' wives? And if, as some say, he is talking about deacons' *and elders'* wives, why does he immediately go back to deacons in verse 12?'

'Well, Paul often does that – starts subjects, breaks off and then goes back to them.'

'No doubt, but there are some other interesting facts here. There is the word 'likewise" or "even so". In verse 8 when he moved from elder to deacon he said "likewise", and now in verse 11 when he moves from deacons to women he says, "likewise", showing that these three are parallel. Another thing, there is no verb in verse 11, so it goes with the verb in verse 8. In fact there isn't even a verb there; the verb comes right back in verse 2 – "must be". It sounds as though he is giving three lists of necessary qualifications, things that "must be" in those who would hold certain offices – elders in verse 2, deacons in verse 8 and women in verse 11. This is confirmed if we look at the actual qualifications for these women and compare them with those of the deacons. They are very similar. Both have to be "grave" – dignified I suppose; the deacons are to be "not double-tongued" and the women "not slanderers", which is very much the same thing; the deacons are to be "not given to much wine" and the women "sober" or "moderate", which is the same thing; the deacons should be "not greedy of filthy lucre" and the women "faithful in all things", which means trustworthy, with special reference to money. Now surely this similarity is too close for coincidence. These women who are included with the elders and deacons must have held some kind of office or at least performed some function in the church.'

'Hm!' Alec sighed again. 'It sounds an attractive argument, but it seems rather a big thing to place on just one verse of doubtful interpretation. And it isn't at all clear what this office or function is. Surely if it was something specific he would spell out what it is these women were supposed to be doing?'

'The difficulty is not so great. The fact that the verse occurs in a section on deacons must mean their work is similar, and probably connected with deacons' work. I mean, they may not be women deacons as such, but assistants or associates. Whatever the deacons did, the women helped them, but did not have separate duties. And perhaps he does not spell out their duties because these were already well known to the people. After all, nowhere are the duties of deacons and elders actually listed, but we can deduce them. In any case, if he had listed them, it might not help us much today, since the needs and conditions of churches and people have changed.'

'So, is that the case for the defence then? Or is it the prosecution? Don't you have any witnesses to produce? Any real life women deacons or deaconesses?'

'As a matter of fact I have, and you know very well who . . . That's right – Phoebe of the church in Cenchrea, mentioned by Paul in Romans 16:1 and 2. Now she is actually called a "deacon", although the translations put "servant". But the word is *diakonos*, which is translated "deacon" in Philippians 1:1 and 1 Timothy 3:8. Calling her "servant" is just a piece of male chauvinism to avoid conceding the point that women did serve as deacons in the churches of the New Testament.'

'No, I can't let you get away with that. I've done my homework too, you know, and this was one of the points I made a close study of. The word *diakonos* normally means "servant" and is applied to someone who serves the needs of others. It may be a single act of service or someone in the permanent service of another, a domestic servant, for example. Now I've got all the facts down here. The word is used thirty times in the New Testament. Of these, five are used in a general way in Jesus' teaching about greatness, such as "Whoever will be great among you let him be your *diakonos*" and "Whoever would be the first, the same shall be last of all and *diakonos* of all". Obviously this would not be translated "deacon". In two places it refers to Christ himself as "servant", and he also used the verb: "The Son of Man came to minister," or "serve". Three times it refers to domestic servants, twice to the governing authorities and twice to "Satan's ministers", that is, his evil angels. None of these could rightly be translated "deacon". But the majority of uses – twelve in fact – are given to the apostles and their associates, especially Paul, who is quite fond of using the word of himself, for example, "the gospel, whereof I Paul am made a *diakonos*'. It would be sheer confusion to translate this "deacon". It obviously means "minister of the Word". Then there are three texts which seem to refer to an office in the church, where it appears along with "elder" or "bishop", and these are in Philippians 1:1 and 1 Timothy 3, where it comes twice. That just leaves us with the one about Phoebe. The question is, in what sense is the word *diakonos* used of her? We can rule out things like domestic servant, state official, evil angel and minister of the Word. It seems to me the best way to understand it is in a general sense – that she was someone so devoted to the Lord and the church that she spent her life *serving* their needs. Paul speaks of her being a "help" or "succourer" of many, including himself. That suggests she did for them what the women had done for Jesus and the twelve in the Gospels. They weren't deacons, and neither was she.'

'Wait a minute. You are confusing what she did as "succourer of many", including Paul, with her being *"diakonos* of the church". These are two separate things – well, not completely separate since the qualities which made her a *diakonos* would lead her to succour Paul and others. But even if she had not helped Paul, she would still have been a *diakonos* of the Cenchrea church. Paul was not involved in that church, so she did not acquire the title by helping him. Whatever it means, it's something distinct.'

'All right then, I'll accept that. But it still doesn't mean any more than that she ministered to the needs of people in the church. After all, we are told about widows in 1 Timothy 5, who had a reputation for good works, hospitality, washing the saints' feet and relieving the afflicted. And they weren't deacons. I don't think Phoebe did any more than that.'

'There's still one thing you've not taken account of – that Paul mentions her in his letter to the church in Rome, commending her and asking them to receive her and assist her in the business she had gone there to do. It's pretty obvious she had gone to Rome on behalf of the church in Cenchrea on some unspecified mission. Maybe it was on behalf of Paul himself. Now if we look at other occasions when he wrote these commendations, we find they refer to people like Timothy, as in 1 Corinthians 16:10 and 11, Titus, as in 2 Corinthians 8:16 to 24 and Onesimus in Philemon verses 8 to 21. These men had some official standing as Paul's representatives, and therefore it's very likely Phoebe did as well.'

'It is possible – yes, it is possible. But we still have the problem of what office she held, remembering *diakonos* is a masculine word.'

'Yes, because there was no feminine form of it at that time. But later they did develop a feminine equivalent. I think "deaconess" would be a fair description, and several translations call her a "deaconess" in their footnote.'

'So where does all this get us? We need some kind of summing up. Could we put it like this? There is nothing in the work of a deacon which of itself would preclude a woman from doing it . . .'

'No,' Eve cut in, 'provided they were doing the type of work that the New Testament stipulates for deacons – ministering to the needy, doing works of charity and mercy. The thing is confused because in so many churches deacons are semi-elders and have much power in the church. A woman could not be given a place in that set-up.'

'No, and I'm afraid our church has had that type of background. But we are gradually moving away from it. I've felt lately that if George and Richard came out of the diaconate and were made elders along with the pastor and myself, the remaining deacons could take over the material tasks and leave all leadership issues to the increased eldership. If we did that at present with just two of us it would look too much like dictatorship.'

'That would certainly clarify things, especially now this matter of women deacons has been raised.'

'Anyway, for the sake of argument, we will assume that the deacons are functioning as New Testament deacons. There is no reason why a woman should not do that type of work. Going on from there, if we ask if there is more explicit as opposed to merely implicit evidence, we discover this verse in 1 Timothy 3:11, which places certain "women" alongside the elders and deacons in the church and even sets down qualifications similar to those of deacons themselves. Since these were almost certainly not wives of deacons or elders, nor is there any reason why he should suddenly start talking about the behaviour of women in general, which he had already done in chapter 2 anyway, the likelihood is that it refers to some kind of office, even if we can't be certain it had a name at that time. However, we can go further and confirm that this was done in practice, as well as in theory, from the case of Phoebe. She does seem to have borne the title of "deacon", although later such women came to be called "deaconesses". Still I wonder myself if it wouldn't have been better to have kept the one word and avoid the sex discrimination.'

'Hurray!' shouted Eve. 'I'm all for abolishing sex-discrimination!'

'You've got a job on, especially in churches! However, I think we have a pretty good case here when the subject comes up in the church. I call that a good afternoon's work, and I think we can give ourselves the rest of the day off. What shall we do?'

Sadly, when the time for the meeting came, Alec was unable to attend, as he had become ill a few days before. In fact he was never to attend any more meetings or services. Eve wondered later whether the illness had been there when they were having their discussion at home, causing Alec not to put up more of a fight against her case. However that might have been, she was not able to give herself as wholly to the discussion in the church as she would have liked, and had to leave the meeting early. In any case they both felt she was too personally involved to present such a clear-cut point of view as the one they had agreed upon. But as they had half expected, the discussion brought out the confusion among the members over what the office of deacon was really about, and the pastor thought it wise to postpone any further discussion over the position of women in the matter until this had been ironed out. This proved to be more than just an academic subject, since Alec's rapid deterioration in health prevented him from continuing to function as an elder. From his sick-bed he discussed with the pastor his feeling that two of the deacons should be made elders and the division of labour between the offices more clearly drawn. The gatherings of deacons and members for a time became largely taken up with this matter, and shortly before Alec's death the two brethren in question were accepted by the church as elders, and the running of the church was reorganized. Although the deacons thereafter functioned on New Testament lines by confining themselves to material needs, the question of appointing women was not raised, it being felt best to let things settle after what had been quite an upheaval in the church.

In any case, Eve now found herself in a new position – she was a widow. She had for some time been conscious of the place given to the widow in the Bible, but now was forced to face up to it in practice. Alec's final illness had lasted only a matter of weeks, during which she was fully occupied with nursing him, so that when he died she was not really prepared for the new situation in which she found herself. During those first months of her widowhood the pastor was a fairly frequent visitor to her home, and he helped her collect her thoughts.

His first few visits were directed to helping her come to terms emotionally with her bereavement. Eve had always

realized that the chances were she would outlive Alec. For
one thing, he was ten years her senior. For another, he had
spent his middle years in a tropical climate and a primitive
society, during which he had contracted a severe illness
which had weakened his constitution. But since returning to
England he had enjoyed fairly good health and had reached
his seventieth birthday with no signs of an imminent
breakdown. And even when he suddenly became ill Eve had
no thoughts that this might be terminal, since she did not
know how much his previous illness had weakened his
resistance to the onset of old age. It was only two weeks
before his death that she was told he would not recover,
although she could expect to have him for a few more months
at least. So his rapid deterioration and death, in spite of the
facts she knew, came as a shock for which she was not too well
prepared, and she needed all the support of family and
friends. This was indeed forthcoming, but, of course, could
not compensate for the loss of the one she had lived with and
loved for a quarter of a century. Only one Person could make
this up to her – the Lord himself.

The pastor therefore devoted himself to strengthening her
assurance of the special relationship that exists between God
and his widowed children who are left solitary. He took her
through many of the promises made to widows: 'If they cry at
all unto me, I will surely hear their cry' (Exod. 22.23); 'He
doth execute the judgement of the fatherless and widow'
(Deut. 10:18); 'A father of the fatherless and a judge of the
widows is God in his holy habitation' (Ps. 68:5); 'The
Lord . . . relieveth the fatherless and widow' (Ps. 146:9). He
referred to some of the many laws God had given Israel for
the protection of widows, and showed how in the New
Testament the church had inherited this labour of love. They
looked together at cases of widowhood in the Bible, such as
Naomi in the book of Ruth, the widow of Zarephath in the
ministry of Elijah, Anna the prophetess, who gathered a little
band of believers in Jerusalem to encourage them to expect
their Messiah (Luke 2:36–38), the nameless 'poor widow'

famous for being observed by Jesus casting her mite into the temple collection box and, most of all, Mary the mother of Jesus, who seemed to have been widowed some time before her first-born son left home. On the basis of all this and much more, the pastor encouraged Eve with Jeremiah's words: 'Let thy widows trust in me' (Jer. 49:11).

Eve also did her own research into what the Bible said about this new chapter in her life. Some of the passages puzzled her a little and she sought the pastor's help over these. 'Looking at what the Bible says about widows,' she said to him one day as they talked, 'it doesn't seem to bear a lot of resemblance to what happens today. For one thing, their families formed a much larger unit than our so-called "nuclear family", and they seemed to remain in the same community, and even the same house, so that a widow rarely found herself completely alone. Even Naomi, who was left utterly desolate, not only bereaved of her husband but also her sons, comes back home and spends her time trying to get herself and Ruth taken in by relatives, however distant they were. They had this rule about "levirate marriage", which virtually put the widow's brother-in-law under an obligation to marry her if he were still single. It all seems a bit foreign to our system where, if a widow is left desolate, she goes into a home.'

'Yes, and, of course, that system you've been describing arose because the law of Moses said that the eldest son of the family inherited the lion's share of the estate, whereas the daughters came under the care of their husbands. If her husband died she again became the responsibility of her original family. In principle this position was similar to that of the New Testament church. Levirate marriage was not continued, but in any case it had so many loopholes that by the time of Christ the system had virtually broken down. But basically the New Testament principles are very similar. The younger widows are advised to remarry, just as they did under the levirate system. The difference, of course, is that this was not compulsory, since they might have a call to remain single for the Lord's sake and the gift of continency to go with it, and also, instead of marrying someone in their husband's literal family, they were to marry "in the Lord", that is, to marry a brother in the church.'

'Oh I see!' exclaimed Eve. 'I'd not seen the connection between those things, but it's clear now. I somehow don't think I shall get married again, though. No one would call me young at sixty-two!'

'People marry older than that, so you never know! However, to come back to the New Testament, the older widows were to be provided for by their closest relatives, especially if these were Christians. But if they had no close relatives, or they refused to support them because they were pagans and would have nothing to do with a Christian, even a relative, then they became the care of the church. This, of course, was the origin of the diaconate we've been talking about so much lately in Acts 6. Quite likely those women the church was providing for had been cast off by their families when they became Christians. They were utterly destitute and so the Christians pooled their resources and took them over. Paul then regularized the practice in 1 Timothy 5, but he is careful to exclude spongers, and says they must be "widows indeed", that is, real widows, who are utterly cast on God, having no one at all.'

'But does this ever happen today, with our social security and welfare schemes?'

'That, of course, is the big change that has come about since those times. Society in general, through the state, has taken over the care of all sorts of people, who at one time depended on voluntary help and what was called "charity". The desolate widow is a thing of the past in the material sense. In fact the boot is on the other foot. The churches would not be able to afford to keep widows, even one widow. Instead of doing what the first Christians did and pooling our resources, we have indulged the luxury of denominations, with the result that a town has far more church buildings than it needs, most of which are half full at best. Small groups of Christians have the burden of maintaining these buildings and trying to support a pastor at the same time. Take our town: if two or three of us got together into one building we would save any amount on overheads, and could support two full-time pastors. We would also be able to do more for the needy and for missions, without having to make special appeals. So it's not so much that the widows need the church to support them, as that the church needs the support of the widows! If they didn't give their mites out of their pensions, allowances and savings, our collections would be a good deal lower. However, we mustn't be too depressed about the change. In one way it's a victory.' He looked over at Eve as he said this, and she asked, 'How do you mean?'

'Well,' the pastor replied, 'in the early days the church *had* to look after its widows because no one else would, because the gospel divided families in a way it rarely does in our day and our country. So great was the need in Jerusalem after Pentecost that the apostles had to appoint seven men to tackle the problem. Later on, as he wrote to Timothy, they had to draw up a roll of widows who qualified for support. I suppose by that time corruption had set in, and relatives were dumping the responsibility on to the church, or perhaps some of the widows were pretending they were destitute when they weren't. So Paul laid down certain qualifications as to who was eligible. She had to have turned sixty, and her marriage and home life had to have been worthy of Christ. She was to be noted for her hospitality to strangers and her service of Christians. The means test had nothing on Paul's conditions! But I'm digressing. The point I'm trying to make is that the example of the church in these matters and its widespread influence has gradually awakened society to its responsibility. Now it's the state that has to draw up the roll and see that widows are provided for. And in a way that's a good thing, because the churches only looked after their own widows, not those of the unbelievers. Some of these probably fared badly. Of course, in practice when the church became monolithic and all-embracing, it was rich enough to open its doors to all the needy. In any case the "Christian nation" concept meant that everyone was regarded and treated as a Christian. But if we look at the church in the New Testament sense, as a small group in the midst of a hostile world, we can understand why the apostles only expected it to care for its own widows. And in this it has been "the salt of the earth", because there is no doubt society has learned this responsibility from the church, just as it has learned a lot of other things. Of course, it doesn't give the church the credit – that goes to evolution!'

'It's rather wonderful when you look at it like that, isn't it? It puts a totally different complexion on it. You feel something has been achieved after all during these long weary centuries of struggle. But it doesn't mean the churches now have nothing to do in the relief of the needy, does it?'

'No, not at all, because there are always special cases which bureaucracy passes over, and this is where the personal approach of Christians comes to the rescue. But I think our main task now is on more spiritual lines. A person needs more than material provision. You can have that and be lonely, worried, depressed, and so on. The state cannot really deal with these conditions. Nor can doctors or psychiatrists, even friends and relations. I often feel our church should be more active in this field.'

He looked straight at Eve as he said this, but she remained silent, so he resumed. 'You've done a great deal for quite a few people in our church and even outside, Eve. Now I think you're going to be even better suited. You have the experience of bereavement and widowhood to add to all your other experiences. And being the kind of person you are, you will treat it positively; it will strengthen you and you will strengthen others.'

'I wish I felt that confident! I'd more or less decided I shall be one of the passengers from now on – put out to grass.'

'You'll never be that, if I know you. So long as there is work to be done, and you have any strength left in your body, you'll be up and doing. And there are plenty of people around who need that help – help I can't give, or even my wife. There's always a slight feeling that a pastor and his wife are outsiders. You can work from inside. Unfortunately not everyone approaches things in a spiritual way. The New Testament recognizes this when it warns Christian women about becoming gossips and busybodies, idlers who do nothing but annoy other people and hold up their work. There are plenty of those around. But people like you can set the right example; you can even talk to these others about their behaviour. And with your accumulated wisdom you can be a great help to younger women. You've done that already, I know. All I'm saying is, go on doing it. You're not finished yet.'

'I certainly don't want to vegetate, and I can see there are real needs. I think these will increase. Paul talked about young widows, but they are a rarity these days. The problem now is unmarried mothers, deserted wives, neglected children – people like this. Then there are younger girls growing up without much parental guidance, getting into moral difficulties. But I'm afraid the generation gap is widening so much I don't know whether I can make contact with them.'

'I don't know. They sense it where someone is really sympathetic, where their wisdom and experience are combined with understanding and tolerance. I think you'll do a lot among us yet. And I haven't forgotten that suggestion that was made that you should come on to the diaconate. I know that came to nothing and I'm not proposing to renew it, but you can do the job even if you don't have the office and name. Now that we have reorganized ourselves, the deacons are devoting themselves to material matters, with a special brief for works of mercy and charity. But they do need someone who is in close touch with people, especially women, to keep them informed and advised. You're the ideal person, and I know you're not ambitious for office, so that pride won't keep you back.'

'That shows how little you know about me! But I can

easily do that kind of thing if the deacons want it. I don't want to interfere if they think they can handle it.'

'Between you and me, I think some of them would have liked you to join them. But it can work almost as well with you operating from the outside.'

So this was how it came about that Eve found herself working alongside the deacons in their ministry to the needy. It brought her into contact with a number of people, some of whom she was also able to help more spiritually. She always made a point of praying with the people she dealt with, as well as spending much time in prayer for them on her own, following what Paul said a true widow should do. But her usefulness was by no means confined to widows or people in material need. These were the more straightforward cases. It was not difficult to become aware of people who were short of cash or needed help in the home, with the shopping or such things. It was the more deep-seated problems that were hardest to get to grips with. Like cancer, they didn't show up until it was virtually too late to remedy them. And they caused far greater misery than did even poverty or physical handicap.

Eve had always been very sensitive to the feelings of women and knew that married or single, young, middle-aged or old, many suffered from maladjustment to their situation, their relationships and even their own femininity. They were often torn between what the Bible said (or what they had been led to believe it said) and the modern movement for women's liberation. This was tending to produce a reaction among evangelical Christians with the result that for not a few the bondage seemed to be tightening. Eve herself, with the help of the Word of God, had long since solved most of these problems for herself, but was well aware that many still had difficulties. There were some like this among the members of her church, and her desire to help them was as great as her desire to relieve the materially and physically needy. But it was always a tricky area, for the problems were nearly always connected with relationships to men,

especially husbands and fathers, and she dare not go behind
the backs of the menfolk. She had to bide her time and await
her opportunity. Her fear was that this would come too late.

This was almost what happened with Phyllis Gatenby. As
a person no one could have had a sweeter or friendlier nature.
She loved company, enjoyed meetings of all kinds and was
happy either to visit or to gather people in her own home. But
she hardly ever did any of these things. For one thing she
always seemed to be having children. Yet her husband was
never at home to take a turn at minding them so that she
could go out. Not only was he ambitious for promotion in his
own profession, but also for as high a rung as possible on the
social ladder. The pressure was increased by his having
bought an expensive house in the most residential area of the
town, which in his view justified seeking promotion in order
to pay for it. Thus if ever he was at home in the evening it was
he who came out to the mid-week church meeting and rarely
Phyllis. Even on Sundays she was not always free to come to
services, since, if one of the children was sick, it was always
she who had to remain at home with it. Not infrequently he
would be away for a whole week-end at a conference.

For a long time Eve observed the strain on Phyllis
mounting and became increasingly anxious for her. When
one day the news came that Phyllis had been taken to
hospital with a nervous breakdown, although she was
shocked, Eve was far from surprised. While she was mainly
concerned about Phyllis, she secretly felt it might have the
effect of waking Robert up to realize he had been making too
great demands on his wife and to alter his ways. She knew he
was not likely to see this all in a moment and would need help
from friends. She had long felt someone should have taken
him quietly aside and told him a few home truths. Perhaps if
that had been done before, Phyllis' breakdown would have
been avoided. On the other hand, when all was going well he
might not have been open to advice. Maybe that was why
Alec or the pastor had not tackled him. Perhaps this crisis
had to occur to soften him up and make him receptive to
counsel.

As she made her way round to the house the day after she had heard of Phyllis' removal to hospital, it was Eve's prayer that she would find Robert feeling worried and lonely, looking around for support and encouragement, searching for an explanation as to why this had happened, and what he could do to help her recover and avoid a recurrence. She pictured a scenario in which Robert paced the room, wringing his hands and crying out, 'Have I done anything to bring this on her?' Then she would calm him down and quietly point out certain things which could have a bearing on the situation, hoping she would not need to be too brutally frank, but that he would see for himself just what he had been doing to her. In her position she could hardly act the part of Nathan to David and blurt out, 'Thou art the man!' Her prayer to God was that he would prepare Robert's heart, open the way for her to speak, and give her much wisdom when the time came.

When she rang the doorbell, however, much to her surprise, she was greeted by Robert's own mother. Evidently, as soon as she had heard the news, this strong, thick-skinned and efficient though elderly lady had packed her case, driven herself down and taken over where Phyllis had left off – in fact rather before, since Phyllis had neglected a good many things during the days leading up to the breakdown. As for Robert, he seemed as usual. He could leave everything in the very capable hands of his mother, and this matter of his wife's illness need hardly cause a ripple on the surface of his life or interrupt the progress of his career. Only the children seemed at all affected and unsettled and Mrs Gatenby senior was organizing them so thoroughly they had hardly time even to think about their mother.

Eve could see at once that the prospect of a heart-to-heart talk with Robert was right out. There was no way she could get to him; nor, come to that, could anyone else, even the pastor. What chance did Phyllis have of a full recovery and a happier life? Eve could see what would happen. The doctors would get her on her feet, she would return home, settle down again, and then the whole process would be repeated – a

vicious circle. How could it be broken into? Only through
Phyllis herself. She was going to have to see the situation
clearly for what it was, and Robert for what he was. She was
the only one who would be able to get anything over to
Robert. Up to now she had been blind to his faults and
blamed herself if things did not run smoothly. She had come
to feel that everything rested on her – the home, the family
and Robert's work. No wonder she had broken down
mentally! It was too much for anyone to bear. She would
have to be relieved, which meant she would have to take
steps herself to lighten the load. The last thing Eve wanted to
do was to come between wife and husband. But they had
reached the last thing! No other course was open. Something
must be done to break the mould, and done without delay.
There just was not the time for the slow process of diplomacy
and courtesy. So her prayers now went in this direction: that
if this were the right course and she was not mistaken, God
would enable her to speak to Phyllis on the matter during the
time she was away from home and when she could consider it
at leisure.

On her first two visits to the hospital Eve had very little
response from Phyllis other than tears, so that she spent the
time holding her hand and talking about life in the world
outside the hospital. But as treatment and rest began to have
their effect, she started to speak more freely. The principal
theme of her conversation was self-reproach. 'The trouble
with me,' she said to Eve towards the end of her second week
in hospital, 'is that I'm not a very good wife and mother. I
don't really enjoy housework. I suppose I'm bascially lazy,
that's the trouble. Then when Bob comes in and the meal
isn't ready he gets annoyed, and that flusters me and I panic.
Then I make a mess of things,' she sobbed. 'Even little Julie
tells me if there's dust on the mantelpiece, but she doesn't go
and get a duster and do it herself. I resent this, and then
realize I shouldn't feel like that. After all, it's my job to do
these things, isn't it?' She looked at Eve as if appealing to her

to join in the attack and lay the blame on her. But Eve refused.

'I know what you think, Phyl,' she said. 'You think this illness is some kind of judgement on you for not doing your job, or not doing it well enough or willingly enough, or something. You think that if you heap the blame on yourself and get your friends to take sides against you, it will relieve your conscience. You're trying to punish yourself black and blue.'

'Well it must be me. Who else can it be? Everyone else is doing their job. Robert works very hard, and does long hours. It's me that's not pulling my weight. And now he has had to get his mother over to fill in for me because I can't cope – someone twice my age. Yet she's coping splendidly, he says, which is another way of saying she is a better housekeeper than me. I'm the one who's failing.'

Eve felt this was the moment about which she had prayed. She put up a swift prayer arrow to God and spoke. 'That's not the way I see things at all. Your problem is an old one and not uncommon, even today, but it's just as hard as ever to solve. It's the problem of a domineering husband.'

Phyllis stared at her in disbelief. 'Well, that's his right, isn't it? The husband is head of the wife. I accepted that when we got married. I promised to "obey and serve" him, in return for him bestowing all his worldly goods on me. It was a fair exchange. He's carrying out his part of the bargain: he's bought us a lovely house in a pleasant part of the town, and we have a car, and I have a well-equipped kitchen. I can't complain of that. It's me that's not being submissive enough.'

'You've got it all wrong. That's not what submission means. It doesn't mean you've got to mould yourself to the shape of the other person – or worse, let him try to mould you. That's what Robert's trying to do, and you're letting him. But it can't be done. You have a personality of your own, and a very good one too. Everyone thinks that. But

you're crucifying it, and yourself in the process. And there'll
be no resurrection either. The damage will be permanent
unless it's stopped soon – now in fact, before it gets worse.'

Phyllis looked horrified, as if Eve were preaching her some
kind of heresy.

'Look,' Eve resumed, 'there's no point in hiding from the
facts any longer. And that's what has been happening, or, to
put it another way, the facts have been hidden from you. And
they've been hidden behind the safest place anyone can find
– the Scripture itself. Bob isn't really the way he is out of
obedience to the Bible; it's due to his personality. He's a
domineering person by nature. He finds, or thinks he does,
that the Bible is on his side. He can justify anything on the
basis that the husband is the head of the wife and the wife
must just submit. But that does not give him the right to
repress your personality, and that's what is happening. And
that's why you're in here. Listen, tell me, how often does he
consult you about anything?'

'Well, I don't know. I can't think at the moment.'

'You can't think because there isn't anything to think.
The answer is "never", isn't it? For example, did he ever ask
you if you wanted another child?'

'No, but I suppose he didn't have to, did he? He pointed
out to me once where the Bible says that the wife does not
have power over her body, but the husband.'

'I thought so – half a verse. There is the other side too. It's
a mutual thing. You have a say in the matter, and you've got
to exercise your right. You're only thirty, and you've already
got four children. The way things are going you'll end up
with eight. And it will be you that carries the can.'

'But we have to trust God over that, don't we? It's he who
gives the children, and they're his blessing, aren't they? Isn't
that what the Bible says?'

'Bob told you that too, I suppose. It may be true to the
letter of the Bible, but not the spirit. The spirit is Victorian.
In any case the Bible doesn't say that because children are a
blessing from God we have to have an unlimited number of

them. And trusting God does not mean suspending the use of
our minds or ignoring the state of our bodies. Some women
are suited to large families and revel in them. But you're not
one of those, and you know it. It's no good trying to make
yourself what you're not. It would be different if Bob spent
more time at home and less in the pursuit of his career. Then
the burden would be shared.'

'Well, he's good at his work and is getting on well, so
naturally he devotes as much of himself to it as possible. I'm
sure the family will get the benefit. We shall be able to afford
extra education for the children and all sorts of things.'

'At the expense of all sorts of other things – mostly paid by
you. What sort of life are you living? Has your marriage
really fulfilled you? From what I heard, you yourself were
doing quite well in your career and could have got quite high
up. But you've had to abandon it all.'

'I don't think husband and wife can both pursue careers.
The Bible says the woman's calling is to be the man's
companion and therefore she should help him to fulfil his
calling. I don't seem to be doing that very well stuck in here,'
she added sorrowfully.

'I agree that it is difficult for a husband and wife both to
pursue careers, if not impossible, although I suppose it
depends on the careers. But that doesn't mean the wife has to
go to the other extreme and give up virtually everything in
order to enable the man to succeed in his career. There is a
balance somewhere. He has no right to devote himself
entirely to the pursuit of his ambition and expect you to
sacrifice everything to make it possible. That is not what the
Bible means by companionship, I'm quite sure. This is not
how most of our married women live their lives. If it were,
they would hardly get any fellowship or ministry in the
church. And that wouldn't be right, would it?'

'I see what you mean. But I just can't help feeling I'm the
one to blame.'

'That's because you're not well at the moment. I hope I
haven't made you worse by talking as I have. But I believe

it's right to do so, because everything I've said is true, and it's the truth that makes us free, Jesus said. This is what I've found over the years. I was in bondage, as many Christians are. That's because they have only been told part of the story, or they've had a certain slant put on it. This has taken hold of their consciences, and so, if they can't carry out what they've been told or led to believe they ought to do, then they feel guilty and blame themselves. That's just what you're doing, Phyl, and this, plus the run-down condition you were in through overwork has brought you where you are. The only way you can overcome this is by looking again at these half-truths you've been living by and getting the full picture. Then you will be free. So do think about these things deeply, won't you, while you're here? Then we can discuss them again. I would so like to have talked to you like this before, but it didn't seem to be my place. I hope I haven't been too bold now. I know it is not the usual thing to talk to wives about their husbands, and I prayed for and sought opportunities to speak to Robert first. But the door was closed tight, and there was no time to pick the lock! So there was no other course open. The truth must be told somehow; it is the only answer to this problem.'

As Eve walked away from the hospital she could not help feeling a little concerned lest she had said too much too soon, and upset Phyllis even more. On the other hand, she thought too little had been said in the past, hence the present situation. Desperate diseases require desperate remedies. Nevertheless she prayed long and earnestly that God would indeed teach Phyllis the truth and that the truth would make her free, liberating her from her self-immolation, and give her a new outlook. But she prayed even more for Robert, for she knew there could never be a full solution until his eyes were open too, especially to his own faults. This would be a much harder task, because with him the snag was a dominating personality, something to which he seemed quite oblivious. In fact he seemed positively to glory in it, making it out to be scriptural. She could not help wishing Alec were still there to take it up with Robert, which she had not succeeded in doing. There was the pastor, but would he take it from him or would he be offended and give more trouble? It was all a big problem.

That had all happened more than a year before. During that time the improvement, such as it was, had been slow and slight. One of the obstacles was Robert's mother. She was one of those people who never seem to wear out and can cope with any situation. She was like him in many ways and had very little patience with women who could not manage their families and homes. She had brought up a large family in an atmosphere of thoroughness and efficiency, and Robert expected Phyllis to be a carbon copy of his mother. However, he was beginning to listen to friends in the church and cut down his headlong pursuit of career and social position. Also, the doctor managed to persuade him that Phyllis should stop having children, and that he should pay for some domestic help for her, rather than calling in his mother. This was the best that could be done, for there would be no full cure until those truths Eve had laboriously got over to Phyllis also penetrated under his much thicker skin.

'And now,' thought Eve, 'I've got to turn my attention to Susie.' Susan Barrington was an attractive and intelligent twenty-year-old who was taking a dressmaking course at a nearby technical college. Although much sought after by the young men both of the college and her home town she remained aloof from them all. When at school she had taken a leading part in school activities and in the youth fellowship at the church. But during her course she seemed to change and to lose interest in young people's activities, preferring the company of older women, especially the single ones. She formed a friendship with Mary Blake, the middle-aged lady Eve had sought to help a while back, and took a liking to Eve herself. These three usually sat together at services. On more than one occasion Eve noticed Susie with her Bible open at 1 Corinthians 7 before the start of the service. This puzzled Eve at first, then the light began to dawn on her.

One day she leaned over to Susie and whispered,
'Understandest thou what thou readest?'

But Susie did not reply in the way the Ethiopian
statesman had answered the same question from Philip, but,
her eyes lighting up, said, 'Yes, indeed, and I think this is the
word for today. Christians ought to be making a stand
against sexual licence. I wish the pastor would preach on it.'

'Perhaps he doesn't share your enthusiasm for it, or even
your understanding of it,' Eve said.

'What do you mean?' Susie asked. 'It's quite plain, isn't
it? Paul says Christians should abstain from sex unless they
are so weak they can't avoid it.'

'Is that really what he is saying? Supposing we got
together and discussed it sometime?'

'I should like that very much,' said Susie.

And so it was arranged that she should come to Eve's
bungalow that day and they should discuss it over a light
supper.

Eve looked at the clock. She had just over an hour to
prepare the meal and collect her thoughts. Fortunately she
had spent some time in the past two or three days pondering
1 Corinthians 7 and looking up one or two books. She was
pretty sure now that she knew what Susie's problem was. It
had taken a long time to get to the bottom of the change in
her, because it was such a rare thing, in fact something she
had not come across before. It was not unusual that she
found herself dealing with the opposite end of the subject –
girls, even Christian ones, who bordered on the provocative
in their dress and behaviour. She didn't blame them because
they were usually children of parents who had been young
during the "swinging sixties" and had little time for modesty
in dress. There was one girl in particular, nice enough in
herself, who in fact had professed conversion and joined the
baptism class. But she was fashion-conscious and failed to
discriminate between those which were reasonably modest
and those which weren't. Being an art student used to
painting from "real life" models, she had few inhibitions

about the human body. In counselling her over baptism, the pastor had thought it wise to put her on to Eve to guide her on this matter, rather than deal with it himself.

Eve had explained to this girl, whose name was Pat, that the Bible did not have many rules about dress. On the whole it left the individual free to be guided by taste and fashion. Really there were only three dangers to avoid in dressing. One was that of being too showy and drawing attention to things like hair-dos, fancy clothes and jewellery by overdoing these things. Eve had taken her to 1 Peter 3:3–5, showing her that Christians were to concentrate on character and behaviour, and not let these be smothered by too much attention to outward appearance. The same passage warned against over-expensive dressing with costly hair-styles and jewellery. The same point was made by Paul in 1 Timothy 2:9–10. The Bible did not regulate on how much a person spent on her hair, her clothes or decorations; the individual had to judge this for herself. It was not good witness to dress in rags or appear dowdy, which could be a perverted form of exhibitionism, trying to appear more spiritual than was really the case. But there should be some restraint, and a Christian woman should not be trying to outdo everyone and always sporting new and better clothes. But the main principle, Eve had said, was modesty and decency. Eve had begun to make use of the recently published New International Version, especially with the younger people, and it was in this translation she pointed Pat to 1 Timothy 2:9, where Paul says, 'I also want women to dress modestly, with decency and propriety.' Women should not dress in a way that displays their sexuality to such an extent that it made it difficult for members of the opposite sex to refrain from stares or glances, with the resulting lustful thoughts. Obviously she was not completely responsible for what went on in the minds of men, and some would not control their thoughts whatever women wore. But she ought to be careful she did all she could to avoid this.

Pat had accepted all this in good part and then raised the

question of trousers. 'I bought a trouser suit a few months ago and wore that. I liked it, and I wouldn't have thought there was anything provocative and showy about it, and it certainly wasn't expensive. But someone told me I should stop wearing it because the Bible said somewhere – Deuteronomy I think it was – that a woman should not wear what pertains to a man and vice versa.' Pat was referring to Deuteronomy 22:5: 'A woman must not wear men's clothing, nor a man wear women's clothing, for the Lord your God detests anyone who does this.'

'Ah!' Eve replied. 'That was a pity, but it's a very commonly misunderstood verse. What it is really against is transvestism, which I expect all Christians would disapprove of as unnatural and perverse. It doesn't mean that men's clothes and women's should never resemble each other. Life would be difficult if it did! These things are matters of style, fashion and culture. In some parts of the world women wear trousers and men wear a garment like a long dress. Then in our own country it's not all that long since men wore stocking tights and frock coats! Before that they wore doublet and hose, which Mrs Bloomer revived for women! And no one worries about blouses, which aren't much different from shirts, and both men and women can wear socks. So it seems to be stretching a point to forbid trousers to women. 'Mind you,' she added, 'if there are Christians who are so legalistic that their consciences would be really offended by trousers, so that they could not worship or hear the Word, then girls should avoid them until the problem is cleared up. But at the same time something should be done to free their consciences from such bondage. But, of course, what is worse is to be the cause of members of the opposite sex being unable to worship because they are distracted by a girl's appearance.' Pat had been satisfied with this and everything was all right. She took more care how she dressed, especially for church, and kept her trouser suit to wear at home, or when she went out somewhere other than to church.

That had been the kind of situation Eve had come across
more than once. But Susie's case was very different. Eve was
by now convinced that she had formed the idea, from 1
Corinthians 7, that Paul was against marriage for Christians
because there was something unclean and defiling about
sexual relations. She had got hold of some of the statements
in that chapter and exaggerated them to the exclusion of
everything else. For example, 'It is good for a man not to
marry' (verse 1) and therefore equally good the other way
round. 'Now to the unmarried and widows I say: It is good
for them to stay unmarried, as I am' (v. 8). 'Because of the
present crisis, I think that it is good for you to remain as you
are' (v. 26). 'Do not look for a wife' (v. 27). 'From now on
those who have wives should live as if they had none' (v. 29).
From all this she was assuming that since Christians were
new creatures and holy people they should keep their bodies
pure. After all, Christ had been celibate. Those who could
not contain themselves were allowed to marry, since this was
better than fornication, but it was very much a second best
and greatly hampered spirituality and the service of Christ.
Eve was convinced that this was Susie's point of view. 'How
different people are!' Eve thought, remembering Mary
Blake, who was celibate but discontented, whereas Susie
could marry a dozen times over but had not the least
inclination! And Susie was an admirer of Mary!

But the question that faced Eve was how to answer Susie.
She began her preparations by turning back to the beginning
of 1 Corinthians to read right through to chapter 7 and get
the train of thought. She noted first the divisions in the
church in Corinth, centring around the various teachers and
apostles associated with it. Some of these were concerned
with charismatic gifts, but not all. There was a
super-spiritual group who were going 'beyond what is
written' (4:6), or, as the writer of Ecclesiastes put it, being
'righteous overmuch'. These people were claiming to be
'different from anyone else' (4:7) and boasting that they had
all they wanted, were rich and had become kings. Evidently

they regarded themselves as having obtained a kind of moral perfection which they wished to impose on the others. In some cases this outlook make them despise the body altogether, so that they thought it did not matter how they used or abused it. Hence the problems of fornication, incest and prostitution he had to deal with in chapters 5 and 6. And others, she noted, were reacting in the opposite way and becoming ascetic, especially in matters of sex. They were saying, 'It is good for a man not to marry' (7:1). Eve thought Susie was probably making the mistake of thinking those words represented Paul's opinion, whereas clearly he was quoting from their letter. It was these ascetics who were advocating total abstinence from sexual relations. As Eve followed this out through the chapter she noted down how these Christians were applying their principle. From his advice to married couples in verses 2–5 she deduced that they were instructing them to abstain from intercourse with each other. Verses 8–9 implied they were advising widows not to remarry. From verses 10–16 it seemed they even advocated divorce as the way to avoid physical contact, especially in the case of a mixed marriage between Christian and pagan. But Paul was opposed to all these practices and to the thinking behind them. On the first point, advising abstinence from sexual intercourse, he said this was fundamentally wrong, since neither partner has the right to refuse the other. Also it opened the door to temptation (v. 5) and could lead to immorality (v. 2). 'I must stress this point,' she said to herself, 'that this does not represent Paul's total view of marriage – that marriage is just an antidote to immorality. He has a much higher conception of it, and only says this to counter the ascetics.'

As regards Paul's view of widows, while he thought it a good thing for them to remain unmarried, for reasons he gave later in the chapter, he in no way forbade it. Verse 8 ('It is good for them to stay unmarried, as I am') might imply that Paul was a widower himself and by God's grace had no great desire to remarry. He wished they were all like that, but recognized they would not be. If they wanted to remarry, they should. The cross-reference to 1 Timothy 5:11–14 showed he positively advised younger widows to remarry. Coming to the question of divorce (vv. 11–14) he was on very strong ground here, since Christ himself had forbidden it, except for adultery. It is true Jesus had not dealt with the specific situation which confronted Paul in Corinth, and therefore Paul had to appeal to his own authority rather than to the specific teaching of Christ (v. 12). But he was quite sure it would be wrong for a believer to separate from an unbeliever on the grounds that the sexual contact would be defiling. It appeared they were pressing too far the teaching that the church had replaced Israel as God's priesthood, and that since all believers were now priests they should behave like Old Testament priests and avoid contact with unbelievers. But Paul replied that there was nothing morally or spiritually defiling about a believer having marital relations with a non-believer.

The basis of the problem was that they were pressing too far Jesus' teaching on celibacy, as if every Christian should practise it because it was more holy than marriage. Paul's position was that this was not what Jesus had meant by 'making oneself a eunuch for the kingdom of heaven's sake'. He did not mean celibacy was morally superior, only that it was commendable for people to devote themselves to the service of Christ and abstain from marriage as a means to that end if it helped. Paul explained at some length that celibacy did not make a person more holy, but simply left him or her freer to serve God, as he himself had found. There are less earthly cares involved in being single and therefore more time and resources are left for the work of the Lord. He warned that things might become very difficult for Christians, and if they did, the married would come off worse because they would be encumbered by dependents. Paul, like Jesus, taught that the single state is not an obligation but a gift. No one should therefore be compelled or pressurized into remaining single. There was no sin involved in marrying; in fact to refrain from it without the special grace of continence was more likely to lead to sin.

Eve thought she could also tell Susie about her conversation with Mary Blake, when she had counselled her to take a positive view of her single state and not be ashamed of it, as if it were inferior, and also to use the opportunities it afforded to serve Christ. This was the balanced position, whereas Susie seemed to be going to the extreme of taking the ascetic position of the Corinthian Christians. She could also point out to her that Paul actually denounced asceticism in 1 Timothy 4:1–3 in all its forms, including abstinence from food and from marriage. Also, she could take her to Ephesians 5 and show her that 1 Corinthians 7 did not represent Paul's total thinking on marriage, and was only a corrective for a warped view. In Ephesians 5 he brings out the glories of the married state – that it is comparable to the relationship between Christ and the church. She felt that Susie could not really have taken all these things into account. She had just got hold of this one idea and let it buzz in her head like a bee in the bonnet. She was quite young after all, and it was natural when everything was fresh to think that a new discovery was the most important truth there ever was, and everything must be subordinated to it.

She suddenly remembered herself at twenty, when freedom from male domination was the only thing that mattered. She thought of Sarah, passing through a similar stage now. She felt glad she could give these lovely girls the benefit of her experience, so that they would be able to avoid the pitfalls she had stumbled into, rather than having to learn in the hard and bitter way she had had to. But it was wonderful to be free, really free, and still a woman, the Lord's free woman, who could perhaps be the means of liberating others. 'Lord, use these thoughts to free Susie,' she prayed, and at that moment the doorbell rang.

'And I haven't even laid the table!'she said.